FAIR PLAY

FAIR PLAY

SHARE THE MENTAL LOAD, REBALANCE YOUR RELATIONSHIP AND TRANSFORM YOUR LIFE

EVE RODSKY

Quercus

First published in the US in 2019 by G.P. Putnam's Sons,
an imprint of Penguin Random House LLC

First published in Great Britain in 2019 by

Quercus Editions Ltd
Carmelite House
50 Victoria Embankment
London EC4Y 0DZ

An Hachette UK company

A CIP catalogue record for this book is available
from the British Library.

HB ISBN 978 1 52940 018 2
TPB ISBN 978 1 52940019 9
Ebook ISBN 978 1 52940 020 5

Every effort has been made to contact copyright holders.
However, the publishers will be glad to rectify in future
editions any inadvertent omissions brought to their attention.

Quercus Editions Ltd hereby exclude all liability to the extent
permitted by law for any errors or omissions in this book and for any loss,
damage or expense (whether direct or indirect) suffered by a
third party relying on any information contained in this book.

Part opener and chapter opener illustrations by Sandra Chiu

Some names and identifying details of people mentioned in this book have
been changed to protect their privacy. In some cases, composite characters have
been created for the purpose of further disguising the identity of individuals.

10 9 8 7 6 5 4 3 2

Printed and bound in Great Britain by Clays Ltd, Elcograf S.p.A.

Papers used by Quercus are from well-managed forests and other responsible sources.

To Seth:
There is no one on Earth with whom I would rather play
the game of life. Thank you for allowing me to share our
story . . . you are my soul mate and I'm so proud that we have
grown together every damn day. I love you.

To Zach, Ben, and Anna:
I wrote this for you.

To my mother, Terry:
Thank you for holding all of the cards for our little three-
person family . . . lots of sh*t may have fallen through
the cracks but your love never did. And for teaching me that
a life worth living is doing everything you can to change
the lives of others for the better.

CONTENTS

> > **PART III** < <
HOW TO WIN AT FAIR PLAY

Playing for Keeps

CONTENTS

>>>> **PART I** <<<<

THE
PROBLEM

What Is Fair Play?

1.

THE CURSE OF THE SHE-FAULT PARENT

||||||||||||||||||||||||||||||||||||||||||||||||||||||||||||||||||||||||||||||||||||||||||||||||||||||||||

I was ready to fold.

CONSIDER:
THE CASE OF THE MISSING BLUEBERRIES

> I'm surprised you didn't get blueberries.

I stared at my husband's text and imagined him speaking these words in what I call his "porn voice"—breathless, like he gets when he's frustrated or overwhelmed.

Instantly defensive, I thought: *Um, why can't you get the blueberries?*

I'd taken the afternoon "off" in order to spend time with my oldest, who was sorely in need of some mommy reconnection time in the wake of the recent arrival of his new baby brother. After going over my long list of instructions for the sitter (twice), I hustled out the front door to pick Zach up from school—all while balancing the snacks I'd just packed, a bag forgotten by the prior day's playmate, a FedEx package to be dropped off, a brand-new already-too-small pair of children's shoes to be returned, and a client contract that needed a markup before tomorrow morning. I was just barely holding it together when my husband's "blueberry text" arrived, and the tears came so fast and furious I had to pull over to the side of the road.

How had it happened that I'd gone from successfully managing an entire department at work to failing to manage a grocery list for my family? And what self-respecting woman cries over an item forgotten at the market? And, just as alarming: Would a container of off-season blueberries serve as the harbinger to the end of my marriage?

I wiped away the mascara streaks beneath my eyes and thought: *This is not how I envisioned my life—the fulfiller of my family's smoothie needs.*

Hold up. Rewind.

HOW I GOT HERE

My mom and dad divorced when I was three and she was pregnant with my brother. Mom opted to forgo alimony to avoid acrimony and raised my brother and me in a one-parent home while working full-time as a professor of social work in New York City. Not a high-paying job, but she made it work for our family. Or so I thought until the first eviction notice was slipped under our apartment door. Mom had taught classes all day, picked my brother and me up from school, took us to the dentist uptown, dropped us back at home with a sitter downtown, and then . . . went back to work. When I saw the envelope on the floor, I opened it, read the letter inside, and then waited up late for Mom to come home. When she finally walked through the door, I broke the news to her that we no longer would have a place to live. I was eight years old. Mom assured me that she'd simply forgotten to pay our rent, and she would mail a check first thing in the morning.

She followed through on her promise and we didn't have to move, but from that moment on I understood how hard life was for my mom because she carried 100 percent of the burden at home. Throughout my formative years and on too many occasions to count, I remember looking at her at the end of another long, exhausting day—my overworked supermom who tried to do it all—and thinking: *That will never be me. When I grow up, I will have a true partner in life.* Though it wasn't modeled for me, I became determined to build and sustain a 50/50 partnership one day.

I worked hard and got myself through college and then law school, when I met the man who would become my partner. My best friend had set us up. Zoe said about Seth: "He's Jewish and obsessed with hip hop." I instantly flashed back to when I'd surprised guests with a choreographed dance to Slick Rick's "Children's Story" at my bat mitzvah. I had to meet this guy.

I was a first-year associate at a law firm in New York City, which meant logging *long* hours, so for our first date Seth and I agreed to meet at a late-night bar in Union Square. But at 9:30 p.m., I received a client call that kept me on the line for nearly two hours. By the time I arrived at the bar, it was almost midnight and Seth was . . . still there. One of Seth's friends had waited with him until I showed up. Seth told me later what his friend had said when I walked through the door: "She was worth the wait." And so was Seth. I liked him right away.

There was just one snag to our budding romance: Seth lived

in Los Angeles, and I had just taken the New York Bar Exam. We did a cross-country courtship for a year, and on our anniversary, I presented him with *The Best of 2003*, every single email we'd written to each other since the night we'd met. There were more than 600 pages of email exchanges that I'd printed out in the basement of my law firm and bound into a deep red four-volume book set. Seth was touched by my sentimentality (and equally impressed by my meticulous organizational skills). I think we both knew then that this was the *real thing*.

Within the year, I took on the arduous endeavor of studying for and passing the California Bar and uprooted to Los Angeles. And then, when Seth's growing business required an East Coast office, we packed up and moved back to New York as a newly engaged couple. (Getting him back home was my secret plan.)

Our first apartment across from the Midtown tunnel was cramped and always loud, but we didn't care. We were in love, true collaborators in the home, and champions of each other's careers. As a young couple, our dynamic felt equitable, a reciprocal partnership of equals. In between loads of laundry, I marked up his client agreements as his entertainment agency expanded, and Seth gave me business pointers while he unloaded groceries.

He was my right-hand man as I worked my way up the ladder to my dream job—using my legal training, organizational management skills, and mediation background to work with individuals and companies to structure philanthropic organizations. In layman's terms, I advised the wealthy on how to give away tons of money to nonprofits that served the greater good. We were both doing work that we felt proud of, and together we crushed it every step of the way.

Cut to married with children—everything changed.

THE SHE-FAULT PARENT

I became the default parent—or more aptly, the *she*-fault parent—and as such, the only thing I was crushing were peas for my baby. To be fair, Seth eagerly jumped in to diaper change, bottle-feed, and provide middle-of-the-night comfort to his firstborn. But beyond forming this early, critical connection with his son, Seth would frequently say about our new family dynamic: "There's not a lot for me to do."

While my husband is no Neanderthal, he was echoing what a good cave buddy had promised him during my pregnancy: "Relax. Dads don't really do anything for the first six months. It's more of a 'mom' thing."

Like many breadwinner-working fathers, Seth returned to work just one week after Zach was born. I'd been granted three months of maternity leave to "stay home" (as if that term encompasses all that new parents do every day). Looking back, I hadn't anticipated the endless emotional, mental, and physical effort parenthood would require. My cousin Jessica, who lived a quick cab ride uptown and who was also pregnant at the same time, hadn't seen what was coming either. In her third trimester, she'd signed us up for a knitting class because "we'll probably get bored on maternity leave." Bored, yes. Idle, no. I had more than enough to keep my hands occupied without ever picking up a knitting needle or a ball of yarn. Because Seth and I hadn't pre-negotiated how to share in the domestic workload before Zach came along, it defaulted to me. He'd leave for work in the office and I'd spend the next eight hours boiling bottles, doing dishes, folding laundry, restocking the nursery, running to the grocery store, picking up prescriptions, preparing meals, tidying up, *and* entertaining and attending to my little one. In his defense, after returning home from the office Seth would offer, "How can I help?" but I was unable to articulate what I needed. I'd typically reply with a sputter: "I don't know. Just pick *something*!"

I was overtired and quickly became overextended. I also felt isolated and alone.

"My public life is so private now," I confided to Jessica one afternoon at the playground.

"We've become 'single married women,'" she offered, quoting a term coined by Dr. Sherry L. Blake that describes women in committed relationships who singularly bear the lioness's share of family responsibilities. Seth could see that I was struggling in my new role, but he also felt constantly nagged. He made efforts to extend a hand but ultimately retreated because "I can't do anything right." The bickering between us became part of our new family routine, and when I considered returning to work, the idea of juggling a challenging office job with the ever-expanding demands of domestic life seemed impossible.

One afternoon, after an office meeting to discuss my return, I "took ten" in the company stairwell to quietly pump breast milk into plastic bags. As I sat with my back against the wall, I thought: *Does this really count as a non-bathroom lactation space?* And more important, *How the hell am I going to balance it all?* I proposed to my employer that I work full-time, but from home one day a week. That was declined. I offered to work a four-day week for less salary. They didn't go for that either.

In the end, I walked away from my dream job to become an independent ("1099") consultant, a move I don't regret (but I do still think about—*a lot*). In my case, it was because—however supportive my corporate employer was about holding my full-time position for me during my maternity leave—the company didn't have family-friendly systems in place to support parents requiring more flexibility in the early child-rearing years that directly follow. The day I gave notice, a colleague texted me: > **Don't blame yourself** and included the following statistic: *Compared to other developed countries, the United States ranks last in employment-protected time off for new parents.* Shared parental leave was introduced in the UK in 2015, giving parents the right to split up to 52 weeks between them. However, research shows that just 2% of couples take up this option.

Girlfriends who'd also taken a career detour by decreasing their professional workload, or who had exited the traditional workforce entirely, totally understood what I was going through. Tanya, a friend and former colleague who'd already left our company to care for her two children at home, cautioned me, "Juggling work and home is a grind, but if you think you're going to gain *more* time by going part-time, think again. More time at home actually translates to *less* time." How could that be? My new mommy friends were quick to point out that when you free up time spent in an office, you quickly fill it by doing more at home, including more that isn't necessarily kid-related.

They were absolutely right. In addition to the non-negotiable daily grind tasks like making sure there are always clean nappies, once I wasn't working full-time outside the home, I also took on many things that my husband used to do. Tasks like upgrading our insurance policies, bill paying, moving boxes to storage, buying backup batteries for our smoke detectors, and countless other supplementary household sh*t that isn't *really* supplementary. Because after the basics, these other tasks keep domestic life moving forward. Without any negotiation, in my new role as CEO, task manager, *and* worker bee of our family's never-ending to-do list, I performed hours upon hours of work that went unnoticed and unacknowledged by my husband—and sometimes, even by me.

On many days, feeling the full weight of exhaustion that would seize me the moment my baby was down and I was finally offline, I'd wonder, *What* did *I do all day?* When even I couldn't answer the question, there was no doubt in my mind that I'd lost all control of my time.

Sound familiar?

WHY CAN'T WE EVER SEEM TO GET AHEAD OF OUR TO-DO LISTS?

The more I talked with my girlfriends who'd entered motherhood, I realized we were all having trouble getting it all done—and what's more, we were all having trouble identifying exactly what it was we were *doing*. Why were we all so busy?

It turns out this phenomenon has a name—many names, actually. One of the most popular is "invisible work": *invisible* because it may be unseen and unrecognized by our partners, and also because those of us who do it may not count or even acknowledge it as work . . . despite the fact that it costs us real time and significant mental and physical effort with no sick days or benefits. No doubt you, too, have read articles describing this "mental load," "second shift," and the "emotional labor" that falls disproportionately on women, along with the toll this domestic work takes on our lives more broadly.

But what are we really talking about here? Sociologists Arlene Kaplan Daniels and Arlie Hochschild started giving us the language to talk about these deeply felt (but largely unarticulated) inequities in the 1980s, and since then, plenty of intelligent women have advanced the conversation and the popular vernacular.

Mental Load: The never-ending mental to-do list you keep for all your family tasks. Though not as heavy as a bag of rocks, the constant details banging around in your mind nonetheless weigh you down. Mental "overload" creates stress, fatigue, and often forgetfulness. *Where did I put the damn car keys?*

Second Shift: This is the domestic work you do long *before* you go to work and often even longer *after* you get home from the office. It's an unpaid shift that starts early and goes late, and you can't afford to lose it. *Every day's a double shift when you have two kids' lunches to prep!*

Emotional Labor: This term has evolved organically in pop culture to include the "maintaining relationships" and "managing emotions" work like calling your in-laws, sending thank-you notes, buying teacher gifts, and soothing meltdowns in Target. This work of caring can be some of the most exhausting labor (akin to the day your child was born), but providing middle-of-the-night comfort is what makes you a wonderful and dependable parent. *It's OK, Mama's here.*

Invisible Work: This is the behind-the-scenes stuff that keeps a home and family running smoothly, although it's hardly noticed and is rarely valued. *The toothpaste never runs out. You're welcome.*

In an effort to "physicalize" this heavy burden carried by women yesterday and today, I began collecting every article I could find on the subject of domestic inequality. After amass-ing 250 articles (and counting) from newspapers, magazines, and online sources, it was disturbing to recognize that, since women began writing about this in the 1940s, we haven't made enough progress in sharing the burden with our partners or finding an answer to this problem that men could buy into. Same sh*t, different decade.

According to the most contemporary research, women *still* do the bulk of childcare and domestic work, even in two-earner families in which both parents work full-time and sometimes even when the mother earns more than her partner. As if reflecting a mirror onto my life, I stumbled upon another study revealing that men who stood up for their fair share of housework prior to having kids significantly cut back their contributions after kids—by up to five hours a week.

Wow, even the good guys?

As I considered the vast research and literature, past and present, bravely naming and articulating this problem, I thought: *OK, we know there's an imbalance. But where is the manual with a practical and sustainable solution?* Sure, it's helpful to understand the breadth of the condition and its historic underpinnings, and it felt gratifying to know that I was not alone in this predicament and that plenty of women had been fed up and writing about it for decades. But what can we do to *change* it? I became determined to find out.

VISIBILITY = VALUE

Soon after my second child was born, we moved back to Los Angeles. I caught my breath as a mom and went back to work full-time. I formed my own consulting firm, the Philanthropy Advisory Group, to provide services for private individuals and family foundations. But even with my return to a paid job that took me to an office, I was still shouldering two-thirds of the work required to run a home and raise a family, a statistic

I wasn't aware of at the time but was undeniably living. I was still the she-fault parent charged with doing it all, buying the blueberries and masterminding our family's day-to-day life while my husband—a good guy and a wonderful father—was still not much more than a "helper" rather than a collaborative partner/planner/participant in all that took place for our family.

Late one night, I was using my phone flashlight to find the outlet to plug in the baby monitor. Seth was asleep in our darkened bedroom and I was careful not to wake him up. But when I accidentally bumped my nightstand, upsetting a precariously tall, Jenga-like stack of books that came tumbling to the floor, he snapped awake.

"What are you doing?" he asked with groggy accusation. "Can't it wait until tomorrow?"

No, I thought but didn't say aloud, *all the invisible planning and coordination that happens when you're asleep needs to happen before tomorrow morning in order for our household to function!* In a flash, I recalled a YouTube clip a friend had recently forwarded to me of author Joyce Meyer reading from *The Confident Woman* where she details the endless work that "Mom" attends to before going to bed:

Wash the dinner dishes, set out cereal for the morning, prep the coffee pot, pull meat out of the freezer, fill the dog's water dish, let out the cat, put wet clothes in the dryer, empty the wastebasket, lock the doors, look in on the kids, write a quick note to the teacher, lay out clothes, wash and moisturize her face, and then add three more things to her To-Do list for the next day. Meanwhile, her husband turns off the TV and announces to no one in particular, "I'm going to bed." *And without doing anything else, he does.*

Frustrated and hurt, I crawled into bed. My mind still racing, I lay there considering all that I'd done over the course of my second shift—emailing Zach's teacher about an upcoming field trip, lining up weekend playdates, scheduling the babysitter, registering for mommy-and-me swim lessons, and negotiating the cell phone bill with a 24-hour help line. Suddenly, our situation became clear. What my favorite childhood detective Encyclopedia Brown may have dubbed "The Case of Going Bump in the Night" would invariably continue in my marriage until Seth and I made some serious changes. That night, our options seemed limited. In fact, the only thing that came to mind was moving to a foreign country where Seth speaks the language and I don't (an actual suggestion that made it into the *New York Times*). In this scenario, I'd kick back on the beaches of Ibiza while Seth, the only Spanish speaker in the family, would be forced to take on more domestic tasks and childcare communication. *¡Qué bueno!*

I decided to sleep on it. By the next morning, I felt less tired and cranky and put off my late-night plans to move our family to another continent. Instead, I followed through on the plan I'd set with my girlfriends to do a local walk for breast cancer awareness.

CONSIDER:
THE CASE OF THE 30 CALLS AND 46 TEXTS

Some of my dearest friends, along with their moms, sisters, and nieces, met in downtown Los Angeles to unite as a community to honor breast cancer survivors, including some of our friends and family. We were covered in pink glitter from the signs our kids helped us make, and as we marched through the streets in pink leggings, chanting, "Not just a women's problem," it felt like a true girlfriends' getaway. We all remarked on the palpable sense of high-energy sisterhood and female badassery in the air. That is, until the first text came through around noon: > **When are you coming home?**

It was from Jill's husband, who'd spent the morning with the kids and was already "done." As we watched her type back a prompt response, nearly every woman in the group felt her own phone come to life as a similar message appeared:

> **When is the babysitter coming?**

> **Where did you put Josh's soccer bag?**

> **What's the address of the birthday party?**

> **Do the kids need to eat lunch?**

The mutual experience was remarkable, and we began sharing each message as it came through. "Eat lunch? What do *you* think?" Suzy wondered out loud in amusement-turned-disbelief-turned-irritation.

As we laughed and griped in equal measure, I got my first call:

"Where's Anna's outfit you picked out? She doesn't have any pants."

It was Seth, breathless and frustrated, speaking in his porn voice. Again. "Well, I guess we're not going to the park because *you*"—he emphasized—"didn't leave *me* any clothes."

Really? I'd quietly left them out after he'd gone to bed the night before. As calmly as I could, I suggested, "Try the dresser. Try the laundry hamper. And if you still can't find any pants," I tried not to snap, "put her in *shorts*."

After 30 calls and 46 texts from our husbands and from

the "substitute" women like sitters, neighbors, and mothers-in-law who'd been called in to rescue and cover for our husbands, Charlotte was the first to say what we were all thinking: "Maybe we should just skip lunch and go home?" She was immediately joined by Amy, who suggested, "I probably did leave him with too much to do." Lisa shrugged and said, "It'd just be easier if I were there."

And just like that, the same group of women who—30 minutes before—had marched together in the spirit of "courage, strength, and power" disbanded and returned home to relieve babysitters, find the soccer bag, wrap another kid's birthday present, and prepare lunch.

As I drove home that day, I reflected on a line I'd read somewhere—resentment grows out of perceived unfairness. *Darn right, it wasn't fair!* I was so frustrated on behalf of my girlfriends and all mothers who receive texts that require us to rush home or return a call to educate our husbands about basic stuff they should know or be able to figure out about caring for our kids and the home. The biggest problem in our marriages, it seemed, were the small details. As I pulled into our driveway still fuming, something new occurred to me: **Visibility = Value.**

In a bolt-of-lightning moment, I realized: There was another option to shift the imbalance of work in my home that did not involve moving to a foreign country or joining the 50 percent of marriages that end in divorce (which would leave Seth doing more, but I'd be doing no less). Rather, if I wanted to stop scorekeeping with Seth and have him "own" some share of responsibility for all it takes to make our life happen, I had to stop sneaking around in the middle of the night, elfin-like, silently and magically making sh*t happen. If I expected Seth to be an informed partner, well then, I needed to *first* treat him like one by making the full breadth of what I did for our family *visible*. You can't value what you don't see, right? And neither could Seth. And my girlfriends couldn't expect their men to value it either. But . . . if our partners recognized the small and large details that go into keeping the ship afloat, maybe they'd appreciate all that we do. Heck, maybe they'd even volunteer to take a few things off our lists.

SH*T I DO

Like a woman obsessed, this lightning moment led me to embark on a quest to create a system for domestic rebalance. It began with a list called "Sh*t I Do." From grocery lists and Costco runs to replacing lightbulbs and laundry detergent to making sure the bathroom has at least one back-up roll of toilet paper, I began writing down *every single thing* I did day to day with a quantifiable time component. Tallying every time-sucking detail was no small feat. For any woman who's ever considered sitting down to enumerate *every single one* of her domestic responsibilities but hasn't, let me say: *I get it.* I understand why you may not have gotten much past the inspired idea of letting your partner in on all that you do; the very notion of articulating the hundreds of small and large to-dos of any given day requires more thought and time than you have in an already time-constrained life.

So don't think about it. **Because I did it for you.**

More accurately, my friends and I did it for you. After the breast cancer walk, I sent Jill, Amy, Charlotte, and Suzy the following text: > Ladies, remember all the things our husbands needed our help with that day? I'm working on a master list of all the sh*t we do behind the scenes that our partners don't see, or aren't aware of. Can you help me out?

Their responses were immediate and affirming. My phone started buzzing with texts. Within minutes, Charlotte wrote: > Great timing as I sit here planning Jacob's birthday party—create invite list, find class emails, send Evite, book party room, order cake, pizza, balloons, paper goods, buy the favors, thank-you cards, what else am I forgetting???

Amy jumped on the text chain: > What about school "work": volunteering in the classroom and PTA meetings, buying school supplies, creating posters for Student of the Week, managing back-to-school needs like new clothes and backpack, registration forms, requesting immunization records, setting up parent-teacher conferences . . .

Suzy added: > Don't forget school pictures, teacher thank-you gifts, planning for dress-up days, securing childcare on half days, school closures, and spring break and effing summer camp!

Jill said: > Did anyone say "Make the lunches" every single night? And beyond school, what about medical needs? Wellness checks, flu shots, and being the automatic parent who stays home when kids are sick . . .

Charlotte looped back: > And here's another: buying holiday and birthday gifts for the entire extended family.

Amy added: > And sending them on time!

On and on this went. My eyes widened as the list doubled and tripled in length as my friends contributed to the number of childcare and domestic tasks. I remember staring down at the seemingly endless list, taking in the sheer magnitude of the unseen, unacknowledged, unappreciated, and largely unpaid labor that mothers do, all of the things that weigh us down and encumber both our minds and time. I remember hoping that by showing this list to my husband, I was going to change my marriage for the better, because I'd gotten over a major hurdle that prevented nearly all women from getting this far. **I'd begun to create a comprehensive list that makes** the invisible visible . . . and thereby, quantifiable. (More on the evolution of this master list later.)

A NEW SYSTEM

I emailed my working "Sh*t I Do" list to my husband one triumphant afternoon with the enthusiastic subject line: CAN'T WAIT TO DISCUSS!! I'm not sure what I expected. Roses? A celebration? Grateful tears?

Here's what really happened. My husband was pretty blown away when confronted by all that I did for our family. But not quite in the way I'd hoped. His first response wasn't: "Wow. You do so much. How can I help?" Instead, he sent me back an emoji of a monkey covering his eyes.

Like, you know, just *one* monkey. Not even the courtesy of the full trio.

Regardless, I got the message—he didn't want to see, hear, or speak of it. And that's when I realized, beyond making the invisible visible, if I wanted to stop being the she-fault parent who serves as the chief family nag, and if I truly wanted Seth and I to rebalance our domestic workload, then I had to *really* put it all on the table. I needed to provide my husband with more context, in which every task that benefits our home is not only named and counted but also explicitly defined and specifically assigned.

This was going to be harder than just forwarding him a list.

I ruminated and soon thereafter it hit me: Lists alone don't work; systems do. For more than a decade, I'd consulted with hundreds of families in my professional life by providing my expertise in organizational-management strategy. What if I applied these strategies in the domestic sphere by creating a new home system with delineated roles and clear expectations, along with a measurement of accountability? As Peter Drucker, management guru, always said: "What gets measured *gets managed*." Preach! I began channeling Drucker when it occurred to me: By treating the home as our most important organization, wouldn't my household run more smoothly? *Heck, wouldn't this work for every family?*

I began to fantasize about what my life and the lives of all of my friends would look like if—in partnership with our husbands—we brought systematic function to what was currently a sh*tshow of family dysfunction. I couldn't think of a couple out there who wouldn't benefit from a practical plan of action to optimize productivity and efficiency, as well as a new consciousness and language for thinking and talking about domestic life.

A systematic shift is a tall order for any partnership, but given my professional training, I was eager to give it a shot. And guess what? It actually *did* work. Over margaritas at our favorite taqueria one afternoon, I borrowed a page from the playbook of every great CEO who seeks to inspire change within her organization. I outlined for Seth how we were both positioned to win from engaging in a time- and sanity-saving system for domestic life: far fewer explosions and less nagging, resentment, and control. Less doubling up on efforts and things falling through the cracks. More confidence and trust in each other. More levity. And probably more sex, too.

He was in.

GAME THE SYSTEM

Today, years after the "blueberry text" that almost ended my marriage, the "Sh*t I Do" list evolved into Fair Play, a figurative game played with your partner, with four easy-to-follow rules to be applied sequentially, along with 100 playing "task cards" to represent all of the invisible tasks that go into running a home. The objective—rebalance your home life and reclaim your "Unicorn Space" (as in, the space to develop or rediscover the skills and passions that define you beyond your role of partner and parent). Task cards are dealt strategically between the two players in accordance with the couple's shared values. No player holds any cards by default, each person's responsibilities are transparent, expectations are explicitly defined, and both partners are set up to win.

If even a game sounds like *more* work than you have time for, relax—Fair Play is designed to be easy. And fun! Most important, irrespective of whether you implement all or none of what you'll soon read about, Fair Play provides you with **a new way of thinking** about how work can be shared within your family, creating solution-based, sustainable change **that you no longer have to *think* about**.

Seth and I were the first to "play," and believe me, we made plenty of mistakes along the way. But with a more equitable way to divide the childcare and household workload, we've eliminated breathless texts and "What should the kids wear?" phone calls. It's revolutionized our marriage. I'll rewind and tell you all about our journey from start to finish and exactly what the Fair Play system entails, including stories selected from men and women from nearly all walks of life, family configurations, and income and ethnic groups across the country and the world, many of whom have also tested Fair Play. Along with input from clinical psychologists, neuroscientists, behavioral economists, law, clergy, and sociologists immersed in the subject of invisible work, I've put the Fair Play system to the test. Although this book is written from the perspective of majority social identities and where the wife is doing more at home because that's the most common dynamic, my interviews and conversations with working and stay-at-home men and women, co-parents, blended families, and both hetero and same-sex couples have shown that the Fair Play system works well in any unbalanced situation and can be rebalanced one partnership at a time. I've heard feedback like:

> "My wife and I are both super competent at work yet we were a mess at home—now almost nothing falls through the cracks and if it does it's not a volcanic blowup."
>
> —*Mark from Toledo, Ohio*

> "Before the system, it was easier for me when my husband was 'away.' I would rather do it all myself. There were less mistakes and no need to constantly remind him. And less disappointment when he didn't 'help.' Now when he is gone I feel the loss of him as a partner in a way that I never imagined. He's integral to the Fair Play system."
>
> —*Melissa from Phoenix, Arizona*

> "I truly thought we were 50/50 until we played and I understood all my partner does for our family."
>
> —*Ron from Portland, Maine*

> "Finally, I got the kick in the butt I needed to realize my potential beyond being a wife and mom."
>
> —*Maria from Hartford, Connecticut*

"The system is eye-opening and life changing. We are a different couple now. Even my mother doesn't recognize me!"

—*Tom from Portland, Oregon*

○

"Your OBGYN need only recommend two things: folic acid and Fair Play."

—*Jamie from Los Angeles, California*

○

Now, if you're thinking, *I can barely get my husband to reply to my text messages. You want me to get him to discuss every detail of our home life?* To you I say:

Absolutely.

In the pages ahead, I'll provide you with language to thoughtfully invite your partner to the table and begin "playing" for fairness. Until then, rest assured that I've seen the Fair Play system work for couples of all variations—even those teetering on the brink of divorce. Besides, getting your partner on board with the system (not a list) is the only way Fair Play can work. And don't you deserve a partner who values you and the relationship enough to play with you?

FAIR PLAY WILL HELP YOU LOSE

The mountain of inefficiencies at home

Scorekeeping with your partner and engaging in daily tit for tat

Serving as the default—or *she*-fault—parent

Feeling like an unbearable nag

Feeling disappointed and resentful when your partner lets you down

Burning out from doing *it all*

FAIR PLAY WILL HELP YOU WIN

A new vocabulary that will change the way you think and talk about your domestic life

A system that sets you and your partner up for success in your relationship and your parenting

A sense of feeling valued—by yourself and your partner

A sense of feeling empowered and capable—by yourself and your partner

More time for self-care, friendships, and life passions that go beyond parenting and work

Recapturing some of who you were *before* you had kids

More humor and levity

The gift of serving as healthy role models for your children

2.

THE HIDDEN COSTS OF DOING IT ALL

The deck is stacked against us.

CONSIDER:
THE CASE OF THE MAN ON THE PLANE

My cousin Jessica and I were lined up to board a cross-country flight from JFK to LAX. While we'd been waiting at the gate, I'd told her about the "Sh*t I Do" list I was compiling to make visible all of the unseen and unacknowledged work mothers do. I shared with her a recent study about new mothers. "They expect their men to do more, be more 'progressive,'" but it turns out the reality is much different.

"In other words"—Jessica elbowed me—"'Surprise! I don't do diapers.'"

Now, as we boarded the plane, Jessica turned her attention toward her own list. I listened in as she made a hurried call to the babysitter: "I forgot to tell you that Noah has soccer practice today," she said apologetically. "If you can take him there *now*, I'll call his coach and tell him he's on the way." While Jessica worked to put out her fire at home, I was stamping out one of my own. I'd scheduled the installation of DIRECTV six months before, and today was *the* day. I'd totally forgotten. The install guys were waiting at my house and didn't know which roofline to secure the dish to, and in an effort to be there virtually, I was giving instructions via FaceTime.

"I don't care. Put it anywhere. Just please don't leave my house," I pleaded.

"I'm sorry, ma'am," the satellite guy said earnestly, "but since you're not here, we cannot do the install until you enter your password on the company site to confirm your appointment."

Huh? But I didn't argue. Instead, I flagged the nearest flight attendant. "Excuse me, can you help me with the in-flight Wi-Fi?" I whispered with urgency. "I need to get on my computer *right now*."

"You'll have to take your seat first." She smiled thinly.

Jessica pointed to our seats. As quickly as I could, I jammed myself, along with my carry-on, a bag of gifts for the kids from Hudson News, and my grab-n-go chicken Caesar wrap into seat 20C. "Hold on," I said to the satellite guys. "Are you still there?" My phone was flashing a low-battery warning. "Don't hang up," I urged, pressing my face into the small screen. As I pulled out my laptop to retrieve my password, Jessica went pale. "Oh no . . . where's *my* laptop bag?"

A quick survey of the haul between us confirmed that there was one bag missing.

"I must have left it back at the gate." She looked at me in panic.

Without another word, the two of us were up and out of our seats, pushing against the tide of travelers getting onto the plane, both crying out, "Let us off!" Once we squeezed ourselves back up to the front, Jessica made a run for it. I stood guard, as if I alone could stop the plane from leaving without her.

"Where is she *going*?" called out the flight attendant mixing Bloody Marys for first class. "We're closing the doors in five minutes."

"Hurry!" I yelled after Jessica as she hustled down the Jetway. Within minutes she was back at the door, laptop in hand, panting but relieved. As we boarded the plane for the *second* time, we averted the gazes of passengers no doubt thinking, *Ladies—get yourselves together!*

It wasn't even lunchtime back home and already—like many women who have increased their workload by 21 hours per week after becoming parents—we were both spent. Of course, we were accustomed to some version of this mad dash every day.

"I doubt Noah got to practice on time," Jessica groaned as we lifted into the clouds.

"I definitely lost the DIRECTV guys."

As I made a mental note to add "satellite install" onto my growing "Sh*t I Do" list under the category of Electronics and IT and roll it over to another day and time, the man across the aisle from us caught my attention. I nudged Jessica. Outfitted in a crisp, charcoal-colored suit and wearing a wedding band, he appeared to be traveling with nothing more than his laptop. As we sat crowded amid all our stuff, he easily stretched his legs out in front of him, popped in his earbuds, and flipped open his computer. A screensaver of a cute brunette and three kids smiled back at him and with a click they faded away, replaced by a PowerPoint presentation. For the next two hours, this man worked on what looked like a sales pitch. Then he took a nap. After that, he watched a movie. During the last hour of the flight, he appeared to be solving math puzzles on his computer. For fun, I guessed.

Was I snooping on his business? You bet I was. Jessica and I found ourselves endlessly fascinated by our neighbor. His overall vibe was cool, calm, and competent, whereas the scene on our side of the aisle was very definitely uncool. While we continued to reel from our preflight juggle of service guys, babysitters, our kids' sports schedules—and now, beginning new to-do lists for our arrival back home—this man's mental load appeared comparatively light. Relatively *unencumbered*. He looked almost refreshed, displaying none of the outward signs of decision fatigue many women get while planning five steps, five hours, and five days ahead. Rather, he seemed to be in the moment. Singularly focused. PowerPoint. Nap. Movie. Math puzzles.

As we began our descent, Jessica leaned into me and whispered, "I want to be that man." So did I. And I couldn't think of any working woman/mother/list-maker/planner who wouldn't want to be him either. From where we sat, this man appeared to be enjoying a luxury all of the women we know couldn't imagine: **the freedom to focus on one task at a time.**

"What do you think?" I quietly asked Jessica. "While he amuses himself by solving math problems, what do you think his wife is doing right now?"

"She's solving *every other problem*," Jessica offered.

We laughed because it really was funny, and yet Jessica had just hit on something profound: The man across the aisle from us could be singularly on task because his wife was likely using all of her brainpower to multitask. If she was anything like the rest of us, she was doing all the invisible, in-tangible "off-screen" work required to care for children and run a household, so that he could stretch out his legs. *What a gal!*

This got me thinking. What is the value of an unencumbered mind? A Woolfian *mental* room of one's own? A "she-shed" to unpack all the lists and reclaim what contemporary novelist Claudia Dey poetically calls our "autonomy of mind"? Mental freedom, in the form of more room, more space, and the time to have singular focus should not be reserved for working men/fathers/husbands. The "dad privilege," as I've heard it described in threads online. *Why,* I wondered, *don't women enjoy a similar advantage?* Instead, we continue to take the metaphoric middle seat with a kid on either side, both demanding snacks and a new movie while we hold our bladders until the "fasten seat belts" light goes off—mentally calculating, *In the ten minutes I have before I can get up, what more can I get done?*

THE COSTS TO *YOU*

I thought a lot about that man on the plane in the weeks that followed, and the toll that an encumbered mind was taking on me. It was impacting every aspect of my life, and I wanted to take the discussion wider, beyond my own family and friends. I went into full "quest" mode, asking women everywhere—in airports and coffee shops, in grocery check-out lines, on the playground and Little League fields—to consider the costs of this mental load in several different aspects of their lives. For starters:

Consider the cost to your partnership or marriage, in the form of exhaustion, resentment, and resignation to feeling alone and isolated in your relationship. I posted the following question on social media: *When I think about who does the majority of household work and childcare in my household, I feel_____.*

Out of a pool of 150 women that I sourced from active mommy groups, a version of the following three responses rose to the top:

> "I feel like running away to escape the exhaustion."

> "I feel pissed off at my husband."

> "I feel that this will always be my role."

I found similar sentiments echoed in Twitter feeds, Facebook chats, and social media memes. The groundswell of "The Invisible Workload Is Killing Me *and* My Marriage" messaging was bubbling up in conversations and publications everywhere. In *Glamour*'s revealing series on modern divorce, writer Lyz Lenz shares, "I stopped cooking because I wanted to feel as unencumbered as a man walking through the door of his home with the expectation that something (everything) had been done for him. I wanted to be free of cutting coupons and rolling dough and worrying about dinner times and feeding. I wanted to rest. To be just like him and sit with the kids and play."

When you multiply this feeling of being overwhelmed, resentment, and resignation over and over and over again, it's no shock that a recent study found women who were tasked with more invisible household work than their husbands were more likely to be dissatisfied in their marriages.

Consider the cost to your identity, in the form of a lost sense of your pre-parent self, and a feeling of disconnection from the passions and purpose that make you uniquely *you*. When getting the baby out of the car seat and safely into the stroller, applying sunscreen to sensitive cheeks, placing a lovey and sippy cup onto baby's lap and speaking in your most soothing mama bear voice to suppress a came-out-of-nowhere deafening meltdown—all so that you can walk from the parking lot and into the pharmacy for a fresh tube of nipple cream in the same quasi-pajama pants you wore yesterday (and maybe the day before)—feels like the biggest accomplishment in the world, do you ever think, *Who have I become?* You're not alone.

"It's really a dance where you lean in to take care of your baby, but you have to lean out to take care of yourself," says reproductive psychiatrist Alexandra Sacks. "Because you're still a human being, and you still have to care for your own body, your own emotions, your relationship with your partner, with your friends, your intellectual life, your spiritual life, your hobbies . . . all these other aspects of your identity and your basic needs. Even if you want to just give unconditionally to your child, you can't, because we're humans. We're not robots."

Consider the cost to your career, in the form of the pay gap between *mothers and non-mothers*, which—GET THIS—is wider than the pay gap between men and women. "Whether women work at Walmart or on Wall Street, getting pregnant is often the moment [women] are knocked off the professional ladder," asserted a recent *New York Times* investigative piece. Did you know that you took an economic risk becoming a mother? That's because in our culture, "mom" has been deemed the she-fault, de facto household manager and caretaker. If the school calls, Mom picks up. If a child is sick, Mom stays home. If the dry cleaning/rent check/prescription order needs to be dropped off, Mom gets to work late, even though her workday already began many hours earlier in order to get her children out of bed, fed, dressed, and dropped at daycare.

Then, once at work, up pops an email forwarded from your husband that makes your stomach turn:

Subject: Inspection Reminder for plate number GEG8612

With a hurried note:

This appointment is today. Can't get away from the office. Can you handle?

You take a deep breath and think, *Sure, honey, I'll leave work early AGAIN and spend my afternoon waiting in line at the DMV.*

Imagine if you could forward just a handful of the household and child-related emails you receive to your spouse or partner to "handle"? How much mental relief would that provide to you? When our husbands press forward because they know we will take care of it, they get to stay committed at work and receive the rewards of higher pay for their disproportionate willingness to work longer and less flexible hours. Hop on a plane to Las Vegas for a conference in the middle of the week? No problem for many husbands/fathers. Meanwhile, we fight to stay valuable at the office and also be on call for any daily disruption or domestic interruption at home. I call that double-committed. Well, certainly, overcommitted.

When you consider the "mommy tax" that decreases a mother's earning power by 5 to 10 percent for every child she brings into the world due to missed opportunities for promotions, prestigious assignments, pay increases, and bonuses, then you understand the true price of motherhood. "For most companies, the ideal worker is 'unencumbered,' that is, free of all ties other than those to his job. Anyone who can't devote all his or her energies to paid work is barred from the best jobs and has a permanently lower lifetime income," writes author Ann Crittenden. "Not coincidentally, almost all the people in that category happen to be mothers."

"They don't work as hard," is how a Plano, Texas, doctor explained it in the *Dallas Medical Journal* as to why female doctors' salaries amounted to about two-thirds of their male counterparts'. "Most of the time their priority is something else. . . . Family, social, whatever."

Don't you love that? Clearly he's never done the "whatever."

> We expect women to work like they don't have children and raise children as if they don't work.
>
> — Amy Westervelt

Consider the cost to your wellness, in the form of exhaustion, stress, and compromised mental bandwidth. In a survey done by *Today* that interviewed more than 7,000 moms across the country, most rated their stress levels at an 8.5 out of 10, mirroring a recent report by the scientific journal *Brain and Behavior* showing women are twice as likely to be affected by anxiety disorders as men. In the UK, a joint study by the Universities of Manchester and Essex found that working mothers of two children had stress levels that were 40% higher than working mothers with no children. As I expanded my focus group, I began conducting more rigorous research to explore this "stress gap." Because I'm not a mental health professional or an academic, I sought out expert voices on the subject. Number one on my list was Darby Saxbe, a psychology professor at the University of Southern

California and researcher on the gendered division of labor. Saxbe also lives in Los Angeles, so we agreed to meet at Din Tai Fung to share soup dumplings and swap insights on the health and wellness industry.

Before Saxbe took her first bite, she said, "I'll let you in on a secret. The wellness industry is certainly hip to imbalanced gender roles. How many beauty messages have you received in the last month via email or social media that offer a cosmetic remedy for battling fatigue or overworked and tired skin?" she asked me.

I took a sip of my tea and guessed, "Twenty?"

"At least, right? Women need to ask themselves—what's more transformative to my life? A new serum for dark circles or a more fair and balanced division of labor in my home?"

This got us laughing over a new revolutionary skin care campaign: Hydration or a more helpful husband?

"The latter is a better bet for tackling tired skin." Saxbe smiled. "But joking aside, women are suffering."

I interjected, "Did you see that recent survey by *Healthy Women* and *Working Mother*? Seventy-eight percent of moms say they are so busy maintaining family stability by being constantly available, mentally and physically, to deal with every detail of home life that they aren't taking care of themselves."

"And because so many of us have less unwinding and restorative time," said Saxbe, "we're generating more of the stress hormone cortisol. This is toxic to women's health."

Consider the cost to our society, robbed of valuable productivity and top female leadership and talent as 43 percent of highly qualified women with children take a career detour. This includes college-educated women who invested in an education and who presumably never planned to exit the workforce . . . but many do so anyway, feeling that they grossly underestimated the demands and difficulty of combining work and parenting. "I went from running a company to banging a spoon on my head to keep my baby occupied and entertained," sighed Elaine, who holds three degrees from Ivy League schools.

Today, women earn the majority of undergraduate and graduate degrees and are now breadwinners in four out of ten families—and still a meaningful number of women (like me) significantly scale back or "opt out" of the workforce. A good number of them never return to work outside the home after having children, and those who do, research shows, often return to lower-paying jobs with lower earnings trajectories.

Do you, too, feel that you cannot be as "ambitious" as your male counterparts because you're at mental overload, caring for children and running a household while also working on starting, building, or establishing your career? Then you can get a sense of how many more women in their homes and communities across the country are saying: *How can any of us possibly lean in if we can't rely on consistent contributions from our partners?*

"It's not actually motherhood or kids that derail women's careers and personal ambitions—it's men who refuse to do their fair share," writes author and columnist Jessica Valenti. "If fathers did the same kind of work at home that mothers have always done, women's careers could flourish in ways we haven't yet imagined." My friend Jenny Galluzzo, cofounder of Second Shift, a company that helps women remain engaged and succeed in the workplace, breaks it down like this: "AMBITION gap, my ass. What we're dealing with is an exhaustion gap!"

A THREE-PLAYER GAME?

"I'd rather my wife blame the state than blame me," is what one man I interviewed said.

Hey, I get it.

Hopefully one day, Fair Play will be a three-player game that includes meaningful state and federal policies. And please do speak to your employers and policy makers about hastening this reality. If you're interested in reading about which policies would be most effective, check out the *Fair Play* bibliography for suggested reading. In the meantime, *Fair Play* is a two-player game that requires change to happen *within your own home*. And here's the encouraging news—"individual change, in turn, creates demand for more social, political, and economic change," says Michael Kaufman, author of *The Time Has Come: Why Men Must Join the Gender Equality Revolution.* In other words: It's not an either-or—you can address policy while also taking agency in your own life. In truth, most national governments could do more to help women pick up their careers after having children.

OLD STORY. NEW SOLUTION.

Decline in marital happiness. Power imbalance at home. Loss of identity. Physical and mental health issues. Decades of underutilized education. Fewer women in leadership and executive-level jobs. The costs of a constantly encumbered mind have women hitting the resentment ceiling.

Is this breaking news? Of course not. Women have been grappling with the gendered division of labor since, *you know*, the turn of the last century. This discontent took a turn during the second Industrial Revolution, when many hoped that women's work outside the home would bring about change in the division of labor inside the home.

No such revolution happened.

In fact, according to a recent United Nations report, the modern woman still does nearly three times as much unpaid domestic work as a man. Sure, men are taking on more responsibility than they traditionally have in the past, but even the most well-intentioned men are still not doing their fair share at home.

"This is an injustice on a grand scale, for housework is everything," wrote Megan K. Stack in a powerful *New Yorker* piece. "It's a ubiquitous physical demand that has hamstrung and silenced women for most of human history. I'd love to believe that the struggle for women's equality is concentrated in offices and manufacturing plants, but I've become convinced that this battle takes place, first and most crushingly, at home."

In other words, the unpaid job of scrubbing the toilet still falls on us. It's women's work. This model begins in childhood, when girls begin shouldering 50 percent more of the household work than boys. These "gendered messages are seeping into our tender little psyches" from a very young age, writes Sara Petersen about the early messaging in many children's books that show "anthropomorphized animal mamas wearing cozy aprons and patient smiles" that set girls up to be babysitters and household helpers, and who later become women who assume the majority of the cooking, cleaning, and childcare in their adult homes. And this "women's work" that we do to enhance our family's quality of life and for which we are not directly remunerated—even if others are paid, and often underpaid, for performing these tasks in more formalized work settings—has been assigned a lower value than traditionally male, societal-facing occupations.

POP QUIZ
Who Said It When?

Guess what year these statements were made by working men/husbands? Choose between 1969 in Pat Mainardi's famous piece "The Politics of Housework" or in my 2018 interviews.

A. "I don't mind sharing the housework, but I don't do it very well. We should each do the things we're best at."

B. "You are so much better at the 'home stuff' than me."

C. "We have different standards. Why should I have to work to your standards? That's unfair."

D. "She is in charge of the house; it's not my job."

E. "What great man would have accomplished what he did if he had to do his own housework?"

F. "I make a living. I make her life. Why do I have to do dishes, too?"

(A) 1969; (B) 2018; (C) 1969; (D) 2018; (E) 1969; (F) 2018

MAKE IT COUNT

If you're not getting paid for it, it doesn't count. Walking the family dog and driving the afternoon carpool for school pickups don't hold equal value to, say, your husband's paid working lunch with colleagues.

Do you believe that? I don't either.

Back to the "Sh*t I Do" list.

Like I'd done, I encouraged my friends to enumerate all the unpaid work that jams their brains and zaps their mental bandwidth. I added their data to my growing "Sh*t I Do" list and then made a daring suggestion: Let's send this sucker to everyone we know. What better way to amplify the message to all the other moms out there? We invited our childhood and high school friends, along with distant cousins, college roommates, and colleagues past and present to add to the list and also share it within their own networks.

Within days, countless copies of the "Sh*t I Do" list were circulating online between women/wives/mothers far and wide. Women whom I'd never met began emailing: "Can I have the list for my moms' group, my book club, my church group, the PTA?" The sheer enormity of all that women were doing, and not often recognized for, was resonating deeply. Before long, a community of women, nationally and internationally, were sharing their lists with me and adding to my data pool. I started receiving messages like: "Add holiday cards and Girl Scout cookie sales." "Don't forget Elf on the Shelf!" "Also, allowance!"

It became clear to me how powerful it was for women to not only make the invisible visible and commodify tasks, but to also count and specifically assign to a category all that they were doing with their unpaid "off" time. As the data became more and more granular and refined, I began to organize childcare and household tasks by grouping them together. For example, the tasks of getting the car washed and renewing car registration both fell under the category of "auto," while the separate tasks of applying sunscreen and the annual wellness checkup both fell within the category of "medical and healthy living."

While itemized to-do lists had been circulated by mommy bloggers before, what we were creating was all-encompassing: a comprehensive list crowdsourced and organized with the principles of professional management in mind. As the original "Sh*t I Do" list became too long and detailed to manage, I enlisted my friend Elana, a type-A taskmaster, to help me transfer all the data into an Excel spreadsheet where I could more easily group tasks together and also break them down into their subtasks. For example, "pet care." Consider the totality of work for the person in charge of the family friend:

- Researching the type/breed (or finding rescue/shelter/adoption organization)
- Choosing a pet
- Animal-proofing the home
- Finding a good vet
- Scheduling and attending vet appointments— necessary shots, spayed/neutered, etc.
- Buying proper food, treats, toys, grooming items, bedding, crate or cage, collar, leash, harness, etc.
- Feeding (multiple times per day)
- Training (bathroom, sleeping, barking, and biting)
- Scheduling playtime
- (If dog) Walking twice a day and/or scheduling a walker

- Grooming pets or finding a groomer and scheduling and attending appointments
- Scheduling pet care during travel
- Poop considerations (kitty litter, birdcage, etc.)
- Cleaning up accidents, sickness, fur, mess, etc.

And depending on your unique pet, there's likely *more*!

Once women recognized that for every one task on their to-do lists, they were actually performing an additional laundry list of subtasks, all hell broke loose. Like a splinter in your foot that's nagging you all day, the ever-expanding "Sh*t I Do" list became an all-consuming trigger point. The phone calls, texts, and emails took a turn toward outrage. > **WTF! I had no idea how much I was really doing until I saw it all listed!** my friend Annie texted me. > **No wonder I'm a FREAK show!** Another mom friend called me crying on the way to work. "I'm literally doing it all. At this rate, I don't think I can stay in this marriage."

I started to feel guilty about the major stink my sh*t list had unleashed. I'd created a rant without a solution. Complaining to your girlfriends can feel satisfying in the moment, and yet the bitch buzz wears off quickly once the bottle of rosé is empty and you have to return home to fold laundry (assuming someone has remembered to put it in the dryer as you asked).

ALL TASK CARDS ON THE TABLE

"I started cc'ing my husband's work email account every time I sent a note to the school, the coach, the pediatrician, family dentist, housecleaner, vet . . . so that he could see all that I'm handling when he's singularly focused at the office," reported Leanne from Michigan.

"And what happened?" I asked.

"He told me to stop jamming his inbox."

As was my experience with Seth, many women reported that when they'd introduced their husbands to "the list," the men refused to engage (surprise, surprise).

"Mine wanted nothing to do with it," my friend Clara reported, "so I transferred the list of everything I do onto separate index cards that he could flip through . . . at his leisure," she quipped.

Hmmmm. I liked the idea of cards. I'd been using them as a mediation tool in my advisory practice for years. Perhaps putting every domestic task on a card, something you could literally hold, was a good way to gamify the list and introduce our partners to a new way of talking about what jobs, responsibilities, and traditions often go unseen or unacknowledged yet nevertheless hold value in our homes. *It was worth a try.*

I looped back to my friends who'd originally helped me compile the list. I asked them to transfer their childcare and household tasks onto cards. Well, a funny thing happened. While holding physical cards did help to physicalize the list, this exercise actually created more resentment because my friends quickly recognized that they were holding *all*, or nearly all, the "task" cards for their families. In my own marriage, I quickly tallied how many Seth freely held without me nagging or ordering him around—three: "money manager," "auto," and "fun! and playing," while I was juggling a full 80 or more on an average day. Not exactly what I'd call *fair*. My friends calling me with fresh complaints matched my own frustration: "He's not holding his fair share!" "I put them all on the table, but he won't pick any up!"

At a school fundraiser, my friend Gillian's husband approached me out of earshot of his wife. "So tell me, Eve," he said with an edge of exasperation, "how many 'cards' do I have to take to *not* be a douchebag?"

I took a sip of my drink and suggested with a smile, "More than zero."

A day after this exchange, Seth and I had our weekly "date" at our couple's therapy office.

"What do you want to work on today?" Derek, our therapist, asked.

Oh, look at that. I just happened to have my set of task cards in my purse. Without a word, I pulled them out and threw them at Seth. "What's all this?" Seth raised an eyebrow.

"It's all the sh*t I do," I said coolly. "And it's your turn to take your share."

As he flipped over some of the cards that had landed in his lap, I read them out loud: "End-of-school teacher gifts, weekend meals, homework . . ."

"Slow down, Eve," Derek calmly advised. But I was so desperate to hand over a portion of all the work I was doing that I couldn't slow down. Instead, I picked a card up off the floor and thrust it at Seth. "Thank-you notes—take it!"

"I'm not taking that." Seth sat back in his chair, his body language clearly communicating, *Back off, crazy woman!*

This is when I realized that, just like my first list, the cards weren't helping to alleviate my resentment and, even more disadvantageous, this competitive versus collaborative approach wasn't relieving our workload. *Not really.*

My friend Gillian pulled me aside at school later that week to happily report that she'd made "some progress" when she presented her husband with the cards. "He said, 'I won't take a task, but I'll take a card,' so I suggested he take 'weekend meals.' And"—she paused for effect—"he took it."

"That's great," I said. "Do you think he'll take the same card again next week?"

Her upbeat composure fell. "Probably not." She perked slightly. "Maybe if I remind him?"

Though some men, like Gillian's husband, were taking cards, they weren't holding on to them. Not without reminders. And an "attaboy" for a job completed. *Ahem.* A reminder, in itself, takes tremendous mental effort *by you.* It requires knowing what needs to be done, remembering what needs to be done, and reminding someone to get it done, whereas the person being reminded gets off easy. He doesn't have to remember a thing, nor does he worry about forgetting. And if you think about it, reminding and praising is the daily work of parenting *children*, not *partnering with husbands.*

Over lunch with my friend Lily, I recalled the countless times I'd expected Seth to pick up dirty clothes, shoes, and Legos off the floor, and felt disappointed when he hadn't. His three most-common responses: "You didn't remind me," "It's just not something I think about," and "Why didn't you just ask?"

"Clothes on the floor—I've got that beat," she countered. "Last week when I was on a business trip, my seven-year-old called me, sobbing into the phone: 'Mommy, the tooth fairy didn't come last night!' I thought: Uh oh, the tooth fairy was a no-show? When Jeff got on the line, he blamed *me*: 'How was I supposed to know to leave a buck under the pillow? You should have reminded me!' I thought: Really? This is on *me*? To remind *you* to notice that her tooth fell out? From the windowless conference room in the hotel in *Hong Kong*?!! I tell you," Lily grumbled, "parenting your husband is not sexy."

"Nor is the need to constantly praise," grumbled Carmen, who refers to her ex-husband as a "Facebook Dad." This is when a husband/father only shares in the workload at home when his efforts can be shared and memorialized on social media. "He only helped out for the 'likes,'" complained Carmen. "All of his 'friends' thought he was such a great dad because he'd post pictures of himself at dance recitals, T-ball games, and back-to-school shopping for the kids. The captions were always some version of: 'Look what I did!' Sometimes he'd even include an award emoji. What I wanted to say was: *People, he staged those scenes.* Off screen, I was the one reminding him to take the kids back-to-school shopping and then running back to the mall in the eleventh hour because he hadn't gotten anything on the list—because they'd gone to the movies instead! The public perception of what my husband was doing versus the reality was very different."

CONSISTENT OWNERSHIP

Having to remind your partner to do something doesn't take that something off your list. It adds to it. And what's more, reminding is often unfairly characterized as nagging. (Almost every man interviewed in connection with this project said nagging is what they hate most about being married, but they also admit that they wait for their wives to tell them what to do at home.) It's not a partnership if only one of you is running the show, which means making the important distinction between delegating tasks and handing off ownership of a task. Ownership belongs to the person who *first off* remembers to plan, then plans, and then follows through on every aspect of executing the plan and completing the task without reminders.

A survey conducted by Bright Horizons—an on-site corporate childcare provider—found that 86 percent of working mothers say they handle the majority of family and household responsibilities, "not just making appointments, but also driving to them and *mentally* calendaring who needs to be where, and when." In order to save us from big-time burnout, we need our partners to be more than helpers who carry out instructions that we've taken time and energy to think through (and then who blame us when things fall through the cracks). We need our partners to take the lead by consistently picking up a task, or "card"—week after week—and *completely* taking it off our mental to-do list *by doing every aspect* of what the card requires. Otherwise we still worry about whether the task is being done as we would do it, or done fully, or done at all—which leaves us still shouldering the mental and emotional load for the "help" or the "favor" we had to ask for.

But how do we get our partners to take that initiative and own every aspect of a household or childcare responsibility without being (nudge, nudge) told what to do? Or, to simply figure it out? That's what *I* needed to figure out.

And so I called a time-out! I told my inner circle of early adopters—DO NOT hand out any more cards, tally, trade, or try to negotiate cards. I realized that I owed each of them a set of rules that set up each player for clear, measurable, and consistent success. Absent a user's manual, so to speak, that was thoughtfully inviting to our partners rather than alienating them, the cards would only serve to create more separation and dysfunction in our marriages. If I wanted to change my own marriage for the better and help others similarly change theirs, I needed to literally change the game. But before I could do that, I had to create one.

THE FOUR RULES FOR FAIR PLAY

Something was starting to crystalize for me about the Fair Play system: If we want our partners to feel empowered and capable of succeeding, rather than clueless or helpless until directed, we have to ditch the maternal gatekeeping control (e.g., *It's my way or move out!*) and create *way* more context (e.g., *Here's how it's done from start to finish—and why we've agreed to do it this way*). Couples who adopt the Fair Play system know exactly what task cards are in play within their homes, along with explicitly defined and mutually agreed-upon expectations for each card and clear, delineated roles and responsibilities that help rebalance the domestic workload with fairness. Imagine your home life with such efficiency. It's no longer a sh*tshow!

In the weeks and months that followed, even as I pledged to stop demanding things willy-nilly and on the fly, and even as Seth vowed to step forward and take ownership of more of the day-to-day work it takes to keep our household humming along, we continued to fall into our favorite traps:

Eve: You forgot!
Seth: You didn't remind me!
Eve: You did it wrong!
Seth: Then you do it!

But I used these pitfalls to help me refine the Four Rules for Fair Play—each representing a big lesson we had to learn (sometimes painfully) together. I'll discuss each of the four rules in turn in Part II of this book. Read and absorb all four rules first—then you'll have the context you need to start putting the Fair Play system into action in your own family. Buckle up and get ready for a change—for the better—in the way your family does, well, everything.

THE
SOLUTION

The Four Rules
for Fair Play

3.

RULE #1: ALL TIME IS CREATED EQUAL

Let's call a spade a spade.

CONSIDER:
THE CASE OF THE DRUNK GUY'S JACKET

As I began working to create a system, or a game, if you will, to more fairly distribute the stack of household responsibilities between couples, I was again on the way to the airport for a one-day work trip to Seattle. I was just about to pull up to the curb at Departures when I got the following text from Seth: > Some guy left his jacket and beer bottle on our lawn.

Weird. Gross. And, more important, what am *I* supposed to do about it from the road?

When I returned home 16 hours later and long after the sun had gone down, I'd forgotten about the text until I pulled into my driveway, and there they were, sitting in the dark—

some guy's jacket and beer bottle on our lawn. Seriously? I began to seethe. As I unlocked the front door, I quickly tried to work out why.

I was reminded of the many girlfriends who had described "the text" and its spiritual cousin, "the email forward," as trigger issues in their marriages—an email comes through to both you and your partner from your child's school, coach, music teacher, doctor's office, or the DMV and your partner forwards it to you. The implicit question: *Can you handle this?*

Lugging my carry-on upstairs, I found my husband stretched out comfortably on our bed, cell phone in hand. While I'd spent the day working in another city, my husband also worked at his own job, but then had another four hours after the kids went down, during which he'd worked out, watched *SportsCenter*, and checked Instagram. Plenty of time to decompress from his long day, and yet, somehow, not long enough to clean up the drunk guy's stuff he'd discovered on our front lawn a full *16 hours* earlier. His morning text wasn't a "Can you believe this?" text but the implication: *I don't have time. This is on you.*

That night, standing in the doorway to our bedroom, I understood that my husband expected me to put down my carry-on, grab a trash bag and a pair of rubber gloves, walk outside, pick up the wet jacket and beer bottle, throw them into the bag, walk the whole thing to the bin in the alley, and return home. When I did just that, I made note of how long it took me to do this: 12 minutes. That was 12 minutes of my time. That I'll never get back. I briefly considered these 12 minutes multiplied by thousands of "this is on you's" required to get through each of my days, and began to understand even more acutely why women like me and you are running against the clock from the moment we wake up.

What might not be so clear, because it wasn't to me that night, is: Why *was* this on me?

Was it because we hadn't yet defined clear roles? And absent specific assignments, the job of handling "weird/gross stuff" defaulted to me? Admittedly, we were still working out the kinks in the Fair Play system and I was still holding the majority of the cards (since hastily throwing the full stack at him, I thought it was probably a good call to *pause* before offering to hand over more). But still—why did he just leave it there? All day? Did we simply have different expectations of curb appeal? Or conflicting definitions of lawn art versus garbage?

The answer came to me 12 minutes later, when I returned to our bedroom still wearing rubber gloves as Seth reclined on our bed. Not only did he regard the cleanup as a poor use of his time, but in leaving it for me to do after a workday that happened to be even longer than his, my husband was clearly communicating that it was a good use of *my* time. To boil it down: **Seth was not valuing my time equally to his.**

This, to me, was a staggering aha. If Seth regarded the 12 minutes it would have taken him to clean up our front lawn as more valuable than the same 12 minutes it took me, how could I ever expect him to take on more of the domestic workload? And it turns out my husband is not alone in this thinking. In my interviews and conversations with more than 500 people in connection with this project, both men *and* women overwhelmingly expressed a related idea that contributes to the same outcome: the notion that men's time is finite and women's time is infinite. And in their finite time, men don't want to bother with retrieving a drunk guy's jacket and beer bottle from the front lawn.

This time discrepancy where men's time is guarded as a finite resource (like diamonds) and women's time is abundant (like sand) is at its worst after kids. According to one study, after bringing home baby, men increased their total workload by about 40 minutes a day, whereas women pick up more than 2 hours of additional childcare work per day (on top of their regular housework *and* paid work). These hours add up to an additional 2.6 weeks of 24-hour days over the course of a year. Hours, days, and weeks of time performing tasks that often go unseen and unappreciated by your partner yet contribute to your family's well-being. How could you otherwise spend that time to benefit *you*—enhancing your career or pursuing your creative passions? Or, heck, setting aside your to-do list for a quiet hour on the beach?

IT'S ABOUT TIME FOR CHANGE

Demanding time equality is a message the women's movement missed, and it's about *time*, pardon the pun, we have recognition that **all time is created equal.** While we freely make the point that our time is still not measured equally in the workplace (women earn 80.5 cents to every man's dollar – in the UK they earn 81.6p to the man's pound – and are also expected to order the boss's birthday cake), women speak out less readily about how our time isn't fairly measured at home. This "time tax," where women are burdened with more than our fair share of childcare and domestic work, compromises every aspect of our lives—our relationships, career, sense of identity, and physical and mental health. Our perception of men's time as finite versus women's time as infinite, or weighted differently in any way, must change if we ever want to achieve true liberation. Ahem, getting off soapbox now.

Embracing **Rule #1: All Time Is Created Equal** is required for you and your partner to benefit from the true life and relationship-changing experience of Fair Play. It asks you both to reframe how you value time and then commit to the goal of rebalancing the hours that domestic work requires between two partners.

Before you ask your partner to reimagine the value of time, take a moment to fully buy into it yourself. To do this, answer the following question:

Are the two hours my husband spends on a work conference call more valuable than the two hours I spend holding my child's hand at the doctor? In other words, is time-consuming support given to my family's to-do list off-screen *equal to the time-consuming activity of paid work* on-screen*?*

What's your answer? And how would your partner respond?

The reality is that the heavy lifting in the home will continue to fall on you, the she-fault partner/parent, until you both recognize that time is a limited commodity. It is a finite resource. You are both diamonds. You both only have 24 hours in a day. **Only when you believe that your time should be measured equally will the division of labor shift toward parity in your relationship.**

AN ATTITUDE ADJUSTMENT

Though we can't change time, we can shift attitudes. Sure, this takes true and deliberate effort, but it *is* possible. My smart mother, a professor of social work, says to her students: Changing attitudes starts with the act of becoming conscious—developing awareness of *how you think*. What I discovered in my conversations with couples is that once both individuals, and especially men, were asked to consider domestic tasks specifically in terms of the fairness of time, and isolated out their preference for or distaste of the task itself, their attitude shifted in a big way. They took more cards, and willingly.

Once men recognized the amount of time it takes to, say, make a lunch (ten minutes), administer sunscreen to a crying toddler (three minutes), unload the dishwasher (nine minutes), plus bigger time sucks like being on call for night waking and soothing bad dreams (one to three hours) and filling out school applications (up to three days), they understood how their reluctance to spend their time performing these tasks led to an inevitable imbalance of time within the relationship.

The bottom line is simple: Every domestic task takes time, and the minutes quickly add up. When your partner recognizes that your time is important and that there is value to him or her in relieving you from some of the time burden (less nagging, disappointment, and resentment), he or she is much more likely to share the workload. That's fairness.

CAUTION!
Prepare for Pushback!

Rule #1: All Time Is Created Equal requires an attitude shift (and sometimes a *big* one) by both players. Prepare for pushback when you challenge your partner to reframe the value of time. Prompted by the drunk guy's jacket, I began collecting data from couples over the phone, via social media, and in person everywhere I went on the subject of the gendered division of *time*. In my interviews, I started to track the prevalence of Toxic Time messages.

?

POP QUIZ
It's About Time

How many of these messages have you heard (or said to yourself)?

- My paid hours are worth more than your unpaid hours.
- It's not worth it for you to work.
- What did you do all day?
- Why are you wasting your time doing that?
- You're so lucky you don't have to "go" to work.
- If you don't have enough time, get help!
- I don't have time . . . so can you?
- I'm a better multitasker, so I'll just do it.
- My partner travels/goes to work early, so it's on me.
- In the time it takes me to tell my partner what to do, I might as well do it myself.
- Yes, more time for myself would be great, but I should really clean out the freezer.

If you've checked at least one of these, your time has been compromised. We each must push back on these messages in order to reclaim our time.

TOXIC TIME MESSAGES

>> Toxic Time Message #1: "Time is money."

Male primary breadwinners often explain: "My time is more valuable because I get paid more." This is the "my paid hours are worth more than your unpaid, or lesser-paid, hours" argument. Even men who aren't the primary earners in the household will affirm that time spent generating a paycheck is the most valuable use of their time. In other words, when I'm off the clock, it's not worth my time.

Seth used to refer to his time in the office as his "power hours," inferring that this time shouldn't be interrupted or compromised by unpaid work—even when it was in service to our home and family, like leaving the office early to take our sons to the dentist. For many years, I didn't push back on this messaging because I bought into it, too. I now recognize it for what it is—the "power hours" argument is just a power trip. Seth has since seen the light and no longer uses his paycheck as leverage, or as an excuse to do less at home. One reason why we're still married, and happily.

TIME REFRAME: Time is counted in minutes, not dollars.

>> Toxic Time Message #2: "You don't work. You have more time."

One man I met with told me, "I show up each day to the office with my hard hat and lunch pail, and what does *she* do all day?" *Pardon?* She does all the daily grind work you aren't doing to keep your household and family afloat, in addition to unscheduled tasks (see annoying DMV email) that allow you to stay at work and eat from your lunch pail, rather than inhaling a protein bar in the DMV line.

Even the most resourceful, productive, high-energy stay-at-home moms (SAHMs) I spoke with report feeling underwater every day. Despite devoting all of their extended waking hours to managing the home and caring for their kids, they admit that they still cannot get it all done. And on top of this, they apologize and tend to accept blame for coming up short.

These women confuse their "time tax" with personal failure. Honey, this is not a "you" problem.

Rather, it's a simple arithmetic problem—there are only so many hours in the day, and when you are married or in a partnership, no *one* person should be expected to do it all, or even come close, regardless of whether both people work outside the home. Holding all the cards required to run a household equates to more than a full-time job. As one woman posted on Facebook: "I don't have a 9-to-5 job; mine is more like a 'when I open my eyes to when I close them' job." And within that grinding schedule, forget about squeezing in time for self-care—a doctor's appointment or a haircut for yourself. Despite what their husbands may say, nearly all SAHMs I spoke to reported that they simply don't have the time for these personal-time luxuries: *Thanks for the reminder to schedule some self-care. I'll be sure to add that to the long list of other sh*t I don't have time to get done.* Now compare the traditional household and full-time parenting job to many paid office jobs (I'm talking to you, hard-hat guy) that have built-in personal time, like lunch breaks, in-office mingling, off-site networking, and not to mention paid sick leave and vacation time. Most SAHMs don't enjoy these perks, unless you count negotiating your cell phone contract with an after-hours help line as your social hour.

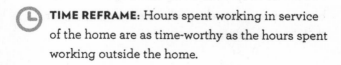 **TIME REFRAME:** Hours spent working in service of the home are as time-worthy as the hours spent working outside the home.

>> Toxic Time Message #3: "If you don't have enough time, outsource or get more help."

Receiving outside support is useful and can be a lifesaver, for sure, and if you're lucky enough to be able to afford an extra hand now and then to babysit or walk the dog, it can help. But what most people forget is the *full amount of time* it requires to find, enlist, schedule, delegate responsibilities, and often train and most certainly pay a babysitter, math tutor, housecleaner, and dog walker, etc. In my interviews, I **found no correlation between soliciting help and less resentment between couples** because hiring someone to help you still takes work. And even asking friends, neighbors, or your mother-in-law to step in and watch the kids and tidy up around the house requires *mental effort* and *real time*. Most mothers know full well that finding and locking down a reliable babysitter, for example, can cost double that amount of *your* time to schedule, plan for, and pull off. A night out without the kids may still be worth it (free tickets to Beyoncé come around only every decade or so, if *ever*), but don't mistake "getting help" with completely crossing a task off your to-do list. And when your "helper" cancels at the last minute or quits, the full task goes right back on you.

> **TIME REFRAME:** Hours spent researching, planning, scheduling, managing, maintaining communication and relationships, and finally handing off responsibilities to someone else and sometimes paying for "help" takes real time.

RULE #1: ALL TIME IS CREATED EQUAL

>> Toxic Time Message #4: "You spend your time doing unnecessary things."

I've often heard men say about their partners: "She's wasting her time on so much unnecessary stuff," suggesting an old trope of the wasteful "professional shopper" who packs the home with unnecessary purchases or the "OCD" woman who is unrealistically focused on keeping the home "perfect."

In an attempt to find out more about this messaging, I began asking men, "Like what? What *stuff* is unnecessary?" Nine times out of ten, I receive a blank stare, or a dodgy, "You know, just *stuff*!" To help my interview subjects articulate their suspicion that their wives are spending time and money not essential to the household, I started presenting to them my growing list of household tasks: Buying new clothes for your kid? What about opening the mail? Fixing the tap when it leaks? Do you see anything on the list that is unnecessary to you?

During one of these exchanges, Matt from Chicago crossed his arms and pointed to "thank-you notes." "OK, *there's* one."

I instantly recalled when my husband had a similar reaction to this particular task of emotional labor. "I'm not taking *that*!" Seth asserted. I interpreted Matt's reaction. "Do you mean to say that thank-you notes are unnecessary—even for birthday gifts or to teachers or special relatives?"

"Well, no, my wife writes those notes."

"But *you* think they're unnecessary?"

"Not *necessarily*," Matt tried to joke, "but it's not something I'm gonna do."

"OK, but if it doesn't get done by you, does it need to get done by her?"

Matt recrossed his arms and exhaled. "Sure, I guess it does."

"And why does it need to be done?" I pressed gently.

"Well, *because*..." Matt said as if it were obvious. "We want to teach our kids to be grateful, and that means saying thank you."

> **TIME REFRAME:** If we decide together that a household or childcare task isn't important to our lives, we'll let it go (after all, it's not necessary to do everything). But if we agree that it holds value or is necessary to keep our family life moving forward, it's not a waste of either of our time.

>> Toxic Time Message #5: "Sure, I'll help you—when I can."

"He says he wants to help, but he doesn't want to be rushed. He wants to 'help' when it's *convenient* for him," griped Rachel as we waited for the afternoon school bus to arrive at our stop. I assured Rachel that she isn't alone in her experience: Research into the gendered division of labor shows that men more willingly take the domestic work that they can perform on their *own time*, while women pick up responsibilities that are difficult to put off or reschedule and inherently forfeit their right to choose when the tasks get done. For example:

School drop-off and pickup
Sick visits to the doctor
Bath and bedtime
Meal preparation
Help with homework

I call these immovable tasks the **Daily Grinds** and—big surprise—they disproportionately fall on women. On any given day, there are 30 of these time-sucking jobs that *must be done* regularly, repetitively, and many at a very specific time. For example, you can't show up at the bus stop when it's convenient for *you*. Unless, of course, you're looking to make friends with the staff of your local Child Protective Services field office.

Now, consider the jobs that husbands/fathers most often opt to do as reported to me in my interviews, because they can choose when they do them or outsource them altogether. In other words, *Sure, I'll help when I can:*

- Landscaping and yard work
- IT and electronics
- Vehicle upkeep
- Storage

This is not to say that these jobs don't hold value, but putting dinner on the table *must happen every day*, consistently requiring more conception, planning, and execution hours, relative to the job of, say, rearranging where the holiday lights are stored in the garage.

> **TIME REFRAME:** My time is worth as much as your time. Fairness is sharing the Daily Grind tasks. When I have more choice over how I use my time, I feel respected.

>> Toxic Time Message #6: "I make her life."

"What does she have to complain about?" was something I heard a lot from men who were the primary breadwinners. "I have the stress of putting food on the table." In other words, his financial contributions "make" his wife and the family's life possible. *But wait a second*—who is actually putting food on the table in terms of meal planning, shopping for groceries, and preparing breakfast, lunch, and dinner? Of the couples I spoke to, it's often the woman who holds these cards and, as one woman countered, "The job of keeping our kids fed and merely alive day in and out—now *that's* a stressful job!"

So perhaps it's the other way around—she makes *your* life. Often the breadwinner/husband/fathers I surveyed are able to have the committed careers they have because their partners carry the majority of the mental and physical load of keeping a functional home life possible. Nowhere is this more apparent than with widowers, who I actively sought out to ask: What changed after your wife passed? The majority admitted that they no longer had the same amount of unfettered time to focus exclusively on their careers. Add to that, highlights Gemma Hartley in *Fed Up*, "widowed and divorced men don't fare as well as their widowed and divorced female counterparts because, without the partners who put time and care into managing their lives, their health, comfort and social bonds suffered."

TIME REFRAME: We each spend time making our life together work for us.

CONSIDER: THE CASE OF GAVRON AND GLOP

As my mother's birthday was approaching, I asked her what she wanted as a gift. "I'd love some more of my favorite Mary Kay cream," she said.

"The orange glop?" I clarified. Mom had been wearing the same Mary Kay overnight cream since I was a kid. I used to watch her slather it on before bedtime, and in the warm light of her bedroom vanity, once topically applied to the skin, it took on an orangish tint. I'd jokingly referred to it as "orange glop." After a few unsuccessful attempts to find it online, I directly phoned a Mary Kay rep to help me find Mom's miracle-skin mainstay.

As Camilla was searching Mary Kay's back inventory of nighttime elixirs, we struck up a conversation and, as it often happens between women, we soon started swapping stories about our personal lives. I explained to her the premise of Fair Play and she lowered her voice, saying, "I could have used that 20 years ago. I'm going through a divorce."

"Oh, I'm sorry."

"Well, that's not the worst of it," Camilla said. "I was issued a Gavron warning."

A what?

Camilla explained: She'd left her paid job as a health aid after she and her husband had kids.

"It wasn't really worth it for me to work," Camilla reasoned. "My yearly income nearly equaled the expense of hiring a nanny or paying for childcare."

I'd heard this argument before. In a *New York Times* opinion piece called "Day Care for All," Katha Pollit writes, "Note the unconscious sexism embedded in that calculation: childcare costs shouldn't be weighed against only the mother's earnings. They're a father's responsibility, too." Pam Stone, a colleague of my mom's and the author of *Opting Out: Why Women Really Quit Careers and Head Home*, offered me a similar rebuttal: "Why is it always the mother's full wages that are attributed to caregiver wages? As if it's the mother's sole responsibility to 'pay' for her replacement in the home. Fathers also benefit from what an outside caregiver brings to the home, so why aren't they sharing in this cost?" I kept this argument to myself as Camilla explained that for 17 years, she performed the uncompensated work of raising their kids and maintaining the household while her husband financially supported the family as a security systems manager.

"We were never rich by any means, but my husband made a decent living that allowed me to stay home with the kids," she said.

And then—after nearly two decades together—they decided to divorce. When they went before a judge to rule on the terms of their settlement, "He told the court that he didn't want to pay any alimony or spousal support, and I panicked. 'What do you mean?' I asked him. 'I left the workforce to raise our family. To be able to pick our kids up from school, drive them to sports, be the homeroom mom, and the list goes on and on.'"

"And what did *he* say?" I asked eagerly.

"He said, 'That was *your* choice,' and the court agreed and issued me a Gavron warning."

"Which is?"

"The duty to become self-sufficient. And I thought to myself: *What am I going to do now? How will I make a living?* I knew I couldn't just jump back into the health industry and earn a competitive salary. After nearly two decades, my skills weren't up to date."

"So what'd you do?"

"I hustled," Camilla said bluntly. "I became a Mary Kay rep Monday through Friday; I'm a Lyft driver on the weekends; and in the evenings, I'm taking online courses to get my nursing degree. I'm making it work, but I have to tell you—when I stood in that courtroom before the judge, I felt like what I did for all those years didn't count. He made it clear that I wasn't the breadwinner contributing monetary worth, but isn't there value to raising good human beings?"

For every hour that her husband worked out of the home, Camilla worked in the home. But when their individual con-

RULE #1: ALL TIME IS CREATED EQUAL

tributions were measured side by side, how Camilla chose
to use her time in service of the family was deemed far less
valuable.

What do you think—is that ruling *fair*?

67

>> Toxic Time Message #7: "It's on me."

We can blame our men. We can blame society. And yet, there's
some accountability women need to take as well. The truth is
that many of us take on an imbalanced share of the domestic load because we've unconsciously internalized some truly
toxic messaging of our own.

When I went back to work full-time after our second child
was born, I took it as *my* responsibility to make my return to
the office a seamless event for our family. I alone arranged for
extra childcare at home and modified my schedule so that I
could wrap up my work meetings and arrive home just after
five. I enjoyed being back in the office and also making the time
to spend evenings together as a family. I was insistent that this
choice wouldn't inconvenience my husband or interfere with
my role as a mom. And that's basically what happened: Seth
continued to leave for the office at 7:30 in the morning while I
delayed my start time to 9:30, giving me more time to feed the
baby, drive my older son to school, try to make a "mom connection" in the schoolyard, and then head to work. Every day,
I struggled to be "on" at the office and still "on call" at home,
and never once did I ask Seth to alter his work schedule to ac-
commodate our two-kid and two-earner household.

Looking back on this now, was I *nuts*?

Why didn't I ask for some help? I mean, he was just as responsible for the creation of these children as I was.

In my case, I reasoned that at the end of the day, my husband made more money than I did (Toxic Time Message #1: "Time is money."). And add to that, my she-fault assumption was that taking care of the house and kiddos was *on me*.

Seth didn't disagree. In fact, he applauded me for "all that you do, babe," a sentiment that came up frequently in my interviews with husband/fathers. I also habitually heard from other men: "I'm so proud of how well my wife balances work with her family life." Hold on—*her* family? I realized that what sounded like a thoughtful compliment was just a better-sounding version of *your time is not equal to mine*.

Back then, I'd internalized the "it's on me" message so deeply that I didn't question what I was doing. I certainly didn't consider that it could be different. And I know I'm not alone. Many of us are unconsciously using the "it's on me" excuse that devalues our time.

> My partner leaves early and works late. I couldn't ask him to _____ [fill in the blank].
>
> My partner travels. When he's out of town, I have no choice but to do it all.
>
> My partner's job is more stressful, so I don't want to ask him to do more.
>
> My partner's in the office all day, so I pick up the slack at home.
>
> He's busy. I don't want to bug or trouble him.
>
> And when school is canceled or the babysitter doesn't show, it's definitely *on me* to make it work.

If you think about it, none of these "he's not available" excuses really fly anymore. Thank you, Tiffany Dufu, catalyst-at-large in the world of women's leadership and the author of

Drop the Ball: Achieving More by Doing Less, for setting us straight on this point. "In the digital age, the 'he's not here' complaint need no longer exempt men from fully participating in homelife," she explains. "The expectation that our husbands cannot be engaged at home because they're at work doesn't take into account that technology can loop them in from wherever they are."

Sure, you can't start a load of laundry using an app on your phone (not yet), but husbands that leave early, work late in the office, or travel up in the air and on the road can certainly use the technology at their fingertips to help with school forms, respond to teacher emails, and make reservations and weekend plans. Heck, with the click of a button, he can have groceries, diapers, dry cleaning, and even a handyman delivered to the front door. I mean, isn't that how we all do it? Didn't I tell you earlier that I attempted to manage a satellite dish installation appointment over FaceTime, *while on an airplane*?!

TIME REFRAME: It's not all on me. It's on us. Our home and family are both of our responsibilities.

›› Toxic Time Message #8: "I can do it better."

I do it better and faster.
I'm an expert multitasker.
I'm wired differently.
I can do it *ALL.*

Guess what? If you're buying any of this, you don't have any time left.

In a survey conducted by *Real Simple* and the Families and Work Institute, 39 percent of women delegate household tasks to their children, while only 26 percent ask their partners to do the same tasks as often. When it comes to sharing the domestic load, we expect more from our children than from our partners. If your husband is guilty of undervaluing your time because he doesn't know the full extent of all that you do, consider that you may be just as guilty. Guilty of undervaluing his capabilities ("I can do it better myself"), of being an enabler to his negligence ("Jeez, I'll just do it myself"), and of failing to relinquish control ("I always do it, so I'll do it again").

Admit it, even though we're super-tired and overextended, we still like to brag about all that we do and how much *better* women are at getting it done. But here's the thing: There is no consistent data proving that women are better at multitasking than men. It's just something we say to our girlfriends over coffee to feel better about all that we've piled on our own plates.

To be sure I hadn't missed some piece of definitive research supporting what I'd always told myself—that I handled more of the domestic work because I had superior executive brain function—I asked one of the preeminent experts on brain science in the country, Dr. Pat Levitt, for his take on the subject. In addition to his PhD, Levitt is also chief scientific officer, vice president, and director of the Saban Research Institute; the Simms/Mann Chair in Developmental Neurogenetics at Children's Hospital Los Angeles; a WM Keck Professor in Neurogenetics; and the editor-in-chief of *Mind, Brain, and Education*.

I figured he must know something. And Levitt saw no reason to humor me.

"I don't know of any research data that shows women are better multitaskers than men," he stated bluntly. "In fact, multitasking is bad for everyone because our brains are not built to deal with more than one complex thing at a time. Even when folks designed studies to prove that women are better at multitasking, nothing was really there. My guess is that women are doing more of the household organization and domestic work not because her biological variation makes her better at it, but because of culture influence. She's bought into the message that she is better at it—and she believes it."

TIME REFRAME: In order to regain some of my time, I must stop identifying with the multitasker role. (The most recent research shows no difference between sexes in terms of executive brain function.) So let's put our heads together to maximize efficiency.

CONSIDER:
THE MYSTERIOUS CASE OF
LOST AND FOUND TIME

Scott and Michelle are acquaintances from my post-college days and co-owners of a television and film production company in Santa Fe, New Mexico. They both budget, schedule, script, scout for talent, hire cast and crew, distribute, and market the company's projects, and at least once a month, they separately travel for work. They literally have the same job and spend the same number of hours running the company. In fact, when they speak about their 50/50 partnership, they're self-congratulatory. On a recent trip to L.A., Scott told me over a burger, "As co-owners, we've always been very intentional about sharing responsibilities fair and square."

At home, though, it's a different story. Scott and Michelle are also married to each other and have three kids between the ages of three and nine. Can you guess who assumes responsibility for the "work" at home?

Michelle. And nearly 100 percent of it. Take a look at her expanded workday as compared to her husband's.

>> SCOTT'S SCHEDULE <<

8:30 a.m. Conference call with line producer to discuss the day's goals

9:00 a.m. Conference call to discuss notes on a script

10:30 a.m. to 1:00 p.m. Casting session

1:00 p.m. Lunch with our director of photography to discuss our camera package

2:30 p.m. Call with the director of film we have on location in Toronto

3:30 p.m. Story call with Amazon Studios

4:30 p.m. Budget call on the film in Toronto

5:00 p.m. Car pickup to LAX

5:30 p.m. Call with writers' room

6:30 p.m. Flight to Toronto

>> MICHELLE'S SCHEDULE <<

8:30 a.m. Conference call with line producer to discuss the day's goals

9:00 a.m. Conference call to discuss notes on a script

***9:30 a.m.** Break away to call the family allergist to reorder asthma inhaler*

10:30 a.m. to 1:00 p.m. Casting session

***Noon** Break away to run to pharmacy*

1:00 p.m. Lunch with our director of photography to discuss our camera package

***1:30 p.m.** Break away to make babysitter-scheduling calls*

2:30 p.m. Call with the director of film we have on location in Toronto

3:30 p.m. Story call with Amazon Studios

***4:00 p.m.** Break away to run to the bank*

4:30 p.m. Budget call on the film in Toronto

5:00 p.m. Leave the office

***5:30 p.m.** Pick up dinner*

***6:30 p.m.** Home to relieve babysitter and eat dinner*

***7:30 p.m.** Bath and bedtime routine with the kiddos*

***8:30 p.m.** Pack for Toronto*

***10:00 p.m.** Lay out clothes for the kids, set out breakfast dishes, and prep coffee*

12:00 a.m. Go to bed

On this particular day, as Scott caught a flight, Michelle went home to finalize the details of moving the family to Toronto "on location" to finish production on a film. She was down to actually packing suitcases, but for the three months prior, on top of what she already accomplished in a single day, she'd spent many additional hours finding and enrolling the kids in temporary schools, securing visas, finding a rental home, and a million other big and small details to pull off a family move without a hitch. And she'd done it all single-handedly.

When I asked her why responsibilities at home are managed so differently than all that they do professionally, Michelle answered earnestly, "You know, Scott's so busy with the company and always stressed that he doesn't have time. I'm better at juggling, so I just do it—to save time."

"But you're spending the same amount of time at work." I pointed out the obvious. "So, how is it that you have *more time* than Scott?"

"I don't," admitted Michelle, "but I guess I find the time."

Reader, one can only "find" time in a world where time is infinite—capable of expanding and collapsing like in a science fiction movie. We don't live in such a world. At the risk of sounding redundant and a bit grim, our time on Earth is finite. We each have only one precious life with limited hours in each precious day. If you find *more* time, please let me know, and I'll pass this scientifically groundbreaking discovery on to Michelle and the other married couples I interviewed who share professions but not an equitable workload in the home.

We'll loop back to whether a couple can realistically split work in the home 50/50, straight down the middle. Spoiler alert: This goal is just as much science fiction as the idea of infinite time. The good news is, it doesn't matter: **The Fair**

Play system facilitates equity, not equality. More on why this is a much better deal later on.

>> Toxic Time Message #9: "I can save time by doing it myself."

"You can understand why someone would think—in the time it takes me to tell my partner how to do it, or redo it, I could just do it. Or, in the time it takes him to do it, I can do it faster myself. This will save time. But the problem with this thinking is that saving time now is making it harder to share the work in the future," reasons Dan Ariely, bestselling author and professor of behavioral economics at Duke University, who took a break from writing his next book to speak with me.

Ariely advises couples to stop thinking short-term. Instead of—*I'll just change the kitty litter right now because I know where to find the scooper and the fresh bag of Tidy Cat*—consider the long-term goal. If some day you want to be free of the kitty-litter job, you must take the time *today* to share what it takes to get the job done, start to finish. Only then can you each "own" the task. Dealing and holding full ownership of the cards (you'll learn how to do this later) not only fosters collaboration, where both partners take fair turns at emptying the kitty litter without nagging reminders, but also—and more important—individual ownership promotes a happy partnership where both people value each other's time equally.

> **TIME REFRAME:** We're both time-starved, so let's work toward being more thoughtful with how we each manage our valuable time—for the long term. By taking time today to engage in Fair Play, we will better share the family's load in the future.

>> Toxic Time Message #10: "I *should* spend my time . . ."

When I get the chance, I like to ask men this question: If you had no choice but to extend your work trip for another day and take an early flight home the next morning, would you feel guilt and shame?

I usually get a deer-in-the-headlights reaction.

So I ask more directly, "Would you feel guilty for failing to come home, for not being there to tuck your kids in, and for not seeing them for another night?"

"Well, sure." They shrug. "I'd miss them, but why would I feel guilt and *shame*?"

Conversely, when I introduce the same scenario to women, nearly all respond with some version of, "Oh, I'd feel terrible" and become regretful at the idea alone.

Of course, we're allowed to miss our children and feel sad over leaving them for work or other obligations and responsibilities, but most women I spoke to identified more closely with guilt and shame, emotions that are so often linked and identified with being a mother, and especially a working mother. Recent research exploring mother's guilt found that working mothers feel far guiltier than working fathers, especially around the idea of missing out on moments when they "should be there." Absent from a child's birthday? *Sacrilege!*

Kim Brooks, author of *Small Animals: Parenthood in the Age of Fear*, really nailed this distinction: "A father who is distracted by . . . his myriad interests and obligations in the world of adult interactions is being, well, a father. A mother who does the same is failing her children." Even today, the so-called good mother is expected to spend as much time as she can in service to her family and is often judged by society, her community, her peers, and her spouse if she chooses to spend her hours differently. Lindsay from Houston recounted how her mother-in-law reacts when she travels for work: *You're leaving your kids again?* "I feel bad enough already before her guilt trip!"

Consider another working-mother scenario: Your colleagues ask you to join them for happy hour. You'd love to take time to casually network over drinks. But, before you say yes to time that will be spent benefiting you and your career, the words, "I really should . . ." come tumbling out of your mouth. This is the cloud of domestic encroachment powered by heavy winds of guilt and shame, moving in to remind you of all the things you should be doing to benefit your family or bring order to your home. Ignore the storm at your own peril. *If I go for drinks, I'll miss bedtime stories with Grace.* Cue the guilt. Or, if you go, cue the shame for not feeling guilty!

If you're not careful, domestic encroachment will trap you every time. The net result is that you spend less time on your career and social outlets, and likely deny yourself mental breathers and important self-care. An hour at the gym, lunch with a friend, or an afternoon pedicure? Not without the stirring winds of guilt and shame. When the national parenting network and publisher Macaroni Kid surveyed more than 8,500 moms, 90.4 percent reported taking better care of their families than they do of themselves, and a full 25 percent admitted they hadn't done anything just for themselves in more than *a year*. Couple that staggering finding with this one: Fathers spend *more time* relaxing while mothers are hard at work performing invisible tasks for the family. Thanks, Mom.

CONSIDER:
THE CASE OF THE BAD PEDICURE

It was a Saturday afternoon and I was sitting in my local nail salon, waiting for an open chair and reveling in a magical hour all to myself to luxuriate in a little well-earned self-care.

"I've been waiting two months for this," I confided to the older woman sitting quietly next to me. "I received this gift certificate for my birthday, but I just haven't been able to take a weekend afternoon away from the kids."

She smiled knowingly. "I have grandkids. How many children do you have?"

I held up three fingers. "That's why it's taken me so long to get here."

"Oh," she said, surprised. "Who's watching them?"

I thought, *Does anyone ever ask a man: Who's watching your kids?* They just assume the mother has it all under control.

"Their father." I said plainly.

"Oh, how nice," she chirped. "He sounds like a good father."

Again, what mother gets a gold star for watching her kids? Why do dads get so much more credit, and audible applause, for parenting? At least she hadn't referred to Seth as "babysitting," as I'd so often heard women refer to their husbands when they were "on watch" with their own children.

Annoyed by the unfair disparity between a mother's and father's time and whose is more valuable, I imagined how rewarding it was going to feel to plunge my feet into soapy water. As I started to relax, a familiar feeling stopped me from unwinding completely. Guilt. *Maybe I was taking too much time for myself?* My confident self answered back: *Seth has this.* I flashed back to the moment right before I left. "Have fun at the playdate," I called as I walked out the door. Now, trying not to fret and enjoy this next hour to myself, I really hoped that Seth had changed Zach and Ben out of their dirty soccer cleats and remembered to comb Anna's hair and—good God—remembered that the playdate had moved from the bowling alley to the roller rink! Before my mounting worry could go into full overdrive, I was called to the next open chair for my pedicure. As I stood up and grabbed my purse, my neighbor said with sugarcoated sweetness, "Enjoy."

> **Twitter @PhillyD:** Best part of being a Dad is I can do almost anything and people are like OMG YOU'RE THE BEST DAD IN THE WORLD!!! I'm like . . . for making my son a PBJ? Meanwhile my wife who does 90% of the work can tweet how she needs an hour for herself to recoup and people will try to shame her.

>> The Shame Shield

The shaming "shoulds" in our cultural conversation are strong. They also happen to be one of the most powerful and effective tools for keeping a woman from reclaiming her time. Anticipating criticism or judgment that may be hurled our way for shirking duties in service to the home and instead spending time on ourselves, many of us go on offense, and typically without realizing it. A review of your social media feed will likely reveal that shame of this kind can be found among countless people close to you. In my own online review, I found a variety of **Shame Shields** that apologize for taking time away from what moms "should" be doing:

So sad to miss the first day of school 😣 #momfail

#collegereunion #missingmykids

My husband's a keeper. Solo dad duty while I'm away #Blessed

A quiet plane and 8 hours to myself . . . love work trips but #mommyguilt

When I looked for similar sentiments posted by men, I found no wealth of #daddyguilt or #dadfails.

🕐 **TIME REFRAME:** I should not feel guilty about how I spend my time. When the cloud of domestic encroachment threatens to trap and shorten the time I've chosen to benefit other aspects of my identity, I remind myself that guilt has been associated with "lower quality parenting." A good mother spends her time in service to her family *and to herself.*

BACK TO DRUNK GUY'S JACKET

The night I returned home and found myself standing at our bedroom door having just retrieved a drunk guy's jacket from the front lawn, I asked myself: *Why* is *this on me?*

Because my husband left too early for work to do it?

Because I should just do it?

Because I'm a better multitasker?

Because I'll be shamed by my neighbors?

Because in the time it takes me to tell him how to do it, I could do it faster myself?

Ding-ding-ding! All of the above.

More important, I realized: I regarded it as a "me" job

because, like my husband, I also believed that his time was worth more than *mine*.

That needed to change.

I sat down next to him on the bed and said in my most patient voice, "Hey, we both have 24 hours in a day. The hours of my life are as valuable as yours and we both get to make choices about how we use our finite time. *OK?*"

No, that's not what I said. That would have been too perfect. What I actually said was a practically inaudible but clearly condemning, "You're welcome," as I peeled off and dropped the plastic gloves at the foot of the bed.

It wasn't my best mediation moment, but within the days that followed, I was able to meaningfully articulate how I'd felt. After the kids were tucked into bed, I sat with Seth on the couch. "Remember when I came home really late from work the other night and picked up that drunk guy's jacket and beer bottle off the front lawn?"

Seth gave me one of those hazy looks of recognition. I continued anyway—

"It felt like you expected me to spend the very last 12 minutes of my day in service of our household. The implication was that I had time to do it and you didn't."

Thankfully, Seth did not dispute my calculation. He acquiesced that in between *SportsCenter* and checking Instagram he had had enough time to slip on a pair of rubber gloves and get the job done, and he let me do it anyway. He agreed this was unfair. And that's when attitudes started to shift within our home. From that conversation forward, Seth began to notice and appreciate that we both have the same number of minutes in a day. (The "All Time Is Created Equal" sign that I posted on the bathroom mirror did help to hammer home the point.) As I said earlier, a reframe in thinking takes deliberate effort. So whenever Seth and I reverted to Toxic Time messages like "I don't have time," "It's on you," or "It's on *me*," I'd attempt to reframe the conversation with words that honor and respect how we each choose to spend our finite time. I finally understood that how I'd spent those particular 12 minutes picking up the jacket and beer bottle was really irrelevant. I wasn't interested in keeping a minute-by-minute scorecard with my husband where each night we tallied and compared how we each spent our days; I simply wanted both of us to value our time equally. Playing for time was a process, but it eventually changed the game.

Once you and your partner reframe how you value time and reimagine a more equitable relationship, a magical thing happens—you will succeed in rebalancing and reenergizing your relationship and your life in ways you haven't felt in years.

With more time and available headspace, just think what you could do.

4.

RULE #2:
RECLAIM YOUR RIGHT TO BE INTERESTING

Don't get lost in the shuffle.

CONSIDER:
THE CASE OF THE FORGOTTEN SKIS

Josie's happy place was on the slopes. When she was eight years old, her parents splurged on a winter ski camp in the Poconos. By the end of the first day, Josie refused to come down off the mountain. She'd found herself at a higher elevation. As she got older, her love for the sport didn't wane and her parents supported her "ski obsession" as much as they could afford to. Josie did what she could, too—working hard throughout school and eventually earning a ski scholarship to the University of Vermont, where she was beyond thrilled to join the alpine ski team.

Cut to marriage and kids—not only had Josie forgone the black diamonds for a single solitaire, she now hardly made time for even the bunny slopes. Nearly ten years into her marriage, she felt a deep loss and longing for her earlier self, so she planned a ski vacation with her family. As the date approached, she became more and more excited to introduce her young ones to the sport she loved so much and to make a long overdue return to her happy place.

The day of the trip, the flight from Tampa to Philadelphia took longer than expected. Long delays and connecting flights made everyone cranky. By the time they began their descent, Josie's two older boys were melting down in the aisles, throwing nut-free snacks at the flight attendants and each other. Her 13-month-old joined the chorus, and right on cue, Josie's nipples began leaking puddles through her shirt. Her husband, usually a helpful guy, was also in a mood.

After collecting their five bags, double stroller, Pack 'n Play, and booster seats from the baggage carousel, all while desperately tearing open a bag of Pirate's Booty to pacify (please, God) her children, Josie realized that her skis had not made it off the plane and onto the baggage carousel. The very equipment that she'd faithfully worn throughout her years in Vermont and that had dutifully transported her for many years and many magical miles were missing.

"They should have come out with the oversized luggage," she said, turning to her husband.

He shrugged and grabbed a handful of Pirate's Booty. "So now what?"

Josie looked down at her tired baby still needing to nurse; her overextended five- and seven-year-olds running in circles through baggage claim like feral animals; and back at her husband, who stared at her blankly. He wasn't withdrawing

permission to go searching for her skis, but he wasn't mag-
nanimously offering it either.

She shrugged back at him and relented, "Forget it. It's not
worth it. Let's just go."

Josie left the airport without her beloved skis, again leaving a part of herself behind. (The skis eventually found their
way back to Tampa, two weeks later.) She spent her ski weekend tending to her baby from inside the resort, while her husband tried to interest their five- and seven-year-olds in begin-
ner ski classes. They quickly grew bored and gave up. We'd
rather make snowmen, they said. After all, skiing is Mommy's
thing. Or, at least, it had been.

RECLAIMING THE RIGHT TO BE INTERESTING

Like Josie, I was already a couple of kids in before I realized
that I'd made "the switch" from my former vibrant self to a
more invisible version. And when I did, I reacted like a woman afraid to confront the truth—defensively. I'd snarl to myself while driving, "But who has *time* to grow a new business
when I'm in charge of school pickups every afternoon, and
at two o'clock on Wednesdays? Who has the free hours to attend evening meetings to help elect more women into public
office when my seven-year-old needs help with homework?
Who has the headspace to think about big-picture goals and
dreams when doctor after doctor still cannot figure out why
my C-section scar hasn't healed—after five years!"

I still felt overworked at home and at the office. And I was
a little bit (OK, a lot) pissed at my husband for behaving as
though, if even unconsciously, the majority of our domestic
workload was "on me." But also I was pissed at *myself*. Where
was the woman I was so proud of being? The woman I was in

love with? I grieved for my old identity. I missed her desperately. And I worried, could I ever find my way back to her in the context of my new kid-filled life?

The first rule for Fair Play is for you and your partner to recognize that all time is created equal . . . whether it results in earning a paycheck or stroking the forehead of a sick child. And once that's agreed upon, let me dangle another shiny bauble in front of you—the most important reason for you to reimagine your life through the lens of Fair Play: It allows you to reclaim your right to be interesting *and* interested.

What do I mean by this? Early on in my research process, I spoke with a woman named Ellen, who'd once had a small but thriving interior design business before she married a real estate investor on his way to becoming a multimillionaire. I was interested in speaking with someone of extreme economic privilege to help me answer the question: *Does money change things? If a woman can "outsource" a significant portion of her childcare and household responsibilities, does she feel less encumbered?* I knew what it was like for my working-class single mom. The daily grind was tough on her. Maybe the weight of invisible work didn't impact the wealthy as heavily?

What I learned over our intimate lunch together was that even women who can get *a lot* of help are still suffering from time deprivation, and in Ellen's case, she was the recipient of nearly every Toxic Time message I'd heard so far. She explained that not long into the marriage, her new husband suggested she stop working. His argument: "It's not worth it." He reasoned that they didn't need her income to maintain their lifestyle, and if she wasn't committed to a job outside the home, she could better use her time to run the household and eventually raise their children.

Ellen hesitated at first. She was proud of the business she'd built. After all, she'd been the first child in her family to receive a university education, by way of a scholarship to a distinguished design program in the Midwest. But maybe her husband had a point? She no longer *needed* to work, and if redirecting her time and energy to the household would make her husband's life easier (thereby making him happier and more successful), perhaps it was a fair trade-off?

So Ellen gave up her design business, along with the client base she'd steadily and thoughtfully built. Her work at home was demanding and exhausting, and in the end, her time amounted to more than a full-time job. For 15 years, Ellen worked tirelessly from inside the home, managing the lives of their two young children and keeping the household afloat on an invisible cloud of competent forward motion. Each and every day, the children arrived at school on time and in a presentable fashion, each with their homework done and displaying the quiet calm of students who know their mom stands at the ready for an unexpected sick day pickup and special treatment back home.

Year after year, thoughtfully chosen and beautifully wrapped gifts appeared on the dates they were required to accompany children to countless birthday parties or to mark milestones in the lives of various family members. Every holiday season, greeting cards that featured professionally captured photographs of the family were printed and posted long before the annual rush. Every summer, camp trunks were magically outfitted and packed off. Naturally, all social engagements, philanthropic commitments, and parent-teacher conferences were promptly scheduled and attended—until the day that Ellen's husband thanklessly asked for a divorce.

When I asked Ellen why her marriage unraveled, she paused in reflection. With sadness behind her words, she said, "Honestly, I believe I lost my permission to be interesting."

She explained that, at first, the role of wife and mother fulfilled her, and she'd lived vicariously through her husband's professional success. But then, more than a decade and a half later, she recognized that she'd lost her earlier identity—the vibrant and passionate woman who she'd worked so hard to become (and who her husband had originally fallen in love with). Over the years, she disengaged from interests and talents beyond motherhood and domestic responsibilities for the family. In effect, she'd stepped into the background of her own life.

The version of who she was *before* her marriage had faded into memory for them both, and Ellen admitted that what she contributed to the relationship as a stay-at-home wife and mother was no longer "interesting to my husband, my community, or myself." She recounted a company retreat she'd attended as her husband's plus-one.

"Nothing I had to say translated in his professional circle," Ellen said. She ran her finger down the "Sh*t I Do" list that I'd brought to our lunch and pointed at "pets" and "school service." "No one wanted to hear about how—back at home—I'd been nursing our sick dog back to health or how I'd planted a community garden at my kid's school. Rather, they were all excitedly focused on a tech innovation I wasn't familiar with and world events I was too exhausted to follow. I felt like I had nothing to contribute. I stood there for hours, barely saying a word, while so many 'interesting' people tried to engage with me. But absent my having anything to add to the conversation, one by one, they excused themselves to refresh their drinks. It was humiliating. I do remember that—occasionally—

someone would ask me, 'Do you think you'll ever go back to interior design?' Defining me by what I *used* to do versus who I was now.

"I had to learn the hard way," Ellen continued with an edge of regret, "nobody needs to give you permission to be interesting. It's a choice you make."

Reader, let me be clear: This is not another SAHM vs. working mom debate. We've all come too far (and worked too hard) to let in-fighting among women destroy us. Ellen's lament was *not* that she stayed home with her kids; it was about the fact that she left so much of herself behind as the years rolled by, unintentionally allowing a vibrant, passionate, engaged, and essential part of herself to disappear.

>> The Permission Paradox

Several years before Ellen's husband asked for a divorce, there was a moment when she decided to fight for her *self*, to advocate for her right to be interesting. Ellen found a specialized interior design course that she believed would spark the once passionate woman now dormant inside her. The problem? Rewind to the halcyon days before the ubiquity of social media and distance learning—the course was only offered in Milan, Italy. Still, Ellen was determined to make it happen. Charged with an "it's on me" diligence, she arranged for her mother to come and stay at the house while she was away. She began the arduous process of hiring babysitters, dog sitters, and afterschool tutors to be on standby should additional help be required, and she created an extensive list of to-dos on a whiteboard calendar to ensure that absolutely nothing would fall through the cracks in her absence. But when she presented her husband with her plans, he reacted with outrage: How could she leave her six- and nine-year-olds? *For two weeks?* What if they needed her? Her job was at home. Again, Ellen's husband reasoned that she didn't "need" the course and definitely didn't need the additional money from restarting her career. When Ellen turned to her closest girlfriends and fellow mothers to weigh in on her plans, they reacted similarly. Taking a design course in another country was a fantasy, they lectured. *What woman gets to leave her husband and kids for Italy? If only! We'd all be eating gelato in the piazza.*

Shamed by family and friends for the "self-indulgent" suggestion, Ellen relented. She gave up the dream of reigniting her passion. In doing so, she withdrew three levels of permission—from her husband, from her community, and from herself—to spend time outside the home that wasn't essential to her role as wife and mother but that would nonetheless make her feel interesting and alive. Rather than listen to her own voice, one begging to be heard, eagerly assuring Ellen that her plans didn't sound crazy, she instead listened to and acted on the limitations set for her by others. As she reflected on her choice to unpack her bags and stay home those many years ago, Ellen said regretfully, "If I'd gone to Milan, I may have reclaimed my right to be interesting by rediscovering the 'me' I'd left behind. And who knows how this may have changed how I felt about myself, and returned a different person in my marriage."

If I'd gone to Milan.

What's your "If I'd . . ." story? Has a lack of permission from your spouse, partner, family, or friends—either overtly or subtly implied—influenced the permission you give yourself? Have you strayed or even taken a sharp detour from your original vision of what your life would look like today?

At some point after marriage and kids, did you listen to the voices that said, "It's not worth it for you to pursue your passions"? In doing so, did you give up your own permission to be interesting?

When you imagine your before-marriage-and-children self, is that woman still looking back at you in the mirror today? Or, as Ellen discovered, has she faded into the past? When the lack of permission coming from the outside—either perceived or real—influences the permission we grant ourselves, we pay a high price. The thing we don't feel permitted to do is often what has the depth to keep us *interested* and is also the very thing that makes us more *interesting* to our partners and nearly everyone else. This is the Permission Paradox.

The irony for Ellen is that within a year of her divorce, Ellen did finally make that trip to Milan. She reinvigorated her interior design career, reigniting the flame deep inside her that restored Ellen to the most alive version of herself.

BUT HE TOLD ME TO QUIT MY JOB

After all his insistence that Ellen leave her career, stay home, and be a "good mother," her husband ultimately rejected what she'd become. I discovered this uncomfortable truth in many of my interviews. After listening to Ellen's Milan story, I sought out the male perspective. I needed their voices in my data set and I specifically wanted to know: How do men regard this shift in their partners?

"I married a fearless, vibrant woman," whispered Bill of his wife, Josie (remember, from the ski slopes?). "And then one day, I just didn't recognize her anymore."

Ouch. But did this really happen "one day"? Had Josie's former self been snatched overnight, off the top of a mountain, by a hovering alien aircraft? Of course not, but this is the bait and switch many of our partners report. And they're just as confused by how it happened as we are. What my interviews continued to reveal was that despite what a husband expresses overtly ("just quit your job"), or insists ("the kids need you at home"), or even alludes to his preference for (a "retired wife"), our partners desperately want us to have interests beyond the home. Yours just might not know it yet.

When my husband and I started dating, I was an ambitious, dynamic woman who challenged the status quo, fought for the underdog, and always had eyes wide open to civil rights issues that shouldn't be left for the next generation. I was engaged. I was passionate. I was *interesting,* damn it.

But after kids rocked our world so completely, I lost some of my spark. One of my more illuminating new mommy moments came when I complained to a seasoned mother of three at the playground, "My baby's nearly six months old and I'm still so tired." I echoed what a girlfriend recently expressed: "And I want to feel something again. Other than exhaustion." As I crawled after Zach on all fours, trapping sand in my thong underwear, I appealed to my new playground pal: "When will I get to sleep in again? I'm just not a morning person."

She laughed out loud at foolish me. "Honey, you'll be getting up at 6 a.m. until your kid's a teenager. Until then, I recommend an afternoon espresso, or two."

I'd catch myself blaming Seth for whatever I didn't like about the new, worn-out me. "Thanks a lot, asshole," I'd mutter in his direction when the baby began to cry at three in the morning. As I'd haul myself out of bed to warm up a bottle, I'd shoot eye daggers at him still sleeping and think: *Why do you still get to be you, while I've become an unrecognizable mommy zombie?*

To be fair, my husband never explicitly said, "Now that we're married with children, you no longer have my permission to be the fullest expression of yourself." Nor did he ever suggest I quit my job. In other words, I received no explicit resistance from him. Rather, it was assumed resistance. I assumed that he wouldn't want me spending time on my career or myself when there were more important things to do, like emptying the diaper pail. In hindsight, *I* was the source of this assumption and the person who unilaterally decided to validate and act on it. And then, just a handful of years after our wedding day, the only "I do" recited around our house—as much from me as from Seth—was: I do not recognize the engaged, passionate, interesting version of Eve anymore. *Where the hell did she go?*

As easy, and often deeply satisfying, as it may be to point the finger at our spouses and partners for obscuring the former, less-encumbered version of ourselves, our partners aren't entirely to blame. We need to hold ourselves accountable for whatever voluntary steps we took toward losing sight of our right to be interesting and turn on our heels and find ourselves again.

FIND YOURSELF AGAIN

If you, too, long for a forgotten version of your pre-parent self, or an evolved and even more interesting version waiting for permission to emerge, then enthusiastically embrace Fair Play's **Rule #2: Reclaim Your Right to Be Interesting**.

And because bait-and-switch spouses manifest in men and women equally, the urgent need to operationalize Rule #2 applies to your partner as much as it does to you. Both of you must reclaim your right to be interesting beyond your roles as wonderful parents and partners, and both must demand more time and space to explore this right.

Does my use of the words "urgent" and "demand" make you wonder where the fire is? It should. You see, more time and available space does not magically appear. In fact, it doesn't f*cking exist—until you create it. Only when you demand the time from your partner, your family, and yourself will you have the ability to enjoy what I call **Unicorn Space**. And like the mythical equine that inspired the name, Unicorn Space is rare, magical, and *essential* in order for you to reclaim the interests that make you uniquely *you*, driving you to be the best version of yourself, and for you to be happy as an individual and in your partnership.

CAUTION AHEAD!

If you think you don't have enough time or space to create more for Unicorn Space, you're probably right. Adding to your already packed schedule will feel like a burden, if not altogether impossible if you already feel as if you're drowning. So begin by taking a breath. Your only added task today is to begin *thinking* about what you *could* do with your Unicorn Space if you had some.

Allow yourself to *dream*. Wouldn't it be great to have more time and space to reconnect with *yourself*?

Asking couples this question pretty consistently results in some combination of "I wish" and an equally emphatic "but there's no way." Unicorn Space will remain the stuff of fairy tales until you and your partner are able to rebalance the workload between you. Like at Thanksgiving dinner, it's only after you remove filler from your plate that you have room to add more of the good stuff (for me that's marshmallow sweet potatoes or another slice of pie). Making room for more doesn't come into play until Rule #4. For now, just dream.

Unicorn Space. I know, the name sounds fanciful and maybe a little too glitter-and-rainbows for something that I am telling you is so essential. But, then again, the thing that makes you interesting is very often the fantasy stuff that brings you to life and makes you sparkle, fortifying you so that you can consistently drudge through the less magical parts of your days. Stand-up comedian Ali Wong twists it this way: "When you're a mom, you need sparkle to compensate for the light inside of you that has died." For a lucky few, your Unicorn Space may be your job, assuming it delivers a Category 5 storm of passion to your life. Some women and men are blessed with jobs and careers that serve as their Unicorn Space—their *dream* jobs (work they would continue doing even if they won the lottery). But for the rest of us, we still need time and space to engage in something outside of the work we do for money that makes us come alive. Something *more* that fuels us to wake up in the morning and power us throughout the day. That *something* is really not a fantasy or a luxury but a critical component of your ongoing sense of self, the health of your partnership, and your ability to convey to your children what a full life looks like. In short, Unicorn Space is essential to your overall happiness and success as a human being with a limited amount of time on this earth. Yeah, I'm laying it on thick and getting existential here because this is a powerful point. In fact, it is *the* point. Creating more Unicorn Space will give your life purpose beyond partnering and parenting.

Being a partner and a parent *is* purposeful. There's no negating that. Being in a relationship with someone you love and who adores and supports you in return is meaningful and can be deeply satisfying. Caring for and raising a child is one of the more miraculous, gratifying, and fulfilling experiences in life, and especially in the early days when you're responsible for keeping a tiny human alive, doing that job well should be your primary focus.

And, still—there can be more.

THE ROLE WE PLAY

After having children, many of us feel that we're no longer seen, *or no longer see ourselves*, for the vibrant individuals we are. Instead, we take on the corresponding identity for the various roles we now play: Spouse. Caretaker. Parent. Household Manager. List Maker. In my own mom circle, many of my friends no longer refer to themselves by their first names. With no apparent irony, they post as #braydensmom, #sawyersmom, #hazelsmom. Some even sign off email correspondence this way. According to the 2018 State of Motherhood survey by *Motherly*, 59 percent of moms report being "most strongly" defined by motherhood. I get it. I'm so proud of the time I've been able to care for and get to know my children, but outside of school, playdates, and kids' birthday celebrations, can't my nonwork identity include something of what made me a good friend, a fun dinner companion, a talented (fill in the blank)? Consider what you were once known for among friends and loved ones, and how often do you identify yourself with that special something *now*?

Being a mom is amazing, important, and—for women who choose it—can feel existentially important. But lest you've forgotten, you were someone else before you became a parent, and you remain more than #sawyersmom today. Losing sight of this comes at a price, described by countless women interviewed by sociologist Orna Donath in her dramatically titled *Regretting Motherhood*. In conversation, Donath and I discussed her interview subjects, many who express loving their children no less, yet also describe not "realizing myself" anymore, "fading away," and "disappearing."

Many of my interviews with mothers mirrored these sentiments. Emma told me candidly, "Being a mom feels necessary, but not sufficient for me." Another confided, "Once I was done having kids, I thought: *Who am I?* I'd gained a family but lost myself." My friend Aspen said, "After kids, I needed to reexamine and find who I was again, and it was hard because even though I'd been on this earth for 30 years, I felt like I was starting over."

And yet, once we pass the milestones of completing school, getting married, and having kids, carving out time for Unicorn Space passions may be more important than ever in order to create *new milestones* that allow each of us to recognize and celebrate personal achievement.

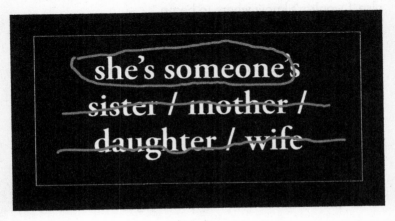

Tovah Klein, PhD, director of Barnard College Center for Toddler Development and an associate professor of psychology, cautions, "Don't let your passion be the perfection of your children. Because when you solely define yourself in relation to another, it's not enough."

Not enough for you, or for your kids, it turns out. New research shows that women who spend time on themselves have a greater capacity to care for their children. Still, expanding our roles beyond the home can feel intimidating. Many women I spoke to said they'd identified as "mom" for so long that they felt unsure they could fill any other role. "I'm not quite sure if I *am* someone else outside of being a parent," reflected Giselle. And without being able to identify what they might do with time set aside for Unicorn Space, many women expressed reluctance to relinquish even some control of the household to their partner, out of fear that they wouldn't be able to replace the success they enjoy in managing their family's domestic sphere. A woman at my kids' school confided, "I'm thinking of having a third child now that my two others are in school. Filling the day scares me. I worry it's too late to think about doing, or being, anything else. I wouldn't know where to begin."

Another friend in the schoolyard added, "It's physics. Bodies in motion stay in motion. And I am *not* in motion. I am an object at rest." She went on to say, "Once you lose your confidence in your abilities outside your role as a mom, it's hard to get the old magic back."

ARE YOU PROUD OF ME?

Once I added men to my interview pool, I crafted a standard set of questions that seemed to easily get them talking. On the subject of Unicorn Space, I'd ask them, "Are you proud of your wife?"

Almost every man I spoke to had this initial and automatic response: "Of course. She's a great mom."

Some would also tack on sentiments like, "I couldn't do it without her," and "It's amazing how she keeps the house running."

I thought it was interesting that when I used the word "proud," men almost always pointed straight to their wives' role as a mother and caretaker. So I reframed the question, and asked, "Beyond her role as a mother or a wife," I clarify, "are you proud of *her*?"

The men whose wives forfeited the focus of their personal passion in the context of becoming a wife and a mom—those women with no connection to their Unicorn Space—had a hard time saying yes. They'd often hedge, hem and haw, then finally land on something their life partners did in the *past* that caused them to feel proud. I call this The Case of the She Used To's, and it's strong evidence that a woman's gone missing.

Conversely, the men with wives who are presently pursuing their unique skills, talents, and passions beyond parenting immediately identify the focus of their partner's Unicorn Space as the source of the great pride they feel—**every single time**.

When I asked Dave if he was proud of his wife, Karen, mother to their twin girls and a dental hygienist by trade, he gushed, "Yes! She's the best *baker*. She makes an amazing strawberry rhubarb. Her pies win competitions."

I received a similar response from Clyde, who works for the Centers for Disease Control and Prevention. His wife, Jan, is a SAHM who carves out time nearly every night after the kids go to bed to work on her oil paintings. The joke among their friends is that at social gatherings where Clyde could easily hold the attention of the crowd with tales of ridding the world of infectious disease, all *he* wants to talk about is his wife's love for art. To him, *she's* the most interesting person in the room. What might be even more interesting is that Jan's never sold a single piece. But this doesn't matter to either one of them, because she doesn't paint for the money. She paints to feed her soul, and her passionate expressions on canvas hang all over the walls of the couple's home. "I always feel supported by Clyde," Jan said.

Once my own husband recognized that writing this book was *my* passion, he became this project's biggest champion, which is kind of funny when you consider the topic and the light it sometimes casts him in. As I got deeper into the research and the writing, I'd overhear Seth talking enthusiastically about my "new solution for the gendered division of labor" at social events. *Can you imagine?* I'm absolutely certain that if someone were to ask him if he is proud of me, he'd skip over my Ivy League degree, my work successes in philanthropy, and my devoted mothering skills. Instead, he'd talk about this book, because this work is my near-single-minded obsession. He's picked up on my passion, and as a result, he's become passionate about it, too.

Recognize that passion flows both ways. Women need their men to be interesting, too. Don't you want *your* partner to be the most alive and passionate version of himself, someone who comes through the door at the end of the day conveying a sense of exhilaration and deep satisfaction?

When I ask women, "Are you proud of your husband or partner?" most will automatically reply with some version of, "He's a great provider," "He works so hard," or "He's a great dad."

As I do with the guys, I push back and ask, "But are you proud of *him*?"

The wives of men who are active in their Unicorn Space easily say yes and reference the interesting activities their husbands engage in beyond the office. The wives of men who aren't connected to a passion beyond making a living tend to respond with a combination of frustration, disappointment, and sometimes resignation. One woman admitted, "Over the years, my husband has become quite boring."

SELF-WORTH, NOT MONETARY WORTH

In my ongoing study of couples who embrace Rule #2, I have found that when men or women signal seriousness in pursuing a passion and ask for Unicorn Space to do so, their partners support them, regardless of the results or whether the passion translates into a paycheck or a sale. Terrell from Redondo Beach said to me in reference to his wife, Jada, "It's not about monetary worth. I want my wife to have *self*-worth." After hearing this sentiment echoed throughout my conversations with men and women, I recognized that the more valuable question to ask individuals is not "Are you proud of your partner?" but "Are you proud of *yourself*?" **Are you making time for activities and interests that elevate your own sense of worth?**

After her second child was born, Evelyn decided to leave her job as a tax accountant to manage her husband Sam's general contractor business. This decision enabled her to tend to their youngest and save money on childcare, while also working from home in a capacity that contributed to her family's financial livelihood. "Continuing to earn money was important to me," Evelyn stressed. "I wanted my husband to recognize my financial contribution." For five years, she worked alongside her husband until one day, she realized her kids were in school and, "I no longer needed to work from home. Sam hired another bookkeeper so that I could pursue something for *me*."

Around that time, a friend of Evelyn's was looking for a partner to help run her boutique laundromat business. She offered Evelyn a 50/50 stake. "It seemed like a great opportunity to make money *and* go into business for myself," Evelyn remembered, "so I jumped on board."

Evelyn soon discovered that managing a laundromat meant long hours, mentally exhausting and physically back-breaking work, and, in her case, not as much financial upside as she'd hoped. Evelyn conceded, "I was so eager to do my own thing that I 'jumped' without really thinking it through. I soon realized that I'd made a wrong choice; the laundromat wasn't the right fit for me." Sam suggested she sell her half of the business and take some time to figure out what would fulfill her.

"That's amazing," I said to her. "Sam sounds like a really supportive guy. So what did you do?"

"When I really thought about it, I realized that what I'd always wanted to do was illustrate greeting cards," Evelyn said, "but that's a hobby, not a way to make a living."

"And is that the point?" I challenged. "To make money?"

"It's certainly important in our family," Evelyn emphasized, "but Sam encouraged me to pursue it regardless."

"And?" I asked.

"I decided to go back to working part-time with Sam, and in my free time, I began creating a line of greeting cards that I eventually donated to our local children's hospital gift shop. I'm working on a second line of cards now." Evelyn beamed.

Evelyn finally understood that having Unicorn Space is not about generating monetary worth. While a two-earner lifestyle is nonnegotiable for her family, Evelyn still created space to pursue something more.

UNICORN SPACE: NOT RESERVED FOR THE RICH

To be clear: Unicorn Space is not reserved for the wealthy. I spoke with many couples who successfully reclaimed or discovered interests and passions beyond parenting without changing their job status at all, such as:

Carrie, a bank teller, who started playing bass guitar in the evenings

Jeff, a middle school teacher, who took up surfing again on the weekends

Ana, a postal worker, who went through her town's volunteer firefighter program

Joseph, a factory worker, who started taking karate (alongside his elementary-school-aged daughter)— today they're both brown belts!

Whoever you are and whatever you do, you still need time and space to engage in something *outside* of the work you do for money to make you come alive. Unfortunately, many of us confuse financial success with personal value, and for this very reason, a large majority of the individuals I spoke to were reluctant to consider carving out time from their schedule for an activity that wouldn't generate income. Some of the most reticent were SAHMs, many of whom are already self-critical of their dollar-value contributions to the home. No wonder. If childcare and housework aren't inherently valued by our society, then engaging in even more activities that "don't pay" is an invitation for scrutiny. Others who often cast off their need for Unicorn Space were busy working moms: How, they asked, were they supposed to fit another activity into their schedule without their work and home life suffering?

Despite these obstacles, those women I spoke to who *have* pursued their passions, irrespective of how it financially contributed to the household, report a bolstering sense of pride and self-worth.

You're next.

5.

RULE #3: START WHERE YOU ARE *NOW*

The stakes are high.

N ow that you understand the value of reclaiming your time and mental space so that you and your partner can reach the ultimate level of Fair Play—two happy people who feel purposeful and fulfilled within and *beyond* the walls of the home—your next move is to start where you are now. The guiding principle of Rule #3 is that you cannot get to where you want to go without first understanding: Who am I? Who am I really in a relationship with? And what is my specific intention for playing the game? Your answers to these fundamental questions, along with an honest assessment of how many task cards you hold today, will serve as your baseline for the Fair Play rules that follow.

As you read through **Rule #3: Start Where You Are *Now***, fill out your Marital Mash-Up.

MARITAL MASH-UP

My name is _____. I currently hold _____ cards. I am a
_____. I am married to a _____. My intention for
playing the game is _____.

GAME CHANGER

The first thing to acknowledge about yourself is that—
whatever your Fair Play personality type (I'll get into those in a
minute)—you have it in you to be a game changer in your marriage. Yes, *you*. When I delivered this assessment to women
of nearly all walks of life, family configurations, income, and
ethnic groups across the country, I was frequently met with
similar resistance. Women interviewees recurrently balked:

> *Why is "making change" on me, too?*
>
> *I already do everything else.*
>
> *Why me . . . and not my partner?*

Dr. Phyllis Cohen can answer that question. She has been a
couples' therapist for more than 40 years and has a postdoc-
toral degree in psychoanalysis and psychotherapy. Her practice is based on the precept: "It all starts with a game changer.
Only one person has to initiate change to proactively change
the entire system."

And that one person is *you*. In fact, you've already initiated
change by picking up this book and investing your valuable
time learning about a new system that promises to renegoti-

ate, rebalance, and reenergize your marriage. Sure, you could wait for your partner to change the old patterns, but then you may be waiting indefinitely. When the dishes, the laundry, and the resentment continue to pile up, one person has to step forward and say: *I don't want to live this way anymore.* "Without one person initiating change, you'll both stay stuck in the same old patterns," cautions Dr. Cohen. And the good news she offers is that, "No matter how many years you've been married or how firmly entrenched your marital patterns or dynamics are, there *is* always the possibility of change."

What if you allowed yourself to believe that the collaborative relationship and the life you want is entirely within reach?

Of course, you will need your partner's willing participation to make sustainable change, but initiating change is your move. Rather than regard this responsibility as more burdensome work, be the courageous one who takes the lead to put an end to the sh*tshow. As Nora Ephron, epic storyteller and all-around cool chick, charged, "Be the heroine of your own life, not the victim." You feel the power in that, right?

THE FAIR PLAY TASK CARDS

Now that you've claimed the title of master game changer, let's get right to it—how much childcare and domestic work are *you* shouldering day to day? How many Fair Play cards are you holding? We'll take an up-close look at what each card entails in Chapter 7. But without further ado, here's the shorthand version of the "100 Cards of Fair Play," all that it takes to keep a household with children running. Do you see now why you're always so busy?

100 TASK CARDS OF FAIR PLAY

🍵 Daily Grind   😊 Happiness Trio

THE HOME SUIT (22 CARDS)	**1.** childcare helpers 🍵	**2.** cleaning	**3.** dishes 🍵
	4. dry cleaning	**5.** garbage 🍵	**6.** groceries 🍵
7. home furnishings	**8.** home goods & supplies 🍵	**9.** home maintenance 🍵	**10.** home purchase/ rental, mortgage & insurance
11. hosting	**12.** laundry 🍵	**13.** lawn & plants	**14.** mail 🍵
15. meals (weekday breakfast) 🍵	**16.** meals (school lunch) 🍵	**17.** meals (weekday dinner) 🍵	**18.** meals (weekend)
19. memories & photos	**20.** money manager	**21.** storage, garage & seasonal items	**22.** tidying up, organizing & donations 🍵

100 TASK CARDS OF FAIR PLAY

☕ **Daily Grind**   ☺ **Happiness Trio**

THE OUT SUIT (22 CARDS)	**1.** auto	**2.** birthday celebrations (other kids)	**3.** calendar keeper ☕
	4. cash & bills ☕	**5.** charity, community service & good deeds (adults)	**6.** civic engagement & cultural enrichment
7. electronics & IT	**8.** extracurricular (non-sports) ☕	**9.** extracurricular (sports) ☕	**10.** first-aid, safety & emergency
11. packing & unpacking (local) ☕	**12.** packing & unpacking (travel)	**13.** points, miles & coupons	**14.** returns & store credits
15. school breaks (non-summer)	**16.** school breaks (summer)	**17.** school forms	**18.** social plans (couples)
19. transportation (kids) ☕	**20.** travel	**21.** tutoring & coaching	**22.** weekend plans (family)

100 TASK CARDS OF FAIR PLAY

Daily Grind   Happiness Trio

THE CAREGIVER SUIT
(22 CARDS)

1. bathing & grooming (kids)

2. beauty & wardrobe (her)

3. bedtime routine

4. birth control

5. clothes & accessories (kids)

6. dental (kids)

7. diapering & potty training

8. estate planning & life insurance

9. friendships & social media (kids)

10. grooming & wardrobe (him)

11. health insurance

12. homework, projects & school supplies

13. medical & healthy living

14. morning routine

15. parents & in-laws

16. pets

17. school service

18. school transitions

19. self-care (her)

20. self-care (him)

21. special needs & mental health (kids)

22. teacher communication

100 TASK CARDS OF FAIR PLAY

☕ Daily Grind   ☺ Happiness Trio

THE **MAGIC SUIT** (22 CARDS)	1. adult friendships (her) ☺	2. adult friendships (him) ☺	3. birthday celebrations (your kids)
	4. discipline & screen time ☕	5. extended family	6. fun! & playing
7. gestures of love (kids)	8. gifts (family)	9. gifts (VIPs)	10. hard questions
11. holiday cards	12. holidays	13. informal education	14. magical beings
15. marriage & romance	16. middle-of-the-night comfort ☕	17. partner coach	18. showing up & participating
19. spirituality	20. thank-you notes	21. values & good deeds (kids)	22. watching ☕

100 TASK CARDS OF FAIR PLAY

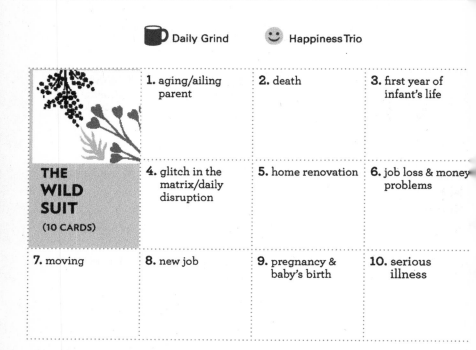

☕ Daily Grind   😊 Happiness Trio

THE WILD SUIT (10 CARDS)	1. aging/ailing parent	2. death	3. first year of infant's life
	4. glitch in the matrix/daily disruption	5. home renovation	6. job loss & money problems
7. moving	8. new job	9. pregnancy & baby's birth	10. serious illness

UNICORN SPACE (2 CARDS)	1. unicorn space (her)	2. unicorn space (him)
	 😊	 😊

RULE #3: START WHERE YOU ARE *NOW*

As I designed it, the Fair Play system consists of 100 tasks, or "cards," that very thoughtfully and intentionally organize the domestic ecosystem into five master suits—**Home, Out, Caregiving, Magic,** and **Wild,** as well as the all-important **Unicorn Space** card that each partner must play.

> *Note!* 60 of the Fair Play cards are not kid-related, which means you can enter the system and begin rebalancing the deck with your partner before having children.

Cards in the **Home** suit include laundry, garbage runs, grocery lists, and other Daily Grind repetitive tasks (noted with a coffee cup), most of which *must happen every day* and many *at a specific time.* Take, for example, the typical morning grind for mothers and fathers who, according to a pop culture report out of the UK, must perform **43 tasks** like packing school lunches and tossing dishes into the sink before even walking out the door—creating an extra 10 hours and 15 minutes of domestic work a week before your 9-to-5 day job begins!

Cards in the **Out** suit include many things done away from home, like transporting kids to school, extracurricular sports, and getting the car's oil changed. Note: Stay-at-home moms will tell you that the bulk of their time is not actually spent *at home,* but *out of the house,* dashing from here to there in a mad effort to fulfill these task cards.

Cards in the **Caregiving** suit are things like potty training, pet care, homework assignments, and the bedtime routine. These are heavy-lifting cards that require a generous hand from your partner or spouse.

Cards in the **Magic** suit include moments of meaningful connection and relationship building. They include birthday celebrations, middle-of-the-night comfort, and leaving a buck for the tooth fairy. It takes many hours of invisible and emotional work to create these moments, and yet it's some of the most rewarding work as parents.

Cards in the **Wild** suit include life-changing scenarios like a job change, losing a loved one, or moving homes. Even if it's a planned and joyful event like having a baby, a **Wild** card—if poorly managed—can disrupt your household, upend your career, and even end your marriage.

CAUTION!
This Is NOT a Score-Keeping Exercise

It will be very tempting for you to look at the "100 Cards of Fair Play" chart and begin keeping score. You may also feel provoked to show it to your partner (e.g., shove it in his face), and swap totals with your girlfriends. This will only do harm, so I strongly advise against it. Making visible and counting all the invisible work you do holds value, but **this is only the starting point. It is not the solution.**

TO HAVE AND TO HOLD

Before we go any further, it's imperative you understand the Fair Play definition of what it means to fully *hold* a card. Within the Fair Play system, holding means you **Conceive, Plan,** and **Execute** every aspect of a domestic task card. Here's an example of how "CPE" works:

Let's say you hold the "groceries" card. Your kid is a big fan of mustard on his hot dog. You notice there is no mustard in the refrigerator or the pantry. That's **Conception**. You add mustard to the grocery list that you create every week. You schedule when you'll go to the store and consult your partner and anyone else helping around the house for any add-ons to the list. That's **Planning**. You go to the grocery store so that mustard is restored to the fridge before your son takes a bite (of what you like to think is the best hot dog in the world, because it's made with love—*and mustard*). That's **Execution.**

Within the Fair Play system, playing for CPE requires that whoever holds a task card Conceives, Plans, and Executes the heck out of it—without reminders, half-ass efforts and excuses, or soliciting a "good job" for completion. If you're thinking: *Yeah, right. That's unrealistic and not the way we do things around here, or would ever do things,* let me stop you. Throughout my extensive beta testing, I observed over and over again that the couples who adhere to the Fair Play CPE approach experience the most dramatic shifts away from dysfunction, resentment, and passive-aggressive behaviors in their relationship and toward more time-saving efficiency and feelings of fairness in the home.

In other words, when both people completely own their sh*t, it's not only more efficient, but there is far less nagging (huge benefit to husbands) and a significant lift in the mental load (huge benefit to wives). The CPE approach is completely transformative. It totally changes the game.

This organizational approach has been helping professional companies for 50 years. Each of the thousands of tasks required to create and bring our favorite products into our homes have assigned *project managers* or *team leaders* whose job it is to Conceive, Plan, and Execute how a given task will be completed. This includes Conceiving of the overall need, Planning how and what is required to get it done completely, and then ensuring that this plan is Executed by someone on the team in a way that meets the product's requirements. All types of project managers will tell you that they live or die by CPE because it's basically the most efficient way to get things done.

Why, then, aren't we applying CPE within our domestic organizations?

CONSIDER:
THE CASE OF THE OVER-REPORTER

Doug, a shipping supervisor from Philadelphia, was one of my first interviewees after I incorporated the CPE approach into Fair Play. I asked him, "What jobs in your home are you solely responsible for?"

He was quick to answer: "I make dinner every night." Doug sounded like a modern man, one who shares more domestic duties with his wife than in previous generations. And yet, given my obsession with the topic, I was familiar with the finding that when self-reporting, men tend to overestimate how much domestic work and childcare they actually do. In a popular *New York Times* piece titled "Men Do More At Home, But Not As Much As They Think," Claire Cain Miller provides evidence that men believe they're taking on more at home than they are in reality. So I pressed Doug to list the specific steps required to perform and complete this daily and time-consuming task. He looked at me sideways. "It's pretty basic, really. I make dinner."

I clarified: "As part of dinner prep, do you also plan the

RULE #3: START WHERE YOU ARE *NOW*

menu and put all the items and ingredients you need on the grocery list?"

"Nah," he said with a dismissive wave of his hand. "That's my wife's territory. She plans the meals and does the shopping. *I'm* the cook." I jotted this down in my Moleskine, noting this as a CPE Break-Up (more on this later), when one person oversees Conception (creating the family meal plan) and Planning (adding those items to the grocery list) and the other handles Execution (cooking). In this particular case, Doug was claiming ownership of "weekday dinners," even though his wife was allocating a sizeable portion of her brainpower to help her husband maintain his *Top Chef* status.

In one interview after another, very few couples reported households where one partner took a CPE lead for any one card in the full deck. With this in mind, for each of the Fair Play cards, I began to look at every one through a CPE lens. I went back to my original "Sh*t I Do" list and reorganized it based on what is required to Conceive, Plan, and Execute each domestic task. I did this so that *anyone*—my partner, my babysitter, or even my mom—understood every part of what was required to meet a single responsibility fully. I put every detail down and left nothing in my head.

Sounds like even more work you don't have time for, right? And yet, providing this amount of context is what someone who is not a mind reader requires to execute in a competent manner. The good news is: **I already did it for you.**

Soon you and your partner will have a thoughtful discussion about who is better to take the lead and CPE each Fair Play card based on your individual preferences, capabilities, and availability. For now, in determining the most accurate assessment of how many cards you alone currently hold, flip back to the "100 Task Cards of Fair Play" chart on pages 108–12 or download the playing cards from fairplaylife.com and count those where you believe you're responsible for the Conception and Planning only. Ignore the Execution for now, even if, *let's face it*, you also do that, too. If there are cards where you think you and your partner are both "holding" some aspect of the "C" and the "P," give yourself half a card for now.

COUNT YOUR TASK CARDS AND RECORD YOUR TOTAL:

_____

MARITAL MASH-UP:
How many cards do you hold?

My name is <u>Eve</u>. I currently hold <u>87 cards</u>. I am a _____. I am married to a _____. My intention for playing the game is _____.

DO NO HARM! Research shows that women shoulder more of the burden of household and childrearing responsibilities than men do, so, ladies: Once you've totaled how many Fair Play cards you currently hold, take a patient breath. Again, I dissuade you from presenting a tallied list to your partner as evidence of who's doing more or less until you actually play the game in Part III, when you will both have the tools to assess who holds what cards with full CPE context.

Q: But really, how many task cards should each partner hold?
A: A fair share. Let me explain . . .

Over lunch with my friend Claire, who loves a good gender wars debate, she asked me pointedly, "Why *fair* play and not *equal* play? You always talk about equal time, so doesn't that also mean sharing equally in the work?"

"Good catch!" I smiled. "I do believe time is created equal, in that everyone holds the right to choose how we spend our time. At the same time, pun intended, when it comes to the actual division of labor, the cards won't necessarily be evenly split because what's fair is not always equal and what's equal is not always fair."

When the "Sh*t I Do" list went wide, prompting women all over the world to complain about their spouses—"He doesn't do *even close* to half"—I recognized that couples who strive for "splitsies," or who demand a 50/50 partnership and don't get it, are highly prone to giving up. **Couples will only win at this game by emphasizing fairness.** How that breaks down by the numbers will come into play later on.

WHAT'S YOUR TYPE?

After talking to hundreds of women on the subject of how they get things done at home, I've found that most describe themselves as predominantly one of the following four personality types based on how many cards they *currently* hold. You may recognize yourself as the intersection of two or more types, but if you had to pick one dominant type, who are you *today*? Recognize that how you self-identify will likely change once you start playing, and depending on how you and your partner negotiate and continue to renegotiate the Fair Play cards.

Who are you?

>> New Superwoman

You are holding at least 60 task cards and you work outside the home full-time. In the 1970s, the "super" term was used as a badge of honor for working mothers. Career, marriage, kids, friendships, hobbies—*Look at all I have!* But if you're one of today's superwomen who has checked all the requisite boxes, spinning yourself into an endless cycle of work-parent-sleep-repeat, and even if your job is your Unicorn Space, you're likely feeling "decision fatigue" and hitting the "exhaustion ceiling" from not only *having* it all but *doing* it all, too. If you're not careful, you may soon be at your crashing point. The New Superwomen I interviewed were some of the most competent, ambitious, and successful women I've met. And still, many were considering opting out of the workforce, and every one of them reported an illness or ailment. Every. Single. One! At the top of the list: insomnia—not a shocker, as sleep disruption is the nighttime manifestation of daytime busy brain.

New Superwomen are often heard saying, "I just can't turn off my mind," along with the all-too-familiar "I have no time for myself," "I'm right on the edge," and "If I have to juggle one more thing . . ." It may feel out of character to delegate full Conception, Planning, and Execution to your spouse, especially if you still believe that your true superpower is your ability to multitask. And yet, something's got to give. It is imperative that you hand over some responsibility before you're dealt a **Wild** card that brings your house down. Imagine substituting the mixed satisfaction you often feel from *accomplishing it all* to the restorative feeling that comes from a blissful eight hours of sleep every night.

>> Accidental Traditionalist

You hold at least 60 task cards and either work part-time or are a full-time stay-at-home parent. You're a traditionalist in the sense that your partner has taken on the role of the primary breadwinner, but you didn't necessarily plan to create a conventional gender divide in your own home. You likely intended to stay in the workforce and may have considered yourself a modern-day superwoman at one point, but now you find yourself joining the 43 percent of highly qualified women with kids who, for a variety of reasons, take a career detour. You enjoy your time at home and are grateful for the flexibility that your spouse and employer have afforded you. Still, you may have the recurring desire to reenergize your career or special skill set. But on days when do-it-all domestic duties consume your waking hours, taking on a second shift—even if for pay—doesn't seem worth the exhausting effort.

The Accidental Traditionalist often says to herself: "This isn't the career + marriage combo deal I thought I'd have," "What's happened to me?" and "Where did my time go?" Imagine what it would feel like to pull the emergency brake on the fast-moving train you now find yourself on and strike a new deal with your partner.

>> Intentional Traditionalist

You willingly hold more than 60 task cards because you made the intentional choice to take on more of the caregiving and domestic workload than your spouse. For as long as you can remember, you've always wanted to dedicate your life to the home. Caretaking brings you great joy and satisfaction, and in your traditional role as wife and mother, you're proud of your fastidious attention to every invisible detail inside the home. Still, on many days, you feel as if there are just not enough hours between sunup and sundown to get it all done.

Because you regard your position at the helm of the household as your sole responsibility (and your spouse likely agrees), you're prone to the heavy winds of guilt and shame that prevent you from asking for help, taking mental breathers, or engaging in important self-care. When a trip to the dentist feels like an indulgence, the idea of carving out Unicorn Space truly seems like a fantasy. In truth, you may desire something *more*, and yet you feel guilty admitting this to other SAHMs. You don't want to appear ungrateful; staying home was your choice. But as the years tick on, the more you consider back-to-me time a slim possibility. The Intentional Traditionalist often says: "I don't have time for *soul* projects," "My passion is my kids," and "Running the household is *my job*." Imagine, though, if you gave yourself permission to expand your role beyond wife and mother to include the joy of rediscovering *you*.

>> Collaborator (Lucky Woman!)

You hold less than 60 task cards. You may have a job outside the home, or you may not. Either way, you easily collaborate and you're lucky to have a partner who willingly handles his fair share of domestic tasks, allowing you to both make time for self-care, friendships, and Unicorn Space (the Happiness Trio). To keep the household humming along peacefully, you and your partner faithfully discuss childcare and home responsibilities. But even you and yours can benefit from Fair

Play. It can start to feel like too many cooks in the kitchen as you both assume a leadership role. Two people unloading the dishwasher won't get the job done faster—you'll only get in each other's way! In your house, play to optimize efficiency.

WHERE DOES YOUR MOON RISE?

Once you determine your dominant Fair Play personality, similar to your astrological sign, consider that you may also have a "moon rising" in one of the following types.

>> My Way or Move Out!

Me: "I need some help around here!"
Also me: "No, not like that . . . here, I'll do it."

Parroting this popular meme, you often complain how you're doing it *all*, and yet you're reluctant to give up control because you believe that the best course of action is *yours*. Even if you feel more competent at Conception and Planning, your tendency to second-guess your partner, call out mistakes, and create a home environment where you micromanage every detail will do more harm than good. Enlisting your partner to merely Execute for Mama's signoff and approval may save some time up front, but in the end, it's exhausting for you and infantilizing for your husband, and contributes to the domestic workload imbalance. For a moment, imagine if you'd allow yourself to relinquish some of your "my way" maternal gatekeeping and empower your partner to CPE more of the domestic workload. Wouldn't you prefer to have a true collaborator instead of someone always asking, "If you just *tell* me what to do, and *how* to do it, I'll help"?

>> I Got It

Regardless of how many cards you hold, you may have a moon rising in this personality type as well. Whether you have a paid job outside the home or work full-time as a SAHM, you're the hardest-working mother you know, and you want points for all that you do. *You're welcome! And you owe me.* And yet, when you're offered help, your reaction is to decline with a long-suffering "It's OK, I got it," because carrying the household burden makes you feel valuable and necessary. You're disinclined to hand off cards to your partner because this might dismantle your sense of worth. Managing the household is a big part of how you identify yourself and popular culture has another name for you: the martyr mom. If you stayed up late helping kids with homework and skipped breakfast to drive morning carpool in your jammies—pause and take a look in the rearview mirror. Can you imagine the *new* version of yourself that might emerge when you reject your I Got It role and work with your partner toward creating more fairness with your combined time?

POP QUIZ
What Fair Play Type Are You?

You want to go away for a weekend with your girlfriends. The following goes through your head as you make preparations:

    A. I have work to do, but I can easily sit poolside and take office phone calls, answer texts from home, and

FaceTime with the kids. It might feel like I've never left town, but being two places at the same time is my superpower. If the sh*t hits the fan and I have to return home or to the office, I've already made prearrangements for an early checkout. After all, I planned and booked this getaway for the whole group.

B. Get me out of here! Maybe in my absence, my partner will see and appreciate all I do. Of course, I didn't leave him totally hanging—the baby's food is prepped, laundry is washed and folded, and my detailed list of daily to-dos is on the fridge so he doesn't have to think. Still, I'm secretly hoping that he fails (just a little!) so he understands how hard it is to juggle domestic life. Meanwhile, I'll be drinking a well-deserved margarita poolside, sucka!

C. I'm not really comfortable handing over my home responsibilities to someone else, and I don't want to inconvenience my husband or the kids. I've asked my mother to come over and help out, and if I need to come home early, I will.

D. I'm so happy to get away with my girlfriends, knowing my spouse can totally handle whatever comes up. As a thank-you, I'll offer to watch the kids for a long weekend so he can get away.

E. Even though I need this trip more than anyone, I rarely leave my kids overnight. They hate it when I'm gone. I'll probably not end up going.

F. I can't believe how much I have to plan ahead of time just so I can leave for two days. I'm sure sh*t will go sideways even though I spent a full hour going over every conceivable scenario and how to handle the big and small details with my husband.

To be sure the house doesn't burn down or my kids go missing, I'll have my phone with me at the pool so I can check in regularly. And believe me, I will.

ANSWERS

If you answered A, you're a **New Superwoman**

If you answered B, you're an **Accidental Traditionalist**

If you answered C, you're an **Intentional Traditionalist**

If you answered D, you're a **Collaborator**

If you answered E, you have a moon rising in **I Got It**

If you answered F, you have a moon rising in **My Way or Move Out**

MARITAL MASH-UP:
What's your Fair Play personality type?

My name is <u>Eve</u>. I currently hold <u>87 cards</u>. I am an <u>Accidental Traditionalist with a moon rising in My Way or Move Out</u>. I am married to a _____. My intention for playing the game is _____.

WHO ARE YOU MARRIED TO?

Some say that one of the most important decisions a woman makes is who she marries, and yet the research shows that you really don't know who you married until you have kids! In my conversations with women about defining roles and responsibilities within the household, they describe their partner/husband/fathers' behaviors and tendencies within these five types. Who are you living with *today*?

RULE #3: START WHERE YOU ARE *NOW*

>> Giant Kid

Your partner is fun, lighthearted, spontaneous, and exciting, but often blurs the lines between himself and the kids, disrespects house rules (even those he sets), and rejects structure and other attempts to formalize time management for the family. He doesn't clean up his own mess or voluntarily sign up to help. This is not because he's incapable (although he may act as if he is and malinger to let himself off the hook). Rather, because you're so clearly capable, the often unspoken implication is that the more laborious, and definitively less-fun, tasks of domestic life are "on you." Instead of being appreciative of all that you do, your partner may instead complain, "You're so not fun" and "Lighten up."

>> Traditionalist

Your partner takes on the role of primary breadwinner, is supportive of your position as keeper of the domestic gavel, and is complimentary of your efforts in the home. On the flip side, irrespective of whether you also work outside the home, he expects domestic duties to follow traditional gender roles and is not particularly flexible or interested in making changes or curious about how the donuts are made behind the scenes. When things go wrong, he's likely to point fingers, and he requires a lot of praise for Executing any task card. He is, after all, doing the *most important work* of earning money. You have a Traditionalist on your hands if you routinely hear any of the following Toxic Time messages:

"What did you do all day?"

"If you don't have enough time, get help!"

"It's not worth it for *you* to go to work, too."

"I make all the money and now you want me to . . ."

>> Where's the Butter?

Your partner is a competent leader at work who can Conceive, Plan, and Execute entirely on his own and also effectively delegate, but somehow he leaves these amazing organizational and time-management skills behind when he steps across the threshold every evening. Once inside of his castle, he seems entirely clueless, relying on you for all domestic navigation. When he opens the refrigerator door, eyeing the shelf where the butter always lives, it's not uncommon for him to ask with feigned helplessness as depicted in the famous cartoon, "Hon, where's the butter?" If this is your guy, you keep hoping he'll *figure it out*, but until he's given more CPE context and encouraged to take the lead, he will continue to make daily excuses like:

"You do it so much better than me."

"You're supposed to remind me."

"I forgot. It's just not something I think about."

"You are the CEO of the house."

>> One Step Forward, Two Steps Back

Your partner has great intentions, is always willing to lend a hand, and would likely agree to take on more control of domestic tasks. Alas, he often bites off far more than he can chew because he has a hard time Conceiving and Planning realistically, often becoming unfocused and falling behind schedule as he works through whatever he launches into, and then he struggles to ask for help or worries that he'll let you down. In the end, and despite all of his thoughtfulness, he often cannot Plan effectively and will fall back on, "It's easier if you just tell me what to do."

>> More Than Most

Your partner already gets it! He inherently values time equally and appreciates that you're both time starved. Because of this, he's flexible in his thinking and with his schedule. A MTM is always happy to Execute a task card without making you feel that he's doing you a favor, and he doesn't point fingers when the inevitable occurs and something falls through the cracks. And yet, like other partners, he may not *fully* comprehend what it takes to keep your household moving forward. The encouraging news: As soon as your guy is introduced to the CPE approach, he will quickly convert from a happy Executor to a full partner of domestic life. I call that an *Even More Than Most*.

POP QUIZ
Who's Your Partner?

You go away for the weekend. When you get home, you're greeted this way:

A. The house will be in reasonable order and the kids will be happy and fed when you walk in the door. Does your domestic landscape look exactly like you left it? Probably not, but count your blessings—you had an uninterrupted weekend away and your husband was happy to be in charge!

B. With the aid of your detailed instructions, the house is still standing. Plan to spend your first evening back delivering high praise to your spouse for "getting it right."

C. The house will be in moderate disarray: an unfinished craft project on the dining room table, a stack of unopened mail, and a heap of clean laundry on the bed—evidence that your husband had the best intentions but not the most successful follow-through. Expect to listen to a long list of reasons for why things fell through the cracks in your absence. "I'm so happy you're home," he says honestly when you walk through the door.

D. The house will most definitely be a mess and the kids will be happily enjoying the "anything goes" vibe—until you walk in the door and ask when the kids last had a bath or a meal away from the TV. Depending on the length of time you were away, there may also be marker scrawled across the living room wall. Expect to hear, "Hey, lighten up."

E. The house will probably look better than when you left it, owing to the housekeeper or mother-in-law who stepped forward in your absence (and that you likely scheduled and paid ahead of time). Because your husband's also had the weekend to kick up his feet, he'll appear relaxed and may say, "We were fine. You should go away more often."

ANSWERS

> If you answered A, you're likely married to a **More Than Most**
>
> If you answered B, you're likely married to a **Where's the Butter?**
>
> If you answered C, you're likely married to a **One Step Forward, Two Steps Back**
>
> If you answered D, you're likely married to a **Giant Kid**
>
> If you answered E, you're likely married to a **Traditionalist**

CAUTION!

Identifying your spouse or partner's Fair Play personality type is really for *your knowledge only.* Labeling your partner without providing him with full context will not help your relationship . . . but it will help you clarify your intention for engaging him in Fair Play. (Between you and me, once you're both onboarded to the Fair Play system and playing for more equity in the home, my guess is that your partner will naturally "level up" to a **More Than Most.** At that point, you can both celebrate what an even *more* awesome guy you married!)

MARITAL MASH-UP:
Who are you married to?

My name is <u>Eve</u>. I currently hold <u>87 cards</u>. I am an <u>Accidental Traditionalist with a moon rising in My Way or Move Out</u>. I am married to a <u>Where's the Butter?</u> My intention for playing the game is _____.

WHAT'S YOUR INTENTION?

Oprah said, "Intention is one with cause and effect. Intention determines *outcome*." Now that you've gained some new self-awareness and understand a bit more about the person you married, **clarify your intention for changing the game.** Your answer will greatly influence how you and your partner eventually discuss and engage in Fair Play.

What is the outcome you want? Here's a peek at what some of the women I spoke to said:

"I want to feel less resentful."

"I want to feel more respected and valued for all I do for our family."

"I want my partner to acknowledge and understand all that it takes to run a home."

"I'm so tired of running at 100 miles an hour; I need help!"

"My partner is really helpful, but we don't always agree on what's most important. We need to reprioritize."

"Our marriage feels equitable but totally inefficient."

"We fight over who's doing what; we need clear roles and responsibilities."

"I want to stop being the 'nag' and family taskmaster."

"I want more time to start working on my *own* projects again."

"I'm ready to go back to work and I need help from my partner to make this happen."

"I just want a mental break."

"I want to have fun again."

MARITAL MASH-UP:
What's your intention for playing the game?

My name is <u>Eve</u>. I currently hold <u>87 cards</u>. I am an <u>Accidental Traditionalist with a moon rising in My Way or Move Out</u>. I am married to a <u>Where's the Butter?</u> My intention for playing the game is <u>to reclaim my time and claim my Unicorn Space</u>.

"THE TALK"

Congrats! You've just completed your Marital Mash-Up. Now you're ready to have your first game-changing conversation. (Remember: Someone must make the first move and that will be *you*.) "Ugh," you reluctantly groan. "Is this when I ask my husband to discuss every detail of our home life? The minute he hears, 'We need to talk,' he'll either tune me out or suddenly have something urgent he *must do*, like organize the junk drawer."

Your spouse may resist any urgent request from you to "talk" because what he likely hears is: *Uh oh. I'm in trouble—again.* Rather than approach him in a way where he may react defensively or dismissively, I will provide you with specific mediation language to help you craft an opening line that your partner is amenable to hearing. After all, it takes two to play this game. Change will not happen without your partner's willing participation, and this begins with a thoughtful and engaging conversation. Still, asking your spouse to join you in creating more efficiency, fairness, and harmony in the home—even if you desperately desire and know you deserve a shift in your dynamic—may still feel provocative.

Doug Stone, who taught my favorite class in law school and wrote a book I've used for countless situations at work and in the rest of my life called *Difficult Conversations: How to Discuss What Matters Most*, offers an explanation for why asking your spouse for a change in your dynamic and the household may feel like a high-stakes game:

> Why is it so difficult to decide whether to avoid or to confront? Because at some level we know the truth: If we try to avoid the problem, we'll feel taken advantage of, our feelings will fester, we'll wonder why we don't stick up for ourselves, and we'll rob the other person of the opportunity to improve things. But if we confront the problem, things might get even worse. We may be rejected or attacked; we might hurt the other person in ways we didn't intend; and the relationship might suffer.

Aspects of these layered and complicated emotions came up frequently in my interviews. You may recognize some Toxic Time messages and personality types buried in here:

RULE #3: START WHERE YOU ARE *NOW*

"I know things need to change, but I worry he won't be open to changing."

"It's too hard. I'd rather not talk."

"I'd almost rather keep doing things my way than have to explain a *new* way to my spouse."

"I'm not used to asking for help; I'm used to doing it all."

"I don't want to admit that I need help—that I *can't* do it all."

"The idea of sitting down with my spouse to discuss all that I do in a day makes me want to scream."

"I don't want to have to tell him what to do."

"I worry that he'll become defensive and we'll end up in a fight."

"I'm not even sure what to ask for."

"I can just hear him now—'I already do more than most guys and now you want me to do more'?"

"I shouldn't have to ask for help; he should be able to figure it out."

"In the time it takes to sit down and talk, I can just do it."

"Maybe I'm scared; maybe I'm proud. Whatever it is, I'm not comfortable asking for help."

"What happens if he says no?"

"What happens if I realize I don't have the partnership I thought I had?"

>> **Just Ask**

When the *Huffington Post* asked divorced women what they wished they'd done differently in their marriages, many said: **I wish I would have asked for help when I needed it.** Blogger Valencia Morton of *Millionairess Mama* somberly expressed, "I thought I had to be this super mom and wife, perfect in every way. To me, this meant doing all the child-rearing, housework, and cooking while attempting to look like I just stepped off a Victoria's Secret runway . . . Looking back, all I had to do was say the words to my ex-husband, 'I need help.' I know now that if I had communicated my feelings, we might have had a better chance at marital life."

If you, too, feel hesitant to take the game-changing lead and clearly communicate your feelings and needs to your spouse, guess what? **You've already started a conversation about your domestic life.** As a mediator, I make this point often to my clients when they resist or shy away from direct dialogue and collaborative problem-solving: "But I don't want to talk to my older brother about Dad's will. It's too hard." To which I'll say, "But you're already communicating through your eye-rolling and silence. When you show up late to every meeting, that says something. Even if you're not talking."

I'm going to take a guess here and say the same very likely holds true for you and your spouse. You're already communicating, if even only nonverbally, which can be the loudest form of communication in the room. As examples:

When her husband challenged, "What do you do all day?" Marian created a time-lapse video of hours and hours of invisible work she performs in the home. "Proof," she said, "that I'm not wasting my time on *unnecessary stuff.*"

RULE #3: START WHERE YOU ARE *NOW*

When the Diaper Genie reaches its full capacity, Lydia drags it into the hallway and walks away. "If I neglect to empty it, maybe he'll get the hint."

Lori turns off her phone when her husband's at Target so he can't reach her to ask: What do we need? And what aisle is that in?

Julia admits to sometimes "playing possum" when her young son comes into their bedroom in the middle of the night. "That way, my husband has to be the one to get up."

Diana posts to-dos for her partner on the bathroom mirror with the following instruction: *Don't forget!*

Stella dumps wet clothes on her husband's pillow when he forgets to put them in the dryer.

If Stacy doesn't receive an "I'm running behind" courtesy phone call or text, she locks her husband out of the house when he arrives home late for family dinner.

"I let him learn by leaving," said Wendy, who makes a habit of walking out the door when her husband isn't ready for events on time. "Meet me there," she'll bark.

Trudy withholds sex until all the dishes are out of the sink.

Face it: You're already having the conversation about who does what in your relationship, in some form or another. Let's take it out of the realm of the unspoken and deal with it head-on.

POP QUIZ
How Do You Communicate?

Passive-aggressive reminders, silent finger pointing, and abandoning our partners, literally and emotionally, to figure it out. This is how many of us are soliciting relief. And when we're unsure we'll receive that helping hand we need, some of us go to extremes to control the outcome we desire. On an "off day," what's your communication vulnerability?

Long-winded: *Wah wah wahhhhhhh.* You're talking and no one's listening.

Sharp commands, *sir*: Your drill sergeant delivery isn't popular with the troops.

Bad timing: You drop your grievances and requests for help into the conversation at inopportune moments. "Thanks for the flowers, honey, but you forgot the dishwashing detergent. Go back out to the store before it closes at ten?"

Toxic word choice: "I wasn't going to say anything, but I really hate it when you . . . Next time, you really need to do it this way..."

All or nothing: "You *never* replace the toilet paper roll. You *always* leave the seat up."

Dredging up the past: "This is just like the last time you forgot to . . ."

Boiling over: "I wasn't going to say anything. I didn't say anything. And now, I'm *really* pissed."

>> Not a Start—a Shift

Recognize that you and your partner have already been communicating about domestic responsibilities, just not in the most positive or constructive way. Jennifer Waldburger, MSW, and a parent educator who's worked with thousands of mothers and fathers around the globe, cautions, "The root cause of many marriage failures is divisive communication." So be the one who now takes the lead to use your voice to shift the conversation away from "he said, she said," "I'm right, you're wrong" competition into the direction of true collaboration.

My interviews with all types of husband/fathers revealed that **most men respond positively to a direct approach, an explicit and collaborative request for help.** "Instead of giving me the 'I'm so disappointed' or 'I hate you' stare as she folds the laundry, I'd rather my wife just ask me for what she needs," offered Mark from San Antonio.

To be clear: By asking your partner for "help," you are not soliciting a "helper" who Executes on your command, but a true collaborator in the system. In *Fed Up*, author Gemma Hartley does a beautiful job of explaining the difference: "Helping means 'this is not my job.' Helping means 'I'm doing you a favor.' Helping means 'this is your responsibility.' Helping implies that the helper is going above and beyond... [Full partnership] means turning away from the idea of help entirely and taking on responsibility in an even manner."

With this important distinction in mind, loop back on your intention for rebalancing the cards and craft this into a clear invitation to engage your partner in Fair Play. Be patient as you communicate. You might say: "Hey, I've been reading this book and it's gotten me thinking about all the work it takes to run our home. I'd like to explore a new way to work *together* [key sentiment!] to dial down the crazy and create more balance and efficiency, and where ultimately we both have more time to pursue interests and activities outside our roles as parents. Are you into that?"

Whatever your specific word choice, aim to keep this first conversation short and upbeat and pick a time when the kids are occupied (that is, don't ask your partner to begin thinking about how to renegotiate the domestic workload when you're both trying to calm a screaming baby and order take-out pizza at the same time). Rather, casually drop your invitation into one of those cherished and fleeting moments when the house is quiet and you're both relaxed.

>> Preparation Is the Key

If my suggestion to craft an opening line hits you as too staged or rehearsed, consider that a few minutes of strategic planning will make a considerable difference in how your words are received. You wouldn't walk into a job interview or give a presentation at the school's fundraiser meeting without having done your prep work, right? How well you communicate directly affects how well you are *heard* out in the world, and this also holds true in your own home. Naturally, you want to sound authentic. Like yourself. You're not trying to sell your spouse an insurance policy. At the same time, it's imperative that you give your word choice meaningful thought and deliver your message in a way that engages and invites your partner into the conversation, rather than alienating him. Furthermore, your invitation is more likely to be accepted if you offer your partner a value proposition that resonates with his personality type.

>> What's My Line?

To help me implement a game that **requires two players,** I offered my own husband the promise of more context, less control, explicitly defined expectations, and a wife who wouldn't scream at him in front of the kids every time the garbage wasn't emptied.

How can you thoughtfully invite *your* spouse to engage in Fair Play in a way that allows you both to win? Depending on who you're in a relationship with, your value proposition may vary.

If your partner is:

Giant Kid: Invite him to play a "game" that will create more efficiency in the home without losing the fun. What's in it for him, specifically? Less nagging and far more levity. You may suggest: "I'd like to explore a new way to work *together* that recaptures some of who we were *before* we had kids."

Traditionalist: Rather than ask him to change, invite him to support *you.* Play up your need for Unicorn Space. You may suggest: "I'd like to explore a new way to rebalance our time that allows me to rediscover my passions beyond the home." What's in it for him, specifically? He'll have a happier and more fulfilled wife at the helm.

Where's the Butter?: Invite your competent guy to learn about a "new home management system" that will alleviate inefficiencies and make domestic life less crazy-making for both of you. What's in it for him, specifically? A partner who empowers him to take the lead.

One Step Forward, Two Steps Back: Invite your go-getter partner to rebalance the domestic workload in a way that sets him up to succeed. What's in it for him, specifically? By providing him with more context, he can easily do his part without being second-guessed for his contributions or criticized for his efforts.

More Than Most: Invite your willing partner to explore an even better way to collaborate for more efficiency at home. He won't need much convincing to jump on board because you already communicate effectively, but it never hurts to play up the promise of more fun and free time together.

>> RSVP

This first game-changing tête-à-tête with your partner should take *less than five minutes*—less than 1 percent of your day. You're not explaining the whole Fair Play system; you're just inviting him to the table. Still, if you begin to lose your nerve, stand your ground and remind yourself that **you deserve a partner who values you and the relationship enough to play with you.**

Every invitation requires an RSVP, so be sure to set up a future date, place, and time where you will eventually sit down to discuss in more detail a new way to collaborate in the home. Commit to your date to begin rebalancing the deck!

INVITATION TO FAIR PLAY

Date:

Place:

Time:

Couples who have already gone through the Fair Play system have reported back that the "right place, right time" is key. Across the board, women swore by wedding anniversary dates, Valentine's Day, birthdays, and weekend date nights as the best times for introducing their spouses to Fair Play. At first, these emotionally charged dates struck me as the worst times to discuss rebalancing the domestic workload, but my testers explained that it was exactly in these settings where their partners were the most willing to participate in conversations about the future of the relationship.

"For our anniversary, we went hiking. Talking about our relationship as we watched the sunset from the top of a mountain was easy because he was already in a collaborative 'we're in this together' state of mind."

"We were out to dinner at our favorite restaurant. Neither one of us were in 'fight mode,' and so the conversation flowed naturally."

"It was my birthday. When he asked me what I wanted, I said—'to come up with a new game plan for creating an even happier marriage.' Well, he couldn't say no to that."

CONSIDER:
THE CASE OF THE WEDNESDAYS

Still not sure that *your* partner will play?

"When my wife asked me to talk about shifting the workload in our home, I resisted at first," admitted the Reverend Dr. Stephen Treat, senior therapist and marriage counselor. "Specifically, she asked me to take over childcare and household responsibilities on Wednesdays, and I thought: But this is *my* day to meet with patients. Wednesdays have always been *on her*. But she really wanted the day 'off' so that she could take a class at the local junior college. I appreciated that she wanted me to step in and I wanted to help her.

"So soon, I took over school pickup, homework, and anything that needed to be done on Wednesdays for our daughter. And guess what I discovered—this time at home didn't take away from my business or me, and more important, my daughter and I grew closer. On my daughter's wedding day over two decades later, she said that the thing she cherished most about Dad is 'our Wednesdays.' I smiled over at my wife of nearly 50 years. Of course, we hadn't had Fair Play back then, but that's exactly what we'd done. We'd 'rebalanced the deck,' and I'm so grateful to my wife for inviting me to make a change."

6.

RULE #4:
ESTABLISH YOUR VALUES
AND STANDARDS

Level the playing field.

ESTABLISHING YOUR VALUES

You've invited your partner to the table, but before you both actually sit down to play, it's essential to comprehend **Rule #4: Establish Your Values and Standards.** This concept is such a hot-button issue for couples that I want to really focus on it here, before you start negotiating cards.

Let's start with value setting. If you've been shouldering the brunt of the grunt work in your household—and especially if you're a New Superwoman—grab hold of this mantra and repeat it again, and again, and again.

I do not have to do it all.

"Many capable people are kept from getting to the next level," suggests thought leader Greg McKeown in *Essentialism: The Disciplined Pursuit of Less*, "because they can't let go of the belief that everything is important."

Chew on that for a moment. What if everything isn't important? What if you let some of it . . . go? What if you choose with intention what you want to do in service of the home and your family based on what's *most valuable* to you and your partner? Rather than doing *more*, or continuing to believe that you should do *it all*, save yourself from burnout and what the millennial generation has termed "errand paralysis" by engaging in a process that systematically lightens your load and allows you to live the life you truly want. In other words, give yourself permission to do less!

You won't actually trim your deck (i.e., take sh*t off your plate) until Chapter 8: Playing the Game, but now is the time to begin taking stock of your domestic ecosystem. When you consider the cards you're currently holding, are there any you want to throw out? And I don't mean hand over to your spouse, but throw out with the bathwater entirely? As an example:

"I'm done. No more classmate birthday parties." As soon as she said it, Sara expected pushback or at least a critical look from her husband.

Instead, her husband, Clark, shrugged and said, "I'm cool with that."

Of course *he* was cool with that because he rarely attended these weekend events at the jumpy gym or the video arcade that sucked up the majority of Sara's daylight hours and left her feeling nearly deaf and drained.

"I mean," she hoped to clarify, "I don't want to attend another kid's birthday party for as long as I live, unless," she conceded, "it's for one of Bennie's very close friends or a family member."

RULE #4: ESTABLISH YOUR VALUES AND STANDARDS

"I agree with you," said Clark. "Those places make me crazy. Why do you think I don't go? And Bennie doesn't really like them either. He's not into big crowds. He always comes home crying because he didn't get 'his turn' or he's melting down from all the sugar and the strobe lights."

Then why am I spending my time and our family's valuable weekend time doing this? thought Sara, although she knew the answer. *Because I should ... because I'm expected to ... because that's what "good mothers" do.* But with the time she could gain back from opting out of the frenzied kids' birthday party circuit, she began to imagine other aspects of her and her family's life that were much more meaningful to her and that she'd willingly give her attention.

"Let's be controversial." Clark winked. "And take birthday parties off our list."

"Rebels." Sara smiled back.

Once Seth and I zeroed in on the cards that were truly adding value to our lives, and what cards didn't hold similar importance, we trimmed our deck. We threw out a handful of cards and began the work of splitting the remaining deck between us. With only those cards left in hand that we both deemed valuable, Seth never again accused me of doing "unnecessary stuff," nor did he make "I don't have time for that" excuses. Not only did the majority of pervasive Toxic Time messages stop driving our daily tit for tat, but my husband was also much more willing to take the lead on many more cards because he recognized their value in our home.

Once more and then we'll move on: **You don't have to do it all.** You don't have to play with a full deck of Fair Play cards. Ditch the peer pressure and societal expectations, and instead make intentional choices about how you want to spend your time and thoughtfully create your life.

Then, after you and your partner determine what cards are in play because they hold value to *your family*, it is an imperative must-must-must that you agree on *how* those cards will be played. Whether it's showing up for the kids, tidying the house, or managing the family budget, each task card requires a mutually agreed-upon Minimum Standard of Care that is aligned with your shared values. And the more you invest in unpacking the details, the more you will be rewarded by the Fair Play system.

THE FAIR PLAY MINIMUM STANDARD OF CARE

The Fair Play Minimum Standard of Care is inspired by something I learned in law school and that is implemented by judges around the world: Any action taken by a citizen should reflect the shared values and traditions of that specific community. Killing an ant is hygienic in the value system of one community and barbaric in another. Wearing shoes indoors is acceptable in one community and considered disrespectful in others. Addressing someone as "Mr." is the rule in one community but considered overly formal in another.

Depending on where you live, your community assigns a Minimum Standard of Care based on its shared societal standards. When a conflict arises in our legal system, judges help people resolve disputes by using a Reasonable Person Test that simply asks: "Given our community's agreed-upon standards, would a reasonable person have ... stepped on the ant ... worn shoes indoors ... addressed the nice gentleman as 'Mr.'?"

As I was creating the rules for Fair Play, I thought, why not borrow this idea to create agreement about the standards within our individual homes? Couples are forever arguing and disagreeing over how things ought to be done!

> **Husband:** Why do we have to do it this way?
> **Wife:** Because that's how we do it.
> **Husband:** No, that's how *you* think we should do it.
> **Wife:** That's right. So do it my way!

In my interviews, many men gruffed that their wives had inflated, often perfectionist standards where women readily expressed disappointment in their spouse's far-from-perfect and sometimes "low" standards. (And in some cases it was the reverse.) What if couples could meet in the middle by creating their own Minimum Standard of Care? And how is this done? **By having a collaborative discussion about what is reasonable in your own home.** To this end, I added into the system the following step: For every card a person holds, how you Conceptualize, Plan, and Execute the domestic task at hand is governed by this question: Would a reasonable person (in this case, your partner, spouse, babysitter, caregivers, parents, and in-laws) under similar circumstances do as I've done? If the answer is yes, you are adhering to your family's agreed-upon Minimum Standard of Care. If the answer is no, you've got a problem.

Here's an example:

Your One Step Forward, Two Steps Back husband holds the "school breaks (summer)" card. For the upcoming summer break, he signed the kids up for YMCA camp. When the last week of camp rolls around, you overhear the kids talking excitedly about Friday's "color war day" and you ask your husband what that's about. "Oh, I think the kids are supposed to wear a certain color," he says offhandedly. "It was in a camp email. I'll go back and reread it." Then late on Thursday night, he admits to spacing on the assignment. He'd forgotten to reread the email, *until now*, and the color combo requirement is a bit more detailed than he'd realized. "But don't worry," he assures you. "We'll work it out." *We?* In the 15 minutes we have in the morning to get the kids up, dressed, fed, out the door, and onto the bus to camp?

You know this is highly unlikely, not only due to time constraints, but also because the colors your children have been asked to sport—canary yellow and lime green—are not wardrobe colors your kids happen to have. At this point, there's no way to improvise without putting your son in his sister's pajama top, and your daughter in a rainbow shirt with a stripe she must point to. ("Look, there's yellow in the rainbow.") You think: *If I were holding this card, there is zero chance this would have happened.* (Old Navy, with its sea of $4 shirts in every color under the sun, is literally around the block, like actually.)

This is a purely hypothetical example, of course.

Because you have a moon rising in My Way or Move Out, you spend the next hour with a flashlight looking to see if there might be something in the back of their closets that will work in a pinch. You feel bad for the kids, who have been looking forward to this fun day, and who are old enough to notice that they don't have the called-for colors when other kids likely will. At the same time, you feel increasingly hostile toward your husband for putting the kids in a position of feeling singled out and embarrassed. Also you begin to worry: *If I can't trust him to pick out the right color T-shirts, how can I trust him with our healthcare directive?!*

Applying Rule #4, did your husband meet the Reasonable Person Test?

It all depends on what you and your partner deem reasonable. Except . . . what if you can't agree? In this case, he says,

"It's just a T-shirt. What's the big deal?" To which you say, "It *is* a big deal!" So how do you decide? Ask yourselves: Would a reasonable person outfit them in the required clothes? If you're still tangled up over the answer, apply the objective test as outlined by Caroline Forell, gender and legal expert on the Reasonable Person Test and whom I tracked down by phone.

"Judges and juries consider two basic questions—did your unreasonable actions (or in this case inaction) cause harm? If so, how bad was the harm?"

In the Case of the Color War, the next day at camp, every kid except yours is wearing the assigned colors. Later that night, your children tearfully express their embarrassment for being in the wrong clothes and feeling left out from the day's fun. The kids were hurt—harm done. What's more, if supporting your children to feel included within their peer group holds value (and only you and your partner can determine this for your own family), then your partner's oversight and inactions were not only unreasonable but also did not meet your Minimum Standard of Care.

Starting to see why establishing a standard is much bigger than a T-shirt? Here's another:

Your family is headed to the beach on a sunny summer day. Your Giant Kid partner accidentally grabs a tube of nappy rash cream instead of sunscreen from the bathroom drawer. Though he can read a label, he applies it to the baby's face anyway, figuring the zinc oxide in this product can double as sunscreen, *right*? Not quite. This particular brand of nappy rash cream includes additional ingredients that cause the baby's cheeks to burn. An argument ensues when you pull the tube out of the beach bag and ask with disbelief: "You didn't use *this* as sunscreen, did you?"

How do you and your partner resolve this? Again, ask yourselves: Would a reasonable person use nappy rash cream in the place of sunscreen? Furthermore, what's the harm? Nappy rash cream and sunscreen are different products, used for different purposes, and applying the former on your baby's face in the hopes that it will prevent her skin from burning isn't reasonable. (And your baby's burnt cheeks prove it.) If you and your partner can agree that using sunscreen to prevent a nasty burn, and presumably to avoid skin cancer later in life, is important to your family, then your partner's actions don't meet your family's Minimum Standard of Care, and you can feel comfortable asking him to step up his game in the "medical and healthy living" department.

One more: Your partner is a professional chef who absent-mindedly threw his knife set in the backseat of the car after a late night at the restaurant. "I swear, they were all in the case," he argues when you ask him about the razor-sharp paring knife you found wedged in the folds of the car seat that transports your eighteen-month-old. An honest mistake? Perhaps. Was there harm done? Potentially. Reasonable? F*ck no! The woman who told me this true-life-is-stranger-than-fiction story made the following argument: "Hey, I'm not an unreasonable control freak; I just don't want my baby playing with knives! That's fair, isn't it?"

WHAT'S REASONABLE?

Of the couples I coached through this process, many were encouraged that they already had agreement and a shared standard in place for many of the childcare and household responsibilities, even though they'd never explicitly discussed or defined expectations. That's fantastic! But before you go congratulating yourselves, I want to spend a few more minutes on the disagreements and the cards that *do* upset the balance in many households. (Big surprise: These tend to be the time-sucking Daily Grinds that must get done on a specific timetable.)

Before we put a minimum standard into place, "garbage" was our most contentious card. Seth agreed to hold this card and yet, on many mornings, I'd walk into the kitchen and find garbage overflowing onto the floor. I'd silently fume at him for ignoring this responsibility, but rather than confront him directly, I'd place a clean garbage liner on the counter next to the coffeemaker. And wait. When he'd pad in to fill his morning cup, I'd glare at him and then very slowly avert my steely gaze toward the bag.

Did this passive-aggressive strategy work? It sometimes stimulated Seth into Execution mode but not without muttering a few PG-13 obscenities as he walked the overflowing can out the back door.

I was frustrated that this one card continued to trip us up. I would nag him for his "unreasonable threshold for filth" and he'd counter that my expectations were too high. *Really?*

And then on the morning I stumbled over an empty pizza box that had fallen off the kitchen counter onto the floor, I remembered a story from Seth's college days. As he told it: In the middle of Seth's freshman year, his roommate Kevin moved out of the dorms to an off-campus apartment. This quickly became home base to watch weekend sports, and Seth and his buddies would cram into Kevin's tiny studio until the beer was gone and the game was over. That spring, they started a friendly competition. How many Domino's pizza boxes could they stack on Kevin's front steps by the end of March Madness? They set a goal of 100 boxes. (Understand that to stack this many boxes meant first eating the pie inside. An extra-large at 8 slices x 100 over 30 days. You do the math.) Did they reach their goal? Of course they did, and Seth still loves to tell the tale. Conjuring the image of 100 boxes stacked on Kevin's front steps, I finally got it: My husband and I didn't share the same standard of kitchen cleanliness. For Seth, a single empty pizza box on the floor is *reasonable*. I further understood that until we established an explicit Minimum Standard of Care within our postcollege home, we'd continue to disagree on how a "reasonable person" behaves on trash day.

Recognize that you and your partner may currently have very different definitions of what's reasonable and acceptable in and around your home. And until you can agree on a Minimum Standard of Care, frustration and disappointment will likely continue to rule the day. To be very clear: I'm not advocating you elevate your expectations, demanding your partner reach them. Nor am I suggesting you lower your standards and settle for less than you're comfortable with or believe is fair. Rather than debate whose standards are better or right, collaborate on what is reasonable within your *own* home.

FAIR PLAY MSC TEST

If you cannot come to an agreement over the Minimum Standard of Care (MSC), ask yourselves:

1. Would a reasonable person (in this case, your partner, spouse, babysitter, caregivers, parents, and in-laws) under similar circumstances do as I've done?

2. What is the community standard, and do we want to adopt this standard within our own home?
3. What's the harm for doing, or not doing, it this way?
4. What is our "why"?

WHAT IS *YOUR* "WHY"?

Later, when you and your partner discuss the Minimum Standard of Care for the cards you choose to hold, thoughtfully **consider the long game** for you and your partner, and for your family. This is where you dig deep and ask: Why *do* we do things the way we do them? What are our values, and are we creating a set of standards we want our children to also buy into? When I look into the future, what's the picture I want to see within our family frame? Most important, are we still in the frame together?

According to the bestselling book *Getting to Yes*, the best win-win negotiations begin over shared interests aimed at achieving a greater goal, such as safety, health, happiness, and building long-term trust. Going back to the garbage disparity in my own home, Seth and I easily arrived at a new standard when we asked ourselves not only what is reasonable but also, "What do we want for our family and why?" Our answer: *We want our family to live in a clean house. We want our kids to value cleanliness. We want to trust each other to create a clean environment for our family.*

The more nuanced discussions come into play when you and your partner focus on the details that are often driven by personal predilection. In our case, what does "clean" mean? Does it mean the garbage goes out every day? If not every day, then at what point, exactly, does the bag need to be tied off and hauled out? (I crossed my fingers that Seth's answer would not be when five pizza boxes are stacked on top of it.)

If this sounds like a lot of nitpicky negotiation, let me assure you that the time you spend with your partner establishing when the garbage needs to head out the door will add hours to your future lives. Once you change the conversation by introducing a standard, you eliminate the need to argue over the garbage ever again. OK, maybe that's overshooting a bit. The topic of garbage will come up far less frequently in your household because you've set mutually agreed-upon expectations and standards, and whoever holds the card knows exactly *what*, *when*, and *how* to do it. And *why* you both agree to do it that way.

Today, Seth and I adhere to the following MSC for garbage: It goes out every night by 7 p.m. How does this new standard work? No more silent brooding or passive-aggressive reminders from me. No more frustrated "get off my back" huffs from Seth. Simply, the garbage goes out every night by 7 p.m.

For real. Change can happen. In your home, too.

CONSIDER: THE CASE OF THE KITTY LITTER

Emily and Paul fought endlessly over cleaning the kitty litter box. When the couple met, Paul had two tabby cats for which he assumed full responsibility. The problem was that once they became a "we," and later after kids, a "three" and then a "four," Paul loosened his grip on the "pets" card. Quite actually, he forgot he was holding it. When I spoke with Emily privately, she complained, "If I'm not there to remind him to buy cat food before it runs out, change the water dish daily, and empty the damn litter box, it won't get done. Which means I usually just do it."

I asked Emily, "Why is it important to you to have clean kitty litter?"

She gave a look like *duh*. "Because cat poop stinks!"

I said: "Any other reason?"

"Well, yeah." She thought. "Because it's not safe for animals or humans to leave it dirty and piling up. The smell can become toxic and make the cats sick if they eat it. And God forbid one of our toddlers stumbles into the garage and decides it's a sandbox worth exploring."

"It sounds like, for you and your family, the most important reason to keep it clean is safety."

"I would agree with that," Emily said.

"And do you think Paul would also agree?"

"Yes, I think he would, but day to day he's not thinking big picture. He sees it as a chore he doesn't want to do, or he doesn't 'remember' to do because there are five minutes left in the game and he thinks, 'It can just wait until tomorrow.'"

I may have audibly gasped when she said "big picture." I flashed back to what author Dan Ariely said to me about long-term thinking. "Consider the long-term goal," he said, "a happy marriage where both people take fair turns at emptying the kitty litter."

Ariely was speaking in the context of valuing each other's *time*, and now I realized: Time is only one component of the fairness equation. Establishing a Minimum Standard of Care—where both partners align with a long-term goal like family safety—encourages a long-term commitment rather than long-term resentment. Instead of regarding it as a daily annoyance, if Paul could shift his thinking and consider the task of emptying the kitty litter as future insurance that his family and pets stay healthy, clean, and safe, he'd be more willing to wield the scooper.

This was my theory, anyway, and I invited Emily to help me test it.

"The next time Paul 'forgot' to clean the litter," Emily reported back, "I held my breath and, when I was calm, I imitated Darth Vader and said something like: 'This is bigger than kitty litter. It goes beyond cat turds. It's about—the future of our family and MY TRUST IN YOU.' Paul laughed at my lame attempt to sound like James Earl Jones, and because I hadn't put him on the defensive, I was able to calmly explain why this one responsibility was important in a big-picture sort of way—to stay healthy, clean, and safe. And save me from killing him."

As soon as Emily outlined the long-term benefit of performing this Daily Grind, Paul's actions and attitude changed. He emptied the kitty litter without reminders or being nagged by Emily because he now appreciated *why* he was doing it.

TRUST WINS

Rule #4 asks you and your partner to make expectations explicit to minimize disappointment and maximize trust in the relationship. For every card that you and your partner deem valuable and worthy of playing (that is, once you start playing in Chapter 8), you will mutually agree upon a Minimum Standard of Care that you both believe serves the best interests of your household short- and long-term, and that you can both trust each other to reach. "It all comes down to trust," asserts Professor Forell. "If you can't trust that the car will stop at the stop sign, you can't feel safe crossing the road. Similarly, if you can't trust your partner to care for the home by meeting your family's minimum standards, then you're not going to feel safe, heard, or met in the relationship."

RULE #4: ESTABLISH YOUR VALUES AND STANDARDS

When I was an Accidental Traditionalist with a moon rising in My Way or Move Out, I used to fall headlong into the "it's just easier for me to do it" time trap because I couldn't imagine my husband CPEing a task in a way that would meet my expectations or standard of care. Many women who served as my early beta-testers also admitted a reluctance to release control for fear that the cards they handed over to their partners wouldn't be done well enough or done at all. As a natural consequence, many of the men I spoke to conceded defeat; they stopped offering to help because they feared being criticized for their efforts. "I stopped asserting myself or taking action without the direction of my wife," admitted Carl from Arkansas, "because however I do it, she'll just redo it."

Establishing a Minimum Standard of Care alleviates this. No more "I didn't know what to do" excuses. **Instead, you can trust your partner to take a CPE lead and follow through with care.** No more "why'd you do it that way?" nagging and scorekeeping. Instead, when you drop the control and replace it with trust, your partner can act with confidence, knowing that a new agreed-upon standard has set him or her up for success. This is what it means for you both to win.

HOW TO WIN AT FAIR PLAY

Playing for Keeps

7.

THE 100 TASK CARDS OF FAIR PLAY

||||||||||||||||||||||||||||||||||||||||||||||||||||||||||||||||||||||||||||||||||||||||||

Set yourself up for a win.

Before you start the game, take a detailed look at the "100 Cards of Fair Play"—what they entail and, crucially, how the Conception, Planning, and Execution (CPE) for each one might play out in your household based on your shared values.

Fair Play consists of 100 task cards that break down the domestic ecosystem into five suits—**Home, Out, Caregiving, Magic**, and **Wild**—as well as the all-important **Unicorn Space** card that each partner must play.

Remember, *all* the Fair Play cards are not necessarily in play for your family. But it's important to know what each of them entails so you and your partner can customize the deck in the best way that works for your household.

Tip! *The task card descriptions that follow are broken down further into list form online at fairplaylife.com. Not everything in these lists will apply to you and your family, but `if you're unclear on how to CPE a card, this is your resource.*

100 CARDS OF FAIR PLAY BY THE NUMBERS:

60 cards—possibly in play for couples only

40 cards—additional cards possibly in play for couples with children

30 cards—Daily Grind tasks split across the full deck

100 cards of FAIR PLAY ™

HOME	OUT	CAREGIVING	MAGIC	WILD
childcare helpers	auto	bathing & grooming (kids)	adult friendships (her) ☺	aging/ailing parent
cleaning	birthday celebrations (other kids)	beauty & wardrobe (her)	adult friendships (him) ☺	death
dishes	calendar keeper	bedtime routine	birthday celebrations (your kids)	first year of infant's li
dry cleaning	cash & bills	birth control	discipline & screen time	glitch in the matrix/da disruption
garbage	charity, community service & good deeds (adults)	clothes & accessories (kids)	extended family	home renovation
groceries	civic engagement & cultural enrichment	dental (kids)	fun! & playing	job loss & money prol
home furnishings	electronics & IT	diapering & potty training	gestures of love (kids)	moving
home goods & supplies	extracurricular (non-sports)	estate planning & life insurance	gifts (family)	new job
home maintenance	extracurricular (sports)	friendships & social media (kids)	gifts (VIPs)	pregnancy & baby's b
home purchase/ rental, mortgage & insurance	first aid, safety & emergency	grooming & wardrobe (him)	hard questions	serious illness
hosting	packing & unpacking (local)	health insurance	holiday cards	
laundry	packing & unpacking (travel)	homework, projects & school supplies	holidays	UNICORN SPACE
lawn & plants	points, miles & coupons	medical & healthy living (kids)	informal education	
mail	returns & store credits	morning routine	magical beings	
meals (weekday breakfast)	school breaks (non-summer)	parents & in-laws	marriage & romance	
meals (school lunch)	school breaks (summer)	pets	middle-of-the-night comfort	
meals (weekday dinner)	school forms	school service	partner coach	
meals (weekend)	social plans (couples)	school transitions	showing up & participating	UNICORN SPACE
memories & photos	transportation (kids)	self-care (her) ☺	spirituality	
money manager	travel	self-care (him) ☺	thank-you notes	
storage, garage & seasonal items	tutoring & coaching	special needs & mental health (kids)	values & good deeds (kids)	
tidying up, organizing & donations	weekend plans (family)	teacher communication	watching	

THE HOME SUIT

def. >> It's mind-blowing how much CPE it takes to run a home with kids: the endless laundry, grocery shopping, meals to prep, garbage runs, cleaning . . . not to mention the 9,000 photos sitting in a cloud that you'd like to put in albums one day. Welcome to the **Home** suit. Someone is supposed to know when you're almost out of toilet paper, where your daughter's favorite doll is, and yep, it's been a year since you last filed your taxes.

CHILDCARE HELPERS

It takes a village, and you're fortunate if your village includes a nanny, babysitter, family caregivers, or others who pitch in with the kids. It can be a lifesaver to have the help, but it still requires someone to Conceive and Plan before Nanny Poppins or Grandma Shirley shows up to help Execute. They don't magically appear when you want them to, so schedules need to be managed, along with payment, delegation of responsibilities, and ongoing communication. Heads up: When your helper cancels or quits, this cardholder is not necessarily the one who drops everything. Rather, engage in Fair Play immediately to re-deal the applicable cards, for example, "transportation (kids)" and "watching."

CLEANING

The pancake batter that fell into the crack on the side of the oven? Last week? It's still there. The pee all over the toilet seat because your toddler can't aim? Still there. The trail of sand in your entryway post-playground? Still there. If you have someone to help deep clean your bathroom and kitchen—lucky you. It's still your responsibility to manage the schedule, task list, payment, etc. Re-deal this card often, as it's a biggie.

> *Tip!* Coordinate with the "home goods and supplies" cardholder so you have cleaning supplies in the house when you need them.

DISHES

It's no wonder so many articles about domestic labor begin and end with dishes—the metaphorical third rail of chores. This cardholder is responsible for washing and drying by hand and/or loading and unloading the dishwasher—for every meal. The upside? Your partner doesn't get to criticize how you put the plates in the "wrong" way. Re-deal this card often to avoid thrown dishes.

DRY CLEANING

Even something as seemingly straightforward as dry cleaning requires step-by-step CPE. This card entails having a bin/bag at home, ensuring the appropriate clothes get into that bin/bag, finding a dry cleaner, knowing when it's open so you can coordinate drop-off and pickup, and taking off the plastic wrapping before hanging clothes back in the closet. If the mutually agreed-upon MSC is that all clothes come back home, this cardholder is responsible for tracking down their spouse's favorite shirt when it goes missing or negotiating a refund. (And maybe finding a new dry cleaner, too.)

GARBAGE

Really, how much darn trash can one family create? Staggering. To CPE this card means, at minimum, you take out the trash before the garbage truck turns the corner of your block (*which day is it again?*). Whoever holds this card is responsible for anticipating when trash bags are running low, and a word to the wise: Don't you dare sit back down on the couch until you put a new bag back in the trash can!

GROCERIES

Your family needs to eat. Can we all agree on that? Good. So how do the pantry and refrigerator get stocked on an ongoing basis? With CPE. This includes noticing what's about to be used up or expire, keeping a running grocery list, and getting to the market . . . ideally before you realize there's not a drop of milk in the fridge. Even if your family orders groceries online and your go-to dinner is frozen pizza, this card requires CPE nearly 365 days a year. Consult the various "meals" cardholders regularly so you can be sure you have taco shells in the cupboard for taco night.

HOME FURNISHINGS

CPEing this card can be as basic as making sure that every bed has a pillow, you have towels in the closet, and the drinking glasses with cracks get replaced before someone chips a tooth. This card is not a one-time deal, as there's regular inventory to be taken and just when you could use that 20 percent off Bed Bath and Beyond coupon, it's nowhere to be found. Kindly discuss with the "points, miles, and coupons" cardholder so you're buttoned up for your next trip to the store.

HOME GOODS & SUPPLIES ☕

This card requires CPE of everything from laundry detergent, batteries, and lightbulbs, to toothpaste, coffee filters, and trash bags! Expect to be astounded by how your parents' generation pulled this off without online delivery services.

HOME MAINTENANCE ☕

How many people does it take to change a lightbulb? In this game, just one, and it's the person holding this card. You're also responsible for unclogging toilets, calling a repairman when the air conditioner breaks (inevitably in the height of summer), finding the manual for the vacuum cleaner that's spewing dust, and every other home maintenance to-do that requires hands-on CPE.

HOME PURCHASE/RENTAL, MORTGAGE & INSURANCE

If you aspire to be a homeowner with a mortgage one day, then when the time comes, you'll need to CPE the purchasing process. If you're already a homeowner with a mortgage, this cardholder oversees title insurance, reviewing an infinite amount of statements, and possible refinancing. If you're looking to rent, then you'll be the one to scour listings, fill out applications, and furnish your credit score. You'll also handle home insurance (whether you rent or own), including evaluating the appropriate policy and filing claims if needed. Grab this card fast if paperwork and record-keeping are your strong suits.

HOSTING

Whether it's a backyard barbecue, potluck dinner, or any other get-together in your home or elsewhere, hosting often entails sending out invites, planning the menu, filling a vase with flowers, and setting the table (and maybe a separate one for the kids). The downside to holding this card: You may forget to have fun at your own shindig as you bend over backward to ensure everyone else does. The upside: no need for a workout on hosting days, as you will probably hit 10,000 steps before you sit down to eat (if you get to at all).

LAUNDRY 🍵

If you haven't ever CPE'd this card, would you like to take a guess at how many loads of laundry your family generates weekly? A freakin' lot, that's my guess. If you never go a day without clean socks and your daughter can always find her favorite rainbow shirt, then be sure to thank this cardholder, who not only throws the load in the washer and dryer but also folds it and puts it all away. If laundry tends to pile up and multiply in your home, it's time to re-deal this card and come up with a new standard before the next cycle begins.

LAWN & PLANTS

If you've got a lawn, a backyard or balcony vegetable garden, or just a struggling succulent by your kitchen window, then you know it takes careful CPE to keep your greenery alive, no less thriving. Even if you have a helpful gardener to lend you his or her green thumb, it's still on you to keep an eye on limp or leggy plants that may need a shot of Miracle-Gro.

MAIL

This cardholder isn't only responsible for grabbing the mail every day on the way in the front door. It's what happens once the mail is *inside your home* that's most important. This CPEer will have a system for retrieving and opening mail in a timely, date-sensitive manner, and then handing off invitations, bills, jury duty notices, health insurance reimbursements, tax refunds, etc., to their rightful owner. Perk: This cardholder gets to choose between the Star Wars or Elvis commemorative stamps for your family's outgoing mail because now it's your job to buy 'em and stick 'em.

MEALS (WEEKDAY BREAKFAST)

One mom I spoke to lamented that she's held this card every single day since her kids were old enough to eat solids. Every. Single. Day. Prepare to frequently re-deal full CPE of this nonnegotiable Daily Grind unless serving oatmeal and toast at breakneck speed is your jam. Dishes left in the sink and milk spilled on the counter isn't "on you" unless you hold the "dishes" and "tidying" cards. Still, be respectful before you zoom out the door.

MEALS (SCHOOL LUNCH)

If you're this cardholder, toss the idea of a relaxing night out the window because it's time to start packing lunch for the kids. Don't let all the #schoollunch pics on Instagram get you down. Your Fair Play Minimum Standard of Care could be a protein bar, an apple, and a bottle of water if that's all your kid will eat. And even if your child's school provides lunch, you still have to take the lead and sign up for this program and provide lunch money to cover pizza Fridays.

MEALS (WEEKDAY DINNER)

If you have never CPE'd dinnertime in a family with kids (particularly young ones), then no words can really do justice to this nightly circus. The ringleader plans a weekly menu, consults the "groceries" cardholder to have the ingredients at home, then cooks, ensures that the food actually gets eaten, and ideally uses this forced family time to have "quality" conversations about everyone's day. Men: Kudos to you if cooking is one of your domestic contributions, but that's just one word on this doozy of a card. Hero status isn't awarded for just pulling out a frying pan.

MEALS (WEEKEND)

Why do weekend meals feel more burdensome than weekday meals? Oh, let us count the ways. Maybe it's because there are twice as many of them than on a school day. Perhaps it's because they amplify the kitchen mess exponentially. Or because when you make it to Saturday night, you're still only halfway there. Weekend meals deserve their own card—who wants it? *Psst.* Serving lunch at 4 p.m. doesn't cut it unless midday meltdowns are your thing.

MEMORIES & PHOTOS

God bless those parents who make photo albums every year and who can rest assured that if the basement flooded, all their old photos are scanned and backed up in the cloud. No need to aim that high, but if you hold this card, your family's lifelong memories are nevertheless in your hands. When a photo collage is needed for "Student of the Week," it's time to cue the music . . . and kiss some of your time goodbye. When the boxes of your child's artwork that you've been collecting since kindergarten threaten to take over every wall in your home, it's time to consult with the "storage" and "organizing" cardholder. *Do we keep it all or secretly recycle?*

MONEY MANAGER

If you're taking the lead on this card, you are intrepid because managing a family's budget is no small feat. Planning for the present and preparing for the future is a good start, but there's so much more to CPEing this card. Short- and long-time budgeting. Paying off debt. Retirement planning. Applying for the kids' student loans. The dreaded tax returns. Day-to-day "cash and bills" is a separate card, and these cardholders will collaborate often.

STORAGE, GARAGE & SEASONAL ITEMS

If you have a storage unit or a garage, do you have any idea what's inside it? If not, now is the time to get it organized and have a CPE plan in place before someone asks, "Where's Zach's sleeping bag? He has a sleepover tonight."

TIDYING UP, ORGANIZING & DONATIONS

This never-ending work includes making beds, putting toys away, finding the Legos under the couch (preferably before you buy a whole new set), and wrapping up the half a banana sitting on the counter before fruit flies infest your home. This card is a hot-button issue for many couples who often disagree on a standard for "tidy," so before one of you claims it, get specific about how long you can both live with the toy closet that's bursting at the seams, all the random crap accumulating under the stairwell, and the donation bags that have been sitting in the trunk of the family car for months. Unless your aspiration is to star on *Hoarders* (and your partner agrees to costar), you may want to binge a few episodes of *Tidying Up with Marie Kondo*.

THE OUT SUIT

def. >> What happens at home stays at home (mostly), so it's your little secret that you're out of clean undies. But when it comes to the **Out** suit, we're talking about being out in the world, so it's time to find a fresh pair and get out the door. The **Out** suit refers to many of the activities that take place outside of your home, or the work that is required to make life outside of the home possible. From getting each kid to their respective extracurricular activities on the right day and time to fulfilling social and civic commitments, CPEing a busy family's life outside the home requires top-notch organization.

AUTO

Do you know what happens if you don't put the new registration sticker on your car? You get a ticket that could have easily been avoided, that's what. This cardholder handles all items relating to your family's car(s), including putting that sticker on in a timely manner, paying for that darn ticket, renewing insurance, handling maintenance, getting car washes, regularly filling up with gas, and getting the oil checked so that you feel safe and secure in the family car.

BIRTHDAY CELEBRATIONS (OTHER KIDS)

From RSVPing to buying presents, the birthday party circuit for your kids is riddled with opportunities for missteps ... like when you're already out the door and realize it's a princess dress-up theme. Oops. And why didn't anyone warn you how many weekend hours you'd be spending at other kids' birthday parties chitchatting with parents you hardly know? Do a happy dance if siblings are invited so you can have two kids in the same place at the same time.

Note! If you have two or more kids who have to be at separate birthday celebrations, you and your partner can both hold this card separately. A Kid Split means you both CPE the same card at the same time but for separate kids. See page 267 for more about splitting cards.

Post Note! This card pairs with the "transportation (kids)" and "gifts (VIPs)" cards. Meaning, if you RSVP'd yes to the birthday party at the trampoline park, you are responsible for getting your son there (gift in hand) and picking him up afterward.

CALENDAR KEEPER ☕

You know how some business executives have an assistant to schedule all their meetings and events? Well, your family is busier . . . but you have no one. It's up to you to create a system that works for your family so everyone knows what's on the calendar day to day and week to week and plans accordingly. Just when you think you've nailed the schedule and hung it on the wall, you'll find out that soccer practice is on the same day as Boy Scouts and you'll be back to square one. Add in your own commitments along with your spouse's, and you've got a job with more moving parts than a millipede.

CASH & BILLS

How darn hard can it be to get to the bank so you have adequate cash on hand (after consulting the "money manager," who can help define the standard for *adequate*)? Enter this cardholder, who will set up a system that prevents all interested parties from ever uttering or hearing, "Sorry, hon, I've only got five bucks." This CPEer also handles the payment (on time!) of all bills, whether online, checks in the mail, or auto-pay, and balances the chequebook (or the virtual equivalent). Cozy up with the "mail" cardholder, who will ensure paper bills come your way.

CHARITY, COMMUNITY SERVICE & GOOD DEEDS (ADULTS)

You want to give back to your community, religious institution, your kids' schools, or whatever causes are meaningful to you or to others who ask for your support. This cardholder is generous with his or her time (making the meatloaf for the neighborhood meal train) and also your family's money, so don't forget to consult the "money manager" before making pledges at the annual school fundraiser you can't afford.

CIVIC ENGAGEMENT & CULTURAL ENRICHMENT

Why do all your friends have tickets to the local production of *Annie*, and you didn't even know about it? Maybe they had someone to CPE this card . . . and now you will, too. From your city council meetings to concerts to a lecture at the library, this cardholder will take it upon him- or herself to research and plan for community events that enhance your family's life experience. Check in with the "calendar keeper" before you purchase tickets to see your favorite redheaded orphan storm the stage.

ELECTRONICS & IT

When your cell phone screen shatters, who ya gonna call? This cardholder! When your Wi-Fi isn't working or your DVR is full, who ya gonna call? This cardholder! You need not work at the cable company or have tech know-how, but you *do need* to have ample time and patience to CPE this card, especially when you have to wait six hours for the cable guy. New cords, chargers, and ink cartridges? Also you. Waiting in line to get your kid his first phone? Still you.

EXTRACURRICULAR (NON-SPORTS) 🍵

Let's say your daughter begs to be in the school play—with rehearsals on the same days that she already has Girl Scouts. This cardholder must sleuth out what the extracurricular commitment entails and how to juggle it within the context of the family calendar.

> **Note!** *This card pairs with the "transportation (kids)" and "packing (local)" cards. Meaning, if you register your daughter for Girl Scouts and also sign her up for the school play, you are responsible for coordinating how she will get to and from both events with both her costume and cookies in hand.*

EXTRACURRICULAR (SPORTS) 🍵

If you think this card means just showing up on the right field at the right time to cheer on your kid, you couldn't be more wrong. While the Execution can be rewarding when you're there to watch your child hit a home run, the Conception and Planning are more tedious and require tremendous fore-

thought. What are the equipment needs? What's the game schedule? And when do you have to provide the team snack?

> **Note!** *This card also pairs with the "transportation (kids)" and "packing (local)" cards. Not only are you responsible for making sure the mitt is in the bag, but you're also on the hook for coordinating how your kid will get to the field on time.*

FIRST-AID, SAFETY & EMERGENCY

Before bringing home baby from the hospital, this cardholder has installed the infant car seat (yep, it's a pain, but it's the law). *Before* a major storm hits, this cardholder will stock up on batteries, bottled water, and other basics. Does your family have an emergency plan for a time when phones may not work and you need to leave the house for a safer place? Working flashlights, candles, and matches for when the power is out? Needless to say, this card is a big one and should be taken seriously.

PACKING & UNPACKING (LOCAL)

If you use the last diaper in the baby's diaper bag and don't replace it, how many diapers will be left the next time you need to change an explosive poop on the go? Exactly. It's got to be restocked, just as backpacks need to be packed (and unpacked) daily with library books, lunch, homework, water bottles, clothes for after-school activities, and about a million other things you'll forget if you don't have a system in place. Bonus duties: packing for sleepovers, packing and replacing the change of clothes in the school cubby as needed, and hitting up the school's lost and found when only one glove makes it home.

PACKING & UNPACKING (TRAVEL)

You're not alone if packing for a trip with kids leaves you questioning if it's worth going on the trip at all. It feels like moving the army, only your troops may be too young to pack and carry their own gear. Rookie mistake if just before takeoff you discover the iPad battery is at 1 percent.

POINTS, MILES & COUPONS

Do you know if you have enough airline miles to fly free on your next trip? And also bring your partner along for the ride? This cardholder keeps track of miles, credit card points, coupons, and all those big money savers. Thoughtful CPE of this card is a must—getting that awesome "buy one, get three free" deal only happens when you have your coupon stash organized and in hand at the checkout line.

RETURNS & STORE CREDITS

If it seems as if there's always something you've bought that needs to be returned or exchanged—typically without the receipt and on the opposite side of town—then this cardholder will be quite busy. Store credit? Gift cards from your mother-in-law? Sure, they were for your kids, but who's gonna know if you used one to buy those cute shoes on sale?

SCHOOL BREAKS (NON-SUMMER)

For your kids' non-summer vacations like winter and spring break, you have plenty of advance notice to plan. Still, don't wait too long. The holidays creep up quickly. But when it comes to parent-teacher conferences, school construction, snow days, smoke days, and every other scenario that has you scrambling for childcare, this cardholder must be able to pivot quickly and CPE like a pro.

SCHOOL BREAKS (SUMMER)

The CPEer of this card may begin researching options for camps or other summer activities months in advance. This workload lasts until the minute all the required forms and fees are taken care of and every day is covered (up to 90 days, but who's counting?).

SCHOOL FORMS

Every freakin' form from school that requires review, including your child's enrollment forms, notices for overdue library books, and permission slips for field trips is now in your hands. School forms may come via email (check your spam folder), crumpled up in your child's backpack, on a school website, or via the school portal, which you're supposed to know how to log onto and navigate by now but remains one of life's mysteries. School forms are enough for this cardholder; direct contact with teachers is the responsibility of the "teacher communication" cardholder.

SOCIAL PLANS (COUPLES)

In theory, it's as simple as texting your friends to get together, picking a date/time/place, and showing up. But that's not how it works in real life, and certainly not how it works after having kids. For starters, you want your partner's buy-in for who you're getting together with, and you'll need to get a babysitter, so consult with the "childcare helpers" cardholder. Then, syncing calendars (pre-bedtime? after the championship game?) will make you question if it's really worth the effort. If you actually make it out the door without cancelling, you have earned a bonus cocktail.

TRANSPORTATION (KIDS)

Full. Time. Job. Whether your kids take a bus, carpool, walk, or have a chauffeur (aka you), managing their transportation can be a beast. On any given day, you could be spending countless hours transporting your kids to school or coordinating with those who are pitching in with drop-offs and pickups. Add on getting them to and from playdates, after-school activities, camp, and every other place they need to be seven days a week and we've come full circle: Full. Time. Job.

> **Note!** The "transportation (kids)" card pairs with "birthday celebrations (other kids)," "friendships and social media (kids)," "extracurricular (non-sports)," and "extracurricular (sports)." Meaning, if you hold any of the aforementioned cards and they involve giving your kid a ride, you are responsible for transporting or arranging for transportation to and from those activities.

TRAVEL

When you're thinking about taking a trip, the who/where/when/how formula has endless permutations. If you add in any extended family, best of luck as you navigate how to get everyone to the same place at the same time on a budget, where hopefully fun awaits. Even a day trip for a friend's wedding requires someone to handle logistics, so just because you're not jet-setting to a white sand beach doesn't mean you're off the hook from CPEing this card.

> **Tip!** *Work closely with the "packing and unpacking (travel)" cardholder to ensure that once you get to your destination, you have the appropriate clothes and amenities in your suitcase.*

TUTORING & COACHING

Take this card if you take the lead on extra school enrichment and/or you are the coach of your kids' Little League teams. Some families utilize school-based options while others pursue tutoring companies outside of school or hire tutors/coaches for kids' academics, sports, or special interests like playing a musical instrument. In every case, this cardholder needs to research the options, confirm availability with the "calendar keeper," and assess progress on an ongoing basis. If your kid still can't hit the ball, it might be time for a new coach . . . or a new sport.

WEEKEND PLANS (FAMILY)

Socializing as a family can check off several boxes, including getting your kids out of the house and off screens, seeing your friends, and your kids seeing their friends. (Lucky for you if you like the parents of your kids' BFFs.) But all this box checking requires much CPE, so think it through before you offer to organize a picnic in the park . . . for *your* BFFs and the twenty kids among them.

THE CAREGIVING SUIT

def. >> Some aspects of domestic life can be outsourced a bit, but that's not the case with the **Caregiving** suit. Both you and your partner are irreplaceable as you CPE the needs of your kids, your family, and your friends, and take care of yourself, too. The **Caregiving** suit may feel like thankless work at times, but these cards matter. A lot.

BATHING & GROOMING (KIDS) ☕

The nature of this cardholder's responsibilities changes depending on your kids' ages, but the point is that your kids need to brush their teeth, bathe, wash their faces, cut their nails, and brush their hair. Over and over again.

> ***Tip!*** *Pay attention to your kids' developing needs. If you notice a suspicious scent every time your teenager is within five feet, it's probably time for this CPEer to buy deodorant and make sure your kid knows how often to use it. Daily!*

BEAUTY & WARDROBE (HER)

Looking and feeling good, especially after children, doesn't come easy. (There's a reason that beauty is a $445 billion industry.) Even if you're a DIY kind of woman, it still takes time to slather on moisturizer, pluck your eyebrows, style your hair, and put on lipstick. Kick it up a notch and you may add mani/pedis, eyelash extensions, and waxing to your beauty regimen. Add in shopping for clothes (in various sizes for pre-pregnancy, post-pregnancy, nursing, and every other reason your weight fluctuates) and you've got a potentially expensive and time-consuming card in your hands.

BEDTIME ROUTINE ☕

It can be super rewarding when nighttime includes bonding over the day's events, cuddling like nobody's business, or lying quietly with your precious child. Not so much when this routine becomes a battle over bedtime. Pleas for just one more glass of water or five more minutes of reading can test your patience and fortitude (no wonder *Go the F**k to Sleep* is a bestselling book). While one person needs to take the CPE lead, the other is not home free (i.e., this is not an ideal window of time for you to hit the couch and start flipping channels). Your collaboration is encouraged. Try this: One partner holds the "bathing and grooming (kids)" card to get the party started while the other is responsible for jammies, stories, and lights out. Keep in mind that this routine won't last forever. Before you know it, your babies will be teenagers and you'll be going to sleep long before them.

BIRTH CONTROL

Why is this a separate card instead of being a component of self-care or medical? Because the woman should not be the she-fault cardholder, meaning either of you can claim this card. If having a baby is not on you and your partner's agenda, this cardholder will research contraception options, which may include buying condoms, the pill, an IUD, or scheduling a vasectomy. (Not sure if being too tired to have sex at all is considered a form of birth control? Ask around.)

CLOTHES & ACCESSORIES (KIDS)

News flash: Your kids' shoes and clothes—in sizes that fit—don't magically show up in their closets. Someone needs to CPE what clothes and accessories to buy, get to the appropriate stores, clean out drawers periodically, and hand off used and outgrown clothes to the "tidying up, organizing, and donations" cardholder. Suggested timeline: If your child's feet have blisters, you've probably waited too long to buy new shoes. Exception: If there is a camp or school one-off clothing need (see Case of the Color War), this responsibility stays with the "school breaks (summer)" or "homework" cardholder.

DENTAL (KIDS)

Your kid's job: Pick out a rubber band color for his braces. Your job: Carve out a boatload of time for orthodontist appointments and pay for it all, too. Regular dental visits will also keep you plenty busy because each child needs regular cleanings and checkups (*it's been six months already?*) along with more time-consuming appointments for getting cavities filled. You get a free toothbrush at the end of each visit, so at least there's that.

DIAPERING & POTTY TRAINING 🍵

Let's be clear: This cardholder will not be the only one changing diapers. Expect to re-deal this card often. While you are the lead, you will, however, be the one responsible for maintaining inventory, including ordering new diapers or washing cloth ones, and getting the soiled ones out of your house ASAP. This cardholder will also oversee potty training your kids, including cleaning up the mistakes along the way. When you're finally a diaper-free home, you may still find yourself wiping the butt of your first-grader, who is perfectly capable of doing it on his or her own. This will end one day—promise.

ESTATE PLANNING & LIFE INSURANCE

Who will take care of your kids if something catastrophic happens to you and your partner? Of course both partners will plan together as you think about long-term security for your family and life-and-death medical decisions, but ultimately this cardholder is responsible for making sure the job gets done so you can all sleep at night knowing there's a worst-case scenario plan (and insurance funds) in place.

FRIENDSHIPS & SOCIAL MEDIA (KIDS)

Do you know who your kids are playing with IRL and online? Unless your children come home from school in tears confiding in you, how would you know if they're hanging with the wrong crowd, feeling left out, or being bullied? Make it your business to plug in (get it?) to your kids' social dynamics online and also help plan and supervise playdates, sleepovers, and any other kid get-togethers.

GROOMING & WARDROBE (HIM)

Imagine a conversation that starts innocently enough with a husband asking his wife, "Babe, where's my black suit?" Then comes, "Never mind. Found it." (Pause.) "Shoot, it doesn't fit anymore." And the coup de grâce is that their best friends' wedding begins in one hour and the clock is ticking while he blames his *wife* for failing to buy or rent him a new one. This scenario is all too common as many women CPE this card for their husbands. That's right, grown men told me they rely on their wives not only to help them get dressed for special events but also to schedule haircuts, hem their pants, and replace their underwear with holes. If that truly works for you both, God bless. Otherwise, please consider taking this card for yourself, mister. You can do it.

HEALTH INSURANCE

It's a blessing to have health insurance. The paperwork that goes along with it? Not so much. Unless you somehow find a medical practice that handles all the billing for you, this cardholder needs to know every time anyone in your family goes to the doctor, makes sure the appropriate paperwork is filed for insurance, keeps track of reimbursements, and steps in when things go awry. Every time you see an envelope from your insurance provider (consult with the "mail" cardholder to ensure you receive), say a prayer that you've been covered.

HOMEWORK, PROJECTS & SCHOOL SUPPLIES

Has homework become a family affair? Even if you swore you'd never be the kind of parent who micromanages and digs in to your kids' assignments, you at least need to be in the know if they don't do their homework and be available if your child needs support. CPEing this card means not only taking the lead on daily assignments but also school projects and enrichment learning at home. If your child needs poster board for "Star Student of the Week" or munchies for "Snack Day," that's also on you, as well as outfitting your child for "Wacky Winter" dress-up day and providing two dozen (hand-signed!) Valentine's Day cards on February 14. This is an endless job, so re-deal this card often.

MEDICAL & HEALTHY LIVING (KIDS)

From stocking up on standard pain relievers and regular checkups at the pediatrician to seeing specialists as needed, your kids' medical care requires tremendous research, coordination, and time. Healthy living may also include buying vitamins and healthy snacks (in collaboration with the "groceries" cardholder) and inspiring an active lifestyle with family exercise or other heart-pumping activities. This cardholder also takes the lead stocking up on items like hand sanitizer, sunscreen, and bug spray. Exception: You're off the hook from dealing with "health insurance" unless that's your card, too.

MORNING ROUTINE

When was the last time you slept in, pooped in peace, or leisurely read the newspaper while drinking coffee in the morning? Before kids, if you're holding this card. This cardholder is prepared for daily combat before sunrise with a baby and early still with school-aged kids who often need rousing from bed and help getting dressed, hair and teeth brushed, sunscreen applied, and ushering out the door. At least the "meals (weekday breakfast)" cardholder takes the lead on getting them fed.

PARENTS & IN-LAWS

Whether your parents and/or in-laws live nearby or thousands of miles away, it's a relationship that can require a fair amount of TLC *and* CPE. Someone's got to call them regularly, help them figure out how to turn on their TV with one of their 100-year-old remotes, and invite them to holiday or birthday celebrations. (Or maybe not.)

PETS

When you got your pet, the deal was that the kids would take on a lot of the responsibility. Ha! Now, here you are with a bundle of furry love . . . and a bundle of work. Your to-do list depends on what kind of animal you have, but across the board this cardholder typically CPEs food, veterinary appointments, grooming, pet supplies, finding a pet sitter for when you're away, and the least fun but most important—taking out the kitty litter or being on the ready with poop bag in hand.

SCHOOL SERVICE

When you agreed to chaperone the museum field trip, it seemed like a worthwhile opportunity to spend time with your child and his classmates. Which it was . . . until you found yourself sitting at the back of a school bus trying not to puke. This card pulls you into a time-sucking vortex that includes reading through a chain of 43 emails (*was "reply all" really necessary?*), school-sponsored lectures (*another one?*), and baking cupcakes (*nut free?*). And what's up with schools requesting volunteers to be class "moms"? Dads make excellent class parents, too, ya know.

SCHOOL TRANSITIONS

If your child needs to apply to a new school (kindergarten through college), this card may include tours, filling out applications, writing essays, ordering transcripts, test preps for the ACT and SAT, and more. And that work only begins after you've completed loads of research about where to apply, considered what might be the best fit for your child, and created your best chances to get in. (*Is the lottery really just a lottery? Better find out.*)

SELF-CARE (HER) & SELF-CARE (HIM)

Each of you gets a self-care card regardless of how many children and other responsibilities you have. For some, a daily multivitamin, a good book, and a hot bath fit the bill. Others may have weekly therapy or wellness appointments, and also set aside regular time to exercise. No guilt or shame allowed. Take this important time for *you* and allow your partner to do the same.

SPECIAL NEEDS & MENTAL HEALTH (KIDS)

Obviously this card needs to be CPE'd with tremendous care if your child has special needs or mental health issues. From identifying the problem to finding the best resources, scheduling appointments, monitoring medication, planning treatment, handling a school IEP, and beyond, this cardholder will steer the ship that guides your child safely and with love. It takes a village, so your Planning should include how to utilize any help from your wider support system to create an environment that fosters progress.

TEACHER COMMUNICATION

Every teacher and child is different, so this cardholder's responsibility could be as minimal as showing up to the parent-teacher conference once or twice a year. Or your communication may involve a weekly email exchange or speaking daily and face-to-face to discuss homework and your child's unique learning needs. As the CPEer, it's up to you to proactively keep tabs on your kiddos in their school environment to identify potential challenges and work with their teachers to help them thrive.

THE MAGIC SUIT

def. >> These aren't the magic cards because you're pulling rabbits out of a hat—far from it when you're the one up at 4 a.m. soothing your child back to sleep after a nightmare. But when you look back on your life, it's these magical moments that you'll remember, and the ones you love most will remember about *you*. Indeed, early childhood researchers at the Simms/Mann Institute posit that how you connect is who you become, but it takes hours of invisible work to ensure those important relationship connections. So for your and your kids' sake, put down your freakin' phone and create some **Magic**. Expect to re-deal these cards often as it takes both parents to sustain it and the rewards are worth sharing.

ADULT FRIENDSHIPS (HER) & ADULT FRIENDSHIPS (HIM) 😊

Each of you gets this card because friends are key to your health, happiness, resilience, career, and sanity. Whether it's grabbing coffee after school drop-off, a dinner date, a networking event, or a weekend trip away, nurturing friendships will reap huge dividends. Friendships are not a luxury you'll make time for in the future so use this card guilt-free now. No partner resentment allowed either, as a girls' or guys' night out is about so much more than a cocktail. It's about cultivating relationships that will support and sustain you along with boosting the health of your marriage.

BIRTHDAY CELEBRATIONS (YOUR KIDS)

Have you ever tried shoving a dozen balloons into the trunk of your car? It's like playing a game of whack-a-mole but you get no prize. How about copying and pasting email addresses for the whole class into your online invitation? Time suck. These are just illustrations of the many tasks you'll handle when planning your child's birthday party. Even if you keep it simple with a family dinner at home, this cardholder might be the one who battles rush-hour traffic to pick up a cake at a favorite bakery before it closes. Don't forget candles, but no need to buy a present unless you're also the "gifts (family)" lead.

DISCIPLINE & SCREEN TIME ☕D

While it's no fun to discipline kids, the **Magic** is in setting critical boundaries and giving them tools that will impact how safe they feel and how they conduct themselves for a lifetime. The goal is not for one parent to be responsible for discipline while the other holds "fun! and playing" forever. That's why this card requires ongoing collaboration between partners, with one cardholder at a time taking the lead. For example, screen time. This came up as the most discussed disciplinary issue within families. It's a biggie, and if you hold this card, you may conduct research about an appropriate amount of screen time for your kids and consult with your partner about reasonable boundaries along with the parameters for taking it away; then you'll each enforce your family's rules and consequences on an ongoing basis.

EXTENDED FAMILY

Someone's got to remember to call Great-Aunt Mary on her ninetieth birthday. Same goes for scheduling playdates with cousins if you want the kids to have a relationship (even if you're the one who always ends up doing the two-hour round-trip drive). Depending on how much you and your partner value this card, this CPEer might plan frequent get-togethers with relatives or just be the one to remember to invite Uncle Norman to Thanksgiving dinner . . . knowing full well he'll have one too many drinks and talk politics all night.

FUN! & PLAYING

Maybe you've forgotten that parenting is fun! So fun that after you take your kids to the indoor water park they begged you to take them to, your ensuing bruised shins feels totally worth it. Seriously, childhood should include interactive playful moments as a family on a regular basis, and those moments and memories are, in fact, magical (bruises notwithstanding). This cardholder will CPE ongoing time for fun, such as arranging to throw a football around in the park at twilight, creating a weekly family game night, or any other activities your kids enjoy. Holding this card can be a blast, so be sure to hand it back and forth regularly with your partner and spread the fun around.

GESTURES OF LOVE (KIDS)

You know that mom who leaves handwritten notes in her kid's lunch box that read "I love you to the moon and back"? Or the dad who drops by basketball practice for a quick hug? With some thought, time, and effort—some CPE, if you will—that parent could be you, making every day a little more special for everyone.

> ***Note!*** *You're both equally capable of having the forethought and spending the time to buy a bouquet of flowers before your child's dance recital, but trust me on this—even gestures of love benefit from one person taking the lead. To ensure that the gesture isn't missed or forgotten, assign one person to pick up flowers for the recital this week, and then re-deal to assign a lead next week.*

GIFTS (FAMILY)

Gift giving is not about buying something because a date on the calendar compels you to. When you get it right, it's about connection and appreciation. The **Magic** here lies in finding gifts and writing cards that will make your family members feel special when a holiday, graduation, birthday, or any other occasion comes around. So the next time you see a card with a message that would resonate with your child, you might purchase it even though his or her birthday is a few months away.

> ***Tip!*** *Re-deal as needed so you don't have to buy birthday gifts for yourself.*

GIFTS (VIPS)

When it comes to Very Important People gift giving, the recipient might be your child's teacher, coach, or the neighbors hosting you two doors down. If regifting is your thing, then CPEing this card can be easy and straightforward. Alternatively, this cardholder may wish to spend more time personalizing gifts and writing heartfelt cards. Either way—or somewhere in the middle—gift giving is an opportunity to connect with and thank the very important people in your life, which requires year-round CPE. Exception: Other kids' birthday gifts stays with the "birthday celebrations (other kids)" cardholder.

HARD QUESTIONS

"Why do I have hair growing under my armpits?" "What does it mean when the other kids talk about 'doing it'?" Enough said. You and your partner may re-deal this card to each other based on the question at hand or which child is asking, but when it's your turn, be prepared as best you can to research and impart thoughtful, accurate, and age-appropriate wisdom. Spoiler alert: The questions get tougher and the stakes get higher as your kids grow up.

HOLIDAY CARDS

Get ready to turn the already chaotic holidays into a job filled with a spreadsheet of personal contacts (*did they move?*), address labels, and the inevitable returned cards that haunt you until next year. The amount of time—even if you go digital with an e-card—is colossal. Not to mention the nearly impossible feat of taking a family picture with everyone looking in the same direction . . . and smiling! But think about it: It's the one time a year Cousin Susie sees a picture of your growing family. In other words, holiday cards can be a meaningful touch point that makes all the CPE well worth it.

HOLIDAYS

Just the time it takes to get holiday ornaments out of storage and unwrap them merits a glass of wine (or three), and that's before the hard work even begins. From cooking to decor to all the logistics, CPEing any holiday is like running an event-planning company—sans the paycheck. When the kids want to attempt their own impossible-to-make (but too-cute-to-resist) Halloween costumes, this cardholder will make the **Magic** happen. Same goes for figuring out who's hosting Thanksgiving, organizing Easter brunch with second cousins twice removed, and every other holiday and special ritual that your family celebrates. Saving grace: "travel," "gifts (family)" and "magical beings" cards are not included in this card. In other words, leaving cookies out for Santa isn't on you.

INFORMAL EDUCATION

Do you remember who taught you how to hold your breath under water? Throw a ball? Ride a bike? Of course you do, and so will your child as soon as this cardholder gets to work. Kudos to you for the countless hours you'll spend hovering over a bike seat with your back wrenched—that's the Execution—but pay special attention to the Conception and Planning, as well. Start thinking now about those special milestone moments and life skills you want to teach your children. (Hint: If your kid is the only one in class still wearing Velcro sneakers, you might want to remedy that by teaching him to tie his shoes.)

MAGICAL BEINGS

By holding this card, you hold the CPE required to keep your child's dreams and imagination alive. When it comes to the

Tooth Fairy, Elf on the Shelf, Santa Claus, the Easter Bunny, the Mensch on a Bench, Saint Patrick's Day leprechauns, the Switch Witch, or any other magical being that you introduce into your family, believing in the unbelievable disappears quickly. Put in the time and effort today to make the **Magic** come to life.

MARRIAGE & ROMANCE

#herofail is what one mom called it when her husband scheduled a series of surprise romantic dinners on Thursday nights . . . not realizing that's when she holds the "transportation (kids)" card for their daughter's play rehearsals. Her husband's heart was in the right place, but this card (like all of 'em) takes Conception, Planning, and Execution—emphasis needed on the Planning in his case. This cardholder might be the one who, for example, initiates a regular date night (on a night that works!). Planning for kid-free time can feel like a logistical nightmare (scheduling a sitter, coordinating calendars, and agreeing on details), but cardholders who pull it off report it's well worth it.

MIDDLE-OF-THE-NIGHT COMFORT

Define "middle of the night" as you see fit, because when daylight savings time hits, you may think of this as the "way too early to be morning" card that leaves you dog-tired and at your wit's end. (It's amazing how just one hour can do so much damage!) Bad dreams at 3 a.m., cries of "I can't sleep!" just when you're curled up in bed to watch TV, and help with trips to the toilet for that stomach bug going around are all in this cardholder's hands. As one woman explained it, "When my husband has middle-of-the-night duty, I refer to this as the 'Don't call Mom' card!"

PARTNER COACH

Every time you help your loved one with his or her work, you are engaging in the highly invisible work of partner coaching. When you edit an email before your husband sends it to his boss, help him plan an important outing with a client, or lie in bed at night thinking through how he could be considered for a promotion, you are doing the loving and often unrecognized work of "coaching" your partner. This card can be one-sided (that is, a wife helping a husband but not the other way around). The aspiration is to hand off the card more equitably so both partners can benefit from each other's support and advice.

SHOWING UP & PARTICIPATING

One dad admits that he spent nearly a month complaining about the daddy/daughter dance at school, dreading everything from the small talk with other dads to the awkwardness of busting out his moves. Ultimately he went, and it turned out to be pure **Magic** for both him and his growing-up-too-fast fourth grader. You've got to show up for and participate in your child's events, big and small, for the **Magic** to happen. Re-deal this card frequently to make sure it does.

SPIRITUALITY

This card looks and feels different to everyone—perhaps even within your own home—so all the more reason you should consult your partner in the Planning to make sure you're on the same page. (Ahem, you don't have carte blanche to join a cult just because it's your card.) It may involve attending church/synagogue/mosque, planning events like communion or a bar/bat mitzvah, establishing a relationship with clergy members, enforcing dietary beliefs, creating a family meditation ritual, or any number of ways you decide to make spirituality a part of your family's life.

THANK-YOU NOTES

Why would the dreaded task of writing thank-you notes be considered **Magic**? Because thank-you notes are an opportunity to express gratitude to people who inspire you to feel it. If you have family dinner with friends, you might send an email letting them know how wonderful it was to spend time together. When a colleague delivers a huge bag of hand-me-downs for your kids, that thoughtfulness merits a note. Imagine a life where sleep-deprived postpartum moms are not saddled with writing thank-you notes for baby gifts. That can be your reality, as either partner is capable of CPEing this card.

VALUES & GOOD DEEDS (KIDS)

You know those families who you look up to because the kids have rock-solid values? This kind of **Magic** takes time and consistency. In other words, one visit to the soup kitchen does not a good kid make. If you want to be the family who feeds the homeless every Thanksgiving, start researching places to volunteer. If you want to make birthdays feel special without any semblance of materialism, start a tradition like a family hug on the time your child was born. (Unless it's in the middle of the night—then wait until the morning.) Soon you'll be the family who everyone else is talking about . . . for the right reasons.

WATCHING 🍺

If you have a little one, then you know that having eyes on your child is endless at the baby/toddler stage. Older children need watching, too, like preventing your ten-year-old from spraying WD-40 all over the living room when he mistakes it for air freshener (true story), or walking by your teen's bedroom door constantly to make sure it's open while a "friend" is over. Good news: It's amazing what can happen when you put down your phone and really watch your kids. Watching a one-year-old may feel uneventful, but this is when you witness your child's first steps!

Depending on what time of day you hold this card and the age of your child, you may also be responsible for taking the lead on a number of other cards, such as "diapering and potty training," "bedtime routine," "meals" "transportation (kids)," and "tidying up." (If you build a fort in your living room while you're on "watch," then it's only fair that you break it down and tidy up before re-dealing this card to your spouse or other caregivers.)

THE WILD SUIT

def. >> Just when you thought you had it together, sh*t hits the fan. SOS! The **Wild** suit includes life-changing scenarios that rock your world. Even if it's a planned and joyful event like having a baby, a **Wild** card is accompanied by a mind-numbing amount of invisible work just to get out of the red and back into the black. So when you hold a **Wild** card (hopefully temporarily), you're entitled to ask for additional help from your partner guilt-free. Your partner is encouraged to reach out to your village for even more support, but the **Wild** cardholder is not the one who handles this delegation because that would be more work, got it?

AGING/AILING PARENT

Sandwich generation, anyone? From managing medications, meals, and doctors' appointments to making visiting a priority, caring for an aging/ailing parent can be all-consuming, not to mention the emotional challenge of this inevitable but often unexpected new caregiver role. Even if you outsource some of the work or can afford in-home or assisted-living support, CPEing this card requires all the love in your heart and a good chunk of your time.

DEATH

As if the loss of a loved one isn't unbearable enough, there are also many important items of business requiring your time, including arranging a funeral, a shiva or other spiritual or religious rituals, and then acknowledging those who paid their respects. If handling any will or estate issues and packing up your loved one's home and belongings are your responsibilities, prepare to be holding this card for quite some time.

FIRST YEAR OF INFANT'S LIFE

Unsettled hormones, sleep deprivation, and a ravaged body are enough to make this a **Wild** card, not to mention that your time has all but disappeared. The days of having even a consecutive two-hour stretch of time to be productive are a vague memory as you drown in nursing/feeding, diaper changing, comforting your baby around the clock, and an innumerable amount of other to-dos all courtesy of your bundle of joy. Make no mistake: The first year of an infant's life is not only a "Mom thing." There's plenty for Dad to do, too. While you're trying to survive another day, let him dig into the Daily Grind cards: "laundry," "dishes," "garbage," "groceries," and taking the lead on "meals (weekday dinner)."

GLITCH IN THE MATRIX/DAILY DISRUPTION

The last thing in the world you have time for is dealing with the unexpected disruption of a fender bender, a computer virus, a flooded basement . . . or having the phone ring and seeing the dreaded school phone number. Your child has lice . . . can you come pick her up? You don't get a vote when a **Wild** card lands in your lap, but you do get to ask for a helping hand from your partner when a daily disruption torpedoes your day. Remember: Leaving work early because of X, Y, or Z is not "on you" unless you currently hold this card.

HOME RENOVATION

Wild cards fall on a spectrum in terms of how life-altering and time-consuming the predicament can be. Obviously installing new toilets or kitchen cabinets is not as serious an endeavor as keeping your newborn nourished or managing a parent's chemotherapy schedule. Still, it sure would be nice to have a working toilet and a functional kitchen, so someone's got to do the work to make that happen.

JOB LOSS & MONEY PROBLEMS

Serious financial issues like unemployment or bankruptcy require heavy lifting that may include networking, job interviews, court appearances, and many other time-sucking items of business. Of course you're both impacted by the stressful issue at hand, but this cardholder takes the lead on resolving it while consulting with the "money manager" so your family's budget can be modified accordingly.

MOVING

There's a reason why moving is typically on the Top 10 list of hellish events; it can be as stressful as the death of a loved one, divorce, or unemployment. The process of purging, packing, relocating, organizing, storing, and living in disarray is all-consuming, disruptive to your family's routines, and basically upends your life. Good news: It's temporary. Bad news: It's a CPE doozy. Who is better equipped to take the lead?

NEW JOB

When you start a new job, you bring your A game daily, which may mean being the first one in, the last one to leave, working weekends, and doing whatever it takes to make an impression. Ask your partner to step up to the plate by taking some of your household and childcare cards while you concentrate on knocking it out of the park at work.

PREGNANCY & BABY'S BIRTH

Never mind how often you're puking and falling asleep on the couch by 6 p.m. Preparing for a baby increases your mental, physical, and emotional load exponentially. While you're going to constant doctors' appointments, registering for baby products that you never even knew existed (a Boppy pillow?) or that you would need (Nursing bras?), and listening to unwanted parenting advice from every other woman shopping in the baby basics aisle, ask your more hormonally balanced partner to take some additional cards. Ask him to hold on to them while you're in labor because, um, you're in labor. And while he's at it, he may just as well hold on to them while you recover from giving birth.

SERIOUS ILLNESS

When a child falls ill, the implications can be life-changing. If you are managing someone else's illness, it can require hours of research, doctors' appointments, treatment plans, and medication monitoring. Thankfully, you can ask your partner to step in and support you. If, however, it's you or your spouse who is ill, the healthier person may need to take on more cards in addition to holding this **Wild** card. Rather than allowing resentment or fear to build, ask for what you need and re-deal as circumstances change.

UNICORN SPACE

def. >> What makes you uniquely you and how do you share it with the world? **Unicorn Space** is about the passion and purpose that drive you to be the best version of yourself, and what's on the line—your identity, fulfillment, and marriage—if you don't nurture what makes you come alive. It may seem like a fairy tale to carve out time to get back to playing piano again or research the business idea that you've back-burnered since becoming a parent, but it's time to reclaim your gifts beyond your career and family without needing permission or feeling guilt. Note: An exercise class, a mani/pedi, hitting a sports bar with a buddy, or catching up on your social media feeds are not **Unicorn Space**. Your career may be if it's a Category 5 storm of passion. Be realistic, but think big as you work to discover or reclaim your essence and talents. Both you and your partner *must* take this card!

8.

PLAYING THE GAME

All cards are on the table.

GAME ON!

Congratulations! You've read the Four Rules for Fair Play. You know all time is created equal. You're excited to reclaim or discover your Unicorn Space. You've set your intention for engaging your partner in the game, and you've started thinking about your family's shared values and the Minimum Standard of Care for the cards you're holding. It's time to kick off your first round of Fair Play . . . and that means bringing your other half fully on board to discuss a new way to think and talk about your domestic life. And as you do, remember what you both stand to gain long-term—time to recommit to meaningful friendships, valuable self-care, and the interests that define you outside of being a parent. And ultimately, for both of you to be happy as individuals and as a couple. **This _is_ the endgame.**

I invite you to play for the next week. Consider these next seven days your trial run, and then assess how you feel. My hope is that the experience will be positively transformative to your relationship and to _you both personally._

You may have already had an initial conversation with your partner about Fair Play, but if not (or if a little more encouragement is needed), I've written a brief note for you to share that outlines all the ways in which you and your partner will win by engaging in a new organizational domestic life-management system, one that shifts the conversation away from competition and toward true collaboration.

To: The stand-up, awesome partner/spouse/husband/father reading this note

From: Eve Rodsky, Organizational Management Specialist, author of this book, and _your_ advocate

---

On behalf of your partner, THANK YOU for showing up to the table. Her invitation to engage you in Fair Play is a testament of her devotedness to your relationship. Your willingness to engage her signals a mutual commitment from you. Hats off to you both. Your joint participation and "two-player" approach is a solid start to what comes next.

Next, you and your partner are going to explore a new way to talk about your family life and work together to dial down the crazy and create more balance and efficiency in your home. Is this some sneaky setup where your partner dumps more sh*t on your plate and where you walk away from the table feeling nagged, _again_? Not this time.

PLAYING THE GAME

In far less time than you spend checking social media in a day, you will learn a new system for domestic life that borrows from proven organizational management principles that does not ask you to necessarily do *more* but instead to consider how to do things differently. (And by optimizing efficiency, you may actually do less.)

While you may have noticed *Fair Play* on your wife's nightstand and regarded it as just another self-help manifesto that has nothing to do with you, make no mistake: I wrote this book so that you both can win. In fact, the game is a bust if you're not both directly benefiting.

Check out what *you* stand to WIN from engaging in Fair Play:

- A new vernacular about home life that speaks to *you* (finally, you and your spouse are speaking the same language)
- Clearly defined roles and expectations; no longer are you in the dark about *who's* doing *what*
- Permission to take the lead, including a partner who trusts you implicitly
- More ownership of the work you do
- Added (guilt-free) time to pursue friendships and personal interests outside your role as partner/ husband/father
- A happier partnership that endures
- A more fulfilling and rewarding parenting experience
- A boost to your brain plasticity and overall longevity

A pretty good value proposition, isn't it? And that's not all. Take a look at what you stand to LOSE by engaging in Fair Play:

- Feeling nagged and bossed around
- Feeling second-guessed and criticized for your efforts
- Arguing over every big and small detail of your domestic life
- Daily scorekeeping over who's doing more, or *doing it better*
- Feeling overscheduled
- Worrying that your spouse has "had enough!"

Wouldn't you freely trade this list for short and collaborative conversations that make daily interactions with your spouse far less contentious, and promote the best reward of all—**happiness as a couple and as individuals, and serving as healthy role models for your kids?**

Assuming you're in, I present to you: Fair Play. The Instruction Manual. (Don't worry; this is far less complicated than Monopoly. You've totally got this.)

FAIR PLAY
THE INSTRUCTION MANUAL

PLAYERS: 2

OBJECTIVE:

A rebalance in the division of labor where 100 cards of child-care and household tasks are dealt strategically between the two players in accordance with the couple's shared values and mutually agreed-upon expectations, as well as the individual's strengths and abilities. No player holds any cards by default, each person's responsibilities are transparent and explicitly defined, and both partners are set up to win.

HOW TO PLAY: 7 Easy Steps

Step 1: SET THE GROUND RULES

Step 2: CUSTOMIZE YOUR DECK (Play for Value)

Step 3: PREPARE TO ONBOARD

Step 4: DEAL YOUR TASK CARDS (Play for CPE)

Step 5: ESTABLISH A MINIMUM STANDARD OF CARE

Step 6: CLAIM YOUR UNICORN SPACE

Step 7: TAKE A *NEW* VOW

DURATION OF PLAY

Deal the first round for seven days; ultimately, the game is designed to be played for a lifetime.

Tip! Stick with it. In time, you'll master the game.

STEP 1:
SET THE GROUND RULES

Before you and your partner lay your cards on the table, set the following ground rules. In my advisory practice, we call this a *community agreement* that guides how you and your partner will engage and play fair. Read the following agreement out loud. Mean it.

> **We agree to**—Listen to each other as we thoughtfully discuss all that it takes to run a home.
>
> **We agree to**—Consider our tone, brevity, and word choice as we share information and our individual perspectives.
>
> **We agree to**—Explore a new way to collaboratively work together as a team to create more efficiency and fairness in our domestic ecosystem.
>
> **We agree to**—Value each other's time equally.
>
> **We agree to**—Keep our phones off the table and focus on each other.

That's it . . . but that's a lot. If you can start from this place of shared intention, it will make the whole Fair Play process much smoother. In fact, it's essential for a win.

STEP 2:
CUSTOMIZE YOUR DECK (PLAY FOR VALUE)

Next, you and your partner will review the "100 Cards of Fair Play" chart on pages 108–12 or, if you prefer, download actual playing cards at fairplaylife.com. **Do not skip this step!** It is essential to the onboarding process. While I appreciate your eagerness to begin rebalancing the workload by divvying up and assigning cards, you must slow your roll. Only by first determining which of the cards are important to and benefit your family will you be able to **customize your household deck**.

REVIEW THE TASK CARDS

Review the task cards one by one across all five suits—**Home, Out, Caregiving, Magic,** and **Wild**—and separately list or start a pile of all those that are essential to your home, starting with:

Nonnegotiable and Daily Grinds: These include the 30 Daily Grind cards (noted with a coffee cup) that are an everyday or highly repetitive occurrence that often happen at a very specific time, like feeding your children breakfast and getting them out the door to school. These cards are a grind, and like it or not, many of them cannot be done at your leisure.

Also included in this round are cards that aren't as time sensitive, yet they're nonnegotiable to your family because you and you partner agree that they still must get done. Ask yourself: Does this task have to get done by someone? Is it necessary to keep our home life moving forward? If so, then it's a valuable use of time, and isn't it fair that you both share in the workload?

Make a value declaration: All time is created equal. My time is as valuable as your time. Fairness is playing with the Nonnegotiable and Daily Grind task cards.

LIST ALL NON-NEGOTIABLE AND DAILY GRIND CARDS IN PLAY:

Card 1. _____

Card 2. _____

Card 3. _____

etc.

Task Cards Both People Value: These tasks may not be essential to the functioning of your home, but both of you value having them in your life; for example, "hosting," "charity, community service and good deeds (adults)," "electronics and IT," and "social plans (couples)" may play to your individual contentment and a happy marriage.

Ask yourself, *what does my family value?* Take this as your opportunity to dial down the chaos of running from activity to activity and feeling obligated to do it all. Get really clear: What cards stay and what cards go? If you don't plan on taking a vacation until your kids can carry their own luggage, or if you don't have a four-legged family member, then, for example, the "travel" and "pets" cards are not in play because they don't apply to or hold importance in your life right now (this could change as circumstances or preferences change). You and your partner must regard this step as an important value-setting exercise where you thoughtfully discuss the aspects of domestic life that are meaningful to your family. Only by *assigning value* to the deck can you determine what cards to play between you.

PLAYING THE GAME

Make a value declaration: We don't have to do it all. We zeroed in on the cards that are important to both of us and threw out the cards that don't serve us. Now that we've added these cards to our deck, let's work toward being more efficient and thoughtful about how we share in the workload.

LIST THE "BOTH PEOPLE VALUE" TASK CARDS IN PLAY:

Card 1. _____

Card 2. _____

Card 3. _____

etc.

Task Cards One Person Values: If a card is important to only one of you, stand up for it! If you believe attending church every Sunday is valuable to your family when your spouse is indifferent about religion, then the "spirituality" card goes in your hand. Create individual "side" lists or piles for the One Person Values cards.

Make a value declaration: The hours of my life are as valuable as yours and we both get to make choices about how we use our time. I will still include you in the planning, but since I alone value it, I will hold the card.

"SIDE" LISTS OF "ONE PERSON VALUES" TASK CARDS:

Card 1. _____

Card 2. _____

Card 3. _____

etc.

YOUR HOUSEHOLD DECK

Combine the **Non-negotiable and Daily Grind Task Cards** and **Cards Both People Value** and total your cards. Collectively, how many cards are you and your partner playing with? Remember: Less is more! The fewer the task cards, the more manageable each person's workload, so **playing with less than a full deck is actually advantageous and recommended.**

> **COUNT YOUR COLLECTIVE TASK CARDS AND ENTER YOUR TOTAL: _____**

Tip! *If, after this value-setting exercise, you and your partner are still holding a hefty deck of 85 to 100 cards, consider if there are any more, if even only one, that you could set aside.*

HALFTIME BREAK!

Hold up! It's often at this point when either one or both partners want to take a halftime break. Check in with each other—do you want to pause or keep playing? You may need some time to ruminate. Heck, just naming and counting all the small and large to-dos in your domestic ecosystem is a giant achievement, especially if you've never done this before! So if you and your partner need a break, take it. Set aside your deck for now and schedule a follow-up date to come back to the table.

CAUTION!

If your halftime break is too long, you run the risk of losing momentum. From what I've observed, men will easily come back to the table twice. If, on the other hand, your partner blows you off or continues to reschedule your second date, remind him what you're playing for: the continuation of your marriage. This simple incentive tends to motivate most guys. Clinical psychotherapist Marcia Bernstein cautions, "So many powerful women bring up what they need once, get shut down, and recoil. They shrink exactly when they should step forward again." When I spoke to Marcia about this specific step of Fair Play, she advised a try-it-twice approach. "If your partner doesn't come back to the table after two tries, convey to him what's on the line if you don't explore Fair Play as a system to rebalance your lives. Use your voice to assert the importance of this exercise—better communication, less resentment, and a way for each person to get what they need."

STEP 3:
PREPARE TO ONBOARD

With your household deck in hand, you and your partner will prepare to onboard and integrate the Fair Play system. **This is another do-not-skip step; some assembly is required!** Before you can negotiate and strategically deal all the cards between the two of you, plan how you will organize your individual "hands" to ensure you and your partner will remember what cards you individually hold (for now). Take some time to experiment and determine what arrangement works the best for you.

Some couples mark up a clean copy of the "100 Cards of Fair Play" chart by initialing the task cards they're separately holding. Others create their own custom "his" and "hers" lists or columns on white boards, chalkboards, and in decoratively designed bullet journals. Couples often use note-taking apps, online calendars, and shared drives for quick access. How you track your task cards is entirely up to you, but I do recommend you follow this general guideline: **Make it highly visible and accessible.** A list that goes missing underneath a pile of junk mail or somehow gets turned in with your child's field trip permission slip will stall the onboarding process. In the long run, creating a task list where roles and responsibilities are transparent will significantly minimize daily reminders and the inefficiencies of unclear, forgotten, or duplicated efforts.

Here's an early version of what our weekly Fair Play list looked like:

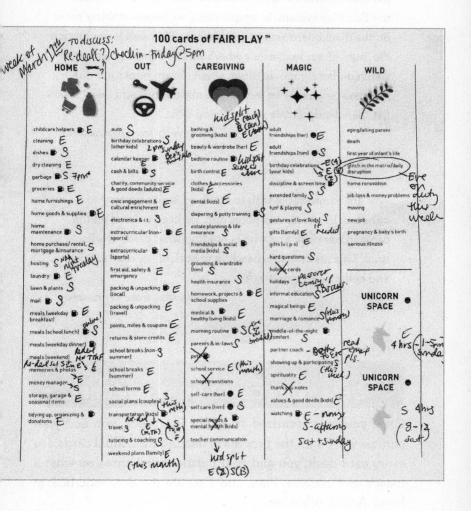

100 cards of FAIR PLAY™

week of March 12th — *To discuss: Re-deal(?) check in - Friday @ 5pm*

HOME
- childcare helpers — E
- cleaning — E
- dishes — S
- dry cleaning — E
- garbage — S 7pm
- groceries — E
- home furnishings — E
- home goods & supplies — E
- home maintenance — S
- home purchase/rental, mortgage & insurance — S
- hosting — S *(Nat night Tuesday)*
- laundry — S
- lawn & plants — S
- mail — S
- meals (weekday breakfast) — E
- meals (school lunch) — S *online!*
- meals (weekday dinner)
- meals (weekend) — Nat M T/Th/F *(Re-deal Sat 5 pm)* E
- memories & photos — E
- money manager — S → E
- storage, garage & seasonal items
- tidying up, organizing & donations — E

OUT
- auto — S
- birthday celebrations (other kids) — S *2pm Sunday*
- calendar keeper — *Barry Mo*
- cash & bills — S
- charity, community service & good deeds (adults) — E
- civic engagement & cultural enrichment
- electronics & i.t. — S
- extracurricular (non-sports) — E
- extracurricular (sports) — S
- first aid, safety & emergency — E
- packing & unpacking (local) — E
- packing & unpacking (travel) — E
- points, miles & coupons — E
- returns & store credits — E
- school breaks (non-summer)
- school breaks (summer)
- school forms — E
- social plans (couples) — S *(this mth)*
- transportation (kids) — *Re-deal* S
- travel — S *(M,Th) (T,W,F)*
- tutoring & coaching — S
- weekend plans (family) — E *(this month)*

CAREGIVING
- bathing & grooming (kids) — *kids split* E (each) E (Ben)
- beauty & wardrobe (her) — E
- bedtime routine — *kid split same as above*
- birth control
- clothes & accessories (kids) — E
- dental (kids) — E
- diapering & potty training — S
- estate planning & life insurance
- friendships & social media (kids) — S
- grooming & wardrobe (him)
- health insurance — S
- homework, projects & school supplies — E
- medical & healthy living (kids) — E
- morning routine — S *(are in breakfast)*
- parents & in-laws ~~(crossed out)~~
- pets ~~(crossed out)~~
- school service — E *(this month)*
- school transitions
- self-care (her) — E
- self care (him) — S
- special needs & mental health (kids)
- teacher communication — *kid split* E (Z) S (B)

MAGIC
- adult friendships (her) — E
- adult friendships (him) — S
- birthday celebrations (your kids) — E(A) E(C) E(B)
- discipline & screen time
- extended family — S
- fun! & playing — S
- gestures of love (kids) — S
- gifts (family) — E *needed*
- gifts (v.i.p.s)
- hard questions — S
- holiday cards ~~(crossed out)~~
- holidays — S *favorite coming up draws*
- informal education — S
- magical beings — S *(this month)*
- marriage & romance — E *(this month)*
- middle-of-the-night comfort — S
- partner coach — *both to E+s plus*
- showing up & participating — S *(this week)*
- spirituality — E
- thank you notes
- values & good deeds (kids) — E
- watching — E - money, S - autumn, Sat + Sunday

WILD
- aging/ailing parent
- death
- first year of infant's life
- glitch in the matrix/daily disruption *(Eve on duty this week)*
- home renovation
- job loss & money problems
- moving
- new job
- pregnancy & baby's birth
- serious illness

UNICORN SPACE — E 4 hrs (-1-5pm Sunday) *read group plus*

UNICORN SPACE — S 4 hrs (9-12 Sat)

"Following your lead, we put a date on the calendar when we planned to deal our deck based on what we learned about the Fair Play system. In preparation, we began making notes on the blackboard wall in our kitchen. This wall is very much the 'hub' of our house—it's where we keep track of what we watch on family movie night, when library books are due, and, now, where we've included a master 'his' and 'hers' task list that clearly shows who is doing what."

—Beverly from Minnesota

○

"We are comfortable with technology, so it was easy to onboard. In our shared notes app, we keep a list of all the cards in our deck and who is holding what cards at what time. This method is accessible to both of us, easy to edit, and helps us stay on track."

—Hudson from Tennessee

○

STEP 4: DEAL YOUR CARDS (PLAY FOR CPE)

Once you've customized your Fair Play deck, you and your partner will begin the process of dealing individual cards. For every card dealt, you and your partner must agree on what it means to Conceive, Plan, and Execute the domestic task at hand. A CPE refresher:

Conception: This is the behind-the-scenes mental load where you assess your family's overall needs and conceive of and define the task that will meet those needs.

Rain season is coming. Find out if the kids have outgrown their rain jackets and boots.

Planning: This is where you do your homework and create a detailed action plan that outlines what is required to get the task done completely. This step may also necessitate management of the plan and possible modifications along the way. Planning also often includes consulting with other stakeholders (your partner, and perhaps your kids, caregiver, parents, in-laws, etc.) for their opinion and buy-in before finalizing this step. *Yup, the kids have outgrown last year's rain gear. Make a list of possible sources: older cousins, secondhand stores, buying new. If buying new, ask kids if they have a color preference.*

Execution: This is the final step to get the job done at an appropriate time while meeting mutually agreed-upon standards and explicitly defined expectations. *As a family, we value staying warm, dry, and healthy, so I will have that rain gear in hand before the first storm of the season!*

As you deal the cards, refer to the descriptions in Chapter 7: The 100 Cards of Fair Play, and **consider what it means to CPE each task at hand.** You are not assigning cards to each other ("Take this one!" "No, *you* take it!"); you're both making thoughtful choices and agreeing to what you each hold in your hand.

Note! As you build your individual hands, discuss with your partner the intended time frame for holding your cards. Keep in mind—there are no strangleholds! It's not forever that you or your partner will be holding any one card; the pre-negotiated window could be for a week, or

*just for a day or even hour by hour. In fact, I encourage
you to frequently re-deal the Daily Grind cards, since
those are particularly taxing. As one father said to
me, "I don't want to be the family chauffeur the rest of
my life!" Who does? Another mother admitted, "If I'm
holding the 'watching' card for more than a few hours
without a break, I start to lose it." I get it! No one should
be stuck with any one card indefinitely.*

OK, time to start dealing! Starting with:

Nonnegotiable and Daily Grinds: Dive right into a discussion about who is better equipped to handle full CPE
of these cards based on individual **capabilities and availability.** These guidelines alone will mean that you or your
partner will be ineligible to pick up some of the cards. For
example, if you leave for work before the morning routine
with the kids even begins, then this Daily Grind won't
be your card this round. To be fair, early-to-work does
not give you an all-around free pass. **There are 30 Daily Grinds and no one person should be responsible for
them all.** Hold your ground as you negotiate these cards
to ensure that neither one of you becomes the default
cardholder in this category. **Each partner should hold a
fair share of the Daily Grind cards, and at least one from
each suit.** This ensures that you are each digging into the
most labor-intensive aspects of domestic life that cannot
typically be done on your own timetable.

Tip! *If you are sharing a card (meaning you "both" do
it), put it in an unassigned pile for now.*

Cards Both People Value: Of the remainder of the cards in the **Home, Out, Caregiving,** and **Magic** suits, discuss who is better equipped to hold them based on your individual **preferences, capabilities, and availability.** Again, it may be clear-cut who will take which remaining cards. If, for example, you're a numbers person who loves to balance a budget, you might serve your family well as the money manager. If you work in tech, you're likely more equipped to handle your home IT department (when the internet crashes, you know how to save the day).

Cards One Person Values: If a card is important to only one of you, claim it. Bring back those "side" lists of One Person Values cards and assign them to your respective piles.

🙂

The Happiness Trio: Self-care, adult friendships, and Unicorn Space. Based on my interviews, these cards are the most important to a couple's and individual's happiness, and they will create strong resentment between you and your partner if you do not both hold them. (Aside from a Kid Split, these are the only cards you hold at the same time.) As it is with time, happiness is an equal right. Both of you deserve and *need* time for meaningful friendships, valuable self-care, and the interests that define you outside of being a parent. If you haven't already, put the self-care and adult friendships cards in your separate piles. For now, set the Unicorn Space cards aside; they will be the last, and most important, cards you each play.

Wild Cards: If you are holding one of these life-changing cards like a job change, ailing parent, or you are the one taking the lead on your home renovation, ask your partner for some guilt-free support (which may mean asking him or her to hold a few extra cards) until circumstances alleviate or change.

CAUTION!
Do Not Leave Cards Unassigned!

If you are left with unassigned cards in your deck, it's likely you've fallen into a Both Trap. Do not leave cards unassigned! If you're unclear who in the partnership should take the CPE lead, refer to the **Fair Play FAQ** on page 233: "What if we're stuck because we each do certain aspects of a card?"

COUNT YOUR INDIVIDUAL CARDS AND ENTER YOUR TOTALS:

Player 1: _____

Player 2: _____

You did it! You've successfully dealt all the Fair Play cards you and your partner deem valuable. If you have unanswered questions about the game so far, flip forward to the **Fair Play FAQs** starting on page 231. Otherwise, move on to Steps 5, 6, and 7 and set yourself up for a WIN-WIN!

STEP 5:
ESTABLISH A MINIMUM STANDARD OF CARE

In addition to clarifying what it means to CPE each card, you and your partner will discuss the Minimum Standard of Care, along with your shared values for each card. This step ensures that you can both trust that all the Fair Play cards in your deck will be **handled on time and with competence and care.** Success!

To be super-duper clear: This step does not give any one player permission to elevate his or her standards and demand his or her partner reach them. Nor is this an opportunity to ask your partner to lower his or her standards. **Rather than debate who has the "right" standards, collaborate on what is reasonable within your *own* home based on your family's shared values.** For every card that you and your partner deem valuable and worthy of playing, discuss your minimum standard, and if you cannot come to a collaborative agreement, use the Fair Play MSC Test:

1. Would a reasonable person (in this case, your partner, spouse, babysitter, caregivers, parents, and in-laws) under similar circumstances CPE this card in this way?

2. What is the community standard, and do we want to adopt this standard within our own home?

3. What's the harm for doing, or not doing, it this way?

4. What is our "why"?

Tip! *To help you unpack this step, revisit Chapter 6:*
Rule #4: Establish Your Values and Standards.

The "Why" We Do It This Way

Damon and Gabe used to argue about the disorganization of
the front hall closet. In their New York apartment, it was the
only option for storage, and as such, it became a catchall for
coats, hats, umbrellas, shoes, and bags of old toys and books
to donate to a local charity. When Gabe also added boxes of
family photos to the clutter, Damon lost it. "Our photos are
being crushed by Teddy's rain boots!" Together, they mutually agreed on a minimum standard: nothing overflowing,
use plastic containers, and the door must shut. Their "why"
for maintaining a manageable closet? Preserving their family's memories with organization and care.

After Alan set up the Christmas tree, strung lights along
the front porch and around the perimeter of the roof, and
then set up an inflatable nativity scene in the front yard, he
exhaustedly asked his wife, "Why do we need to decorate
so much every year?" Jill gave it some thought. Perhaps
the pervasiveness of fresh pine potpourri wafting through
their home, along with her insistence to place an Elf on the
Shelf in every room, including the bathroom, was a bit unreasonable? On the other hand, "holidays" and "magical
beings" were two of her favorite cards. Jill agreed to back
down from her over-the-top standards, and together she and
Alan agreed on what they both mutually valued—creating
a sense of magic and wonder and future nostalgia for their

children. Jill finally understood that she could accomplish this without transforming their home into a holiday theme park.

STEP 6:
CLAIM YOUR UNICORN SPACE

Once you have negotiated and strategically dealt every card in your deck, the last step in your initial implementation of the Fair Play system requires you both to play your Unicorn Space cards. **This is an all-important card that each person must play.** Unicorn Space is essential to your ongoing sense of self, the health of your partnership, and your ability to convey to your children what a full life looks like.

One at a time, you and your partner discuss what your goal of Unicorn Space entails—time, money, and kid-coverage-wise. Please read Chapter 11: Living in Your Unicorn Space to help you each create an actionable, step-by-step plan.

> *Tip!* You must agree as a couple to allow each other Unicorn Space. Your spouse doesn't get a vote in how you spend your time, and you don't get a vote in how he or she spends theirs. Still—you must have a conversation about creating this valuable space for each other. If one partner feels that he or she is still holding too many task cards to reclaim Unicorn Space, go back to the drawing board and re-deal so that you can both hold this essential card. Revisit page 208 for a refresher on the Unicorn Space card and encourage your spouse to read it, too.

STEP 7:
TAKE A *NEW* VOW

Congratulations! You've now both been onboarded to a new system that prioritizes collaboration over competition; clarifies roles, responsibilities, and expectations; and enhances efficiency and harmony in the home. Now that you've rebalanced the domestic workload, you can begin to play fair.

And as you do, make a vow to each other:

> **I will**—Let go of resentment about the past.

> **I will**—Play my cards with full Conception, Planning, and Execution (CPE).

> **I will**—Relinquish control of the cards that are not mine; no messing with your cards in the eleventh hour.

> **I will**—Adhere to our agreed-upon Minimum Standard of Care for each card I take; cut the criticism and nagging when things aren't done "my" way.

> **I will**—Re-deal individual cards as often as needed with clear and collaborative communication.

> **I will**—Claim my Unicorn Space, and support you as you take yours.

> **I will**—Make regular time to check in with you; practice makes perfect.

FAIR PLAY FAQs

Q: I'm confused by CPE and what's all entailed in the Conception, Planning, and Execution of a task card. Help?

A: Oftentimes the invisible work of Conception and Planning is the most time-consuming and mentally draining work. Be sure to consider all that's entailed in each card if you're claiming it. Turn back to Chapter 7 for a snapshot of every Fair Play card including what it takes to Conceive, Plan, and Execute each responsibility. For a more detailed CPE breakdown in list form, go to fairplaylife.com.

Q: If I take a card, how long will it be mine?

A: Some cards you may hold indefinitely, others for an extended period of weeks, or just for a day or even hour-by-hour. There are no strangleholds! Re-deal accordingly.

For example, if your family's system dictates that one of you prepares dinner Monday, Tuesday, and Wednesday, and the other on Thursday and Friday, the re-deal of the "meals (weekday dinner)" card works so long as the lead for any given day is responsible for cooking, and also meal planning and informing the "groceries" cardholder what they need in advance. The lead for the other days is responsible for full CPE when he or she holds the card. Make sense?

As you deal the Fair Plays cards between you, understand that because Fair Play is fluid, you and your partner will regularly check in (see Chapter 9 for the importance of check-ins) and periodically re-deal the cards as negotiated, as needed, and as circumstances change.

Q: Define "re-deal"? I'm not sure I get it.

A: A re-deal is the pre-negotiated, explicit handoff of a card to a partner, given with full CPE. There are some cards like "pets" that may be re-dealt midweek or even day to day.

For example:

When my dad told me that he'd offered to help out my stepmom by handling Monday drop-off and pickup at doggie daycare so she could get to work earlier, I was blunt: "Dad, that's only minimally helpful."

"What do you mean?" he appealed. "I'll probably save her a good hour on the road today."

"That may be true," I acknowledged, "and I'm sure she appreciates your offer to help out. But the question is, will you also make sure Sadie is fed before you leave? Did you pack more food for the day, and remember her special treats and vitamins? And will *you* be the person on call today if someone at the facility has a special question or concern?"

"Well, no," he freely admitted. "Marcia handles all that."

"Then you haven't really taken full ownership of the card. You've taken on one execution aspect of 'pets' by transporting Sadie to and from doggie daycare, but Marcia is handling the time-consuming prep work and is still carrying the mental load. She's anticipating any number of needs Sadie might have today, and she may also be worrying that without a reminder, you'll forget to pick her up."

I explained to my dad that in order to be truly helpful, he had to completely take the task off Marcia's to-do list by Conceiving, Planning, and Executing every aspect of what pet care requires *just for the day*.

"This is your full-dog day. Tomorrow, you'll re-deal the card back to Marcia," I emphasized to my dad, who had become a much more involved domestic partner since I was a kid, and who was earnestly attempting to implement Fair Play. "If you're going to be the primary cardholder on Monday, then take the lead and be responsible for *everything*—Sadie's food, the vitamins, the leash, the carrier, driving her to and from doggie daycare, *and* walking her when she gets home, including poop pickup."

"That's a lot of work," he puffed.

"Exactly." I laughed. "That's the point! But remember, you're only holding this card for one day and then you can re-deal."

Q: **What if we're stuck because we each do certain aspects of a card?**

A: A core tenet of Fair Play is a redefinition of "teamwork." In order for your home to be governed by efficiency and accountability, you must negotiate who will be responsible for the entire Conception, Planning, and Execution for the card at hand. If you're both holding a card and can't agree who will be the lead, you run the risk of falling into a Both Trap—the Double-Up or the Break-Up. More below:

>> The Double-Up

What could be wrong with both of you holding a particular card? Plenty. Consider this scenario:

Maria and Paoula receive an email from the school that the fourth grade is about to start a chemistry unit called Mystery Powders. Their child's teacher includes this note: *Your child has been identified as having a food allergy. Since we will be*

*experimenting with six different Mystery Powders, please fill
out the following school form to be 100 percent sure your child
can touch and experiment with each powder.* Who's holding
this card? Since the "school forms" card hasn't been assigned,
Maria and Paoula both unknowingly fill it out and hit "sub-
mit." Doubly efficient, right? Wrong. What happens next is
that they each get a call from the school nurse because one
of them has indicated that powder #2 is unsafe while the other indicated otherwise. They must now regroup and fill out
a *third* form to clear up the allergy dispute. A day later, they
argue over who should drop off the form to the school office.
The corrected form requires both their signatures and a hand
delivery. If one of them had only filled it out initially, they
would have saved a lot of time and bickering!

Another all-too-common Double-Up: Ali and Ben head to
their local big-box store. "We like to share decision-making
and it's fun spending the time together," they claim. What really happens? Ali takes off down aisle 3 with her list of basics.
Ben heads off to the refrigerated section and returns with
Omaha steaks and a case of ice cream sandwiches. On and
on this goes until the cart is full and two hours have passed.
It's not until Ali and Ben get home, relieve the grandparents
of watching the baby, and start unpacking the bags that they
realize—neither one remembered the diapers!

The risks of the Double-Up are that no one person takes
leadership and the blame game is easily played—*I thought
you were doing it? No! You said you were handling it! Wait,
I already did it. No, I already did it. Oh no, we both did it!*
Again, this two-cardholder approach to dividing the domestic
workload is colossally inefficient, and it signals that you mis-
trust your partner to handle a task independently. Even when
partners double-up in an attempt to be helpful or support-

ive, without specifically assigned responsibilities, it's often a disaster. When you and your partner approach tasks as the royal "we," efforts are duplicated, big and small details tend to fall through the cracks, and neither partner is absolved of the mental load.

>> The Break-Up

When one person oversees Conception and Planning and the other handles Execution for a task, I call that a Break-Up. Avoid at all costs. This way danger lies.

Consider this scenario: Mom selects ABC cleaners because they're the cheapest (and the prior cleaners ruined a shirt). That's Conception. She gathers all the clothes that need dry cleaning and puts them in a bag that she parks at the front door. That's Planning. She then asks Dad to drop them off. Oops! She just dropped the ball on Execution. What happens next? Dad agrees to her request and swings by Monday morning on his commute to work. But when he arrives, he discovers that the shop is closed. He sends his wife a frustrated text: > **Why didn't you tell me the dry cleaner is closed today?**

When there is a Break-Up, no one person has taken full CPE ownership of the task, and the person Executing likely has little context to carry it out successfully. This two-cardholder approach to dividing household tasks is disorganized and ultimately ineffective. When partners don't know who's doing what, it's a wonder anything gets done! In the Case of the Closed Dry Cleaners, if Dad had done the Conception and Planning, he wouldn't have needed to consult his wife; he would have known when the shop was open and used his time more efficiently by dropping off the bag on Tuesday. If Mom had followed through on Execution, she also would have dropped off the clothes on Tuesday and no disgruntled texts would have been sent.

Q: Why can't I ask my partner to execute on my behalf? What's wrong with asking for a little help?

A: Because your house will be infested with RATs. Consider: The Case of the Marvel Legos.

"I'm leaving to pick up Isabella from my mom's," Jill called out to her husband, who was finishing up in the shower. "Luis is playing in the living room. Pick up the Marvel Legos before we get home," she hurriedly instructed before closing the bathroom door.

David turned off the water, quickly toweled himself off, and got dressed. He joined his eight-year-old son, Luis, who was reading a Spider-Man comic in the living room. He'd been looking forward to some Daddy bonding time on a Saturday afternoon. As he sat down next to his son, David scanned the floor and didn't see any marbles. "Mama said pick up the *marbles*, right?"

"Sure, Daddy," said Luis as he closed his comic and trotted off to the kitchen.

For the next several minutes, David looked for marbles on the floor, even lifting up the rug. When he couldn't find a single marble, he went into the kitchen and started making lunch for Luis and Isabella.

Twenty minutes later, Jill returned. As soon as she walked through the front door carrying their six-month-old, the sh*t hit the fan. "I told you to pick up the *Marvel Legos*," she screamed and pointed at some scattered Legos in the entrance hall. "Why are they still on the floor? If Isabella puts any of them in her mouth, she'll choke!"

"I thought you said 'marbles'!" David yelled back.

"Ugh," his wife huffed. "I just asked you to do one thing."

In David's defense, that *one thing* was not communicated clearly and she unfairly handed off Execution, on the fly, instead of carrying it through herself.

Ideally, Jill would have taken ownership for picking up the Legos before she left because she holds the "tidying" card. Instead, Jill delivered a Random Assignment of a Task (RAT) and blamed David when he didn't Execute to her expectations.

If you want your spouse to become a collaborator who can be invested, and also empowered and capable of succeeding, you must retire your habit of issuing RATs. A predominant number of the men I interviewed report being on the receiving end of emasculating finger-pointing on a daily basis.

"I'm sick of being constantly ordered around," said one man.

"The only time she speaks to me is to nag me," offered another.

"My wife jokes that I need better 'training,'" said a third. "Hey, I admit I'm not perfect, but I'm not a *dog*."

While a single RAT will turn up from time to time, when homes become infested with them, guess what happens? At least one person inevitably declares, "I'm not living like this. I'm out of here!" After speaking one-on-one with countless men, the data was clear: Random Assignment of Tasks is **one of the top reasons men resent their wives, admit to affairs, and** express a desire to divorce. *Yikes!* This is a painful reality check and well worth addressing before it gets to the point of no return. Thankfully, RATs become unnecessary when CPE comes into play because **tasks are no longer random.** After pre-negotiating and specifically assigning all the cards, both partners know in advance—actually, at every minute of the day, seven days a week—what they are responsible for so nobody is caught off guard, needs reminding, or is told to figure it out! As soon as you each take full responsibility for the cards you hold, your respective roles evolve beyond the "nag" barking random orders and the "helper" who simply carries out instructions that someone else has taken the time and energy to think through. In your new Fair Play partnership roles that are explicitly defined, both partners are set up to consistently succeed.

Q: If I'm holding a card and really need Execution help, what do I do?

A: On the occasion that either one of you need help reaching the finish line, rather than deliver a RAT—"I just need you to . . . !"—request help from someone in your village *other than your partner* by providing full context and an explicit request. Even though you're responsible for Execution of all the cards in your hand, this doesn't necessarily mean you must physically complete the task. After all, every great project manager enlists help on aspects of a job—just be sure you're not asking your spouse to step in! Ideally, to avoid needing to enlist outside help in the eleventh hour, re-deal the card in its entirety at weekly check-in.

Q: **What if we're stuck because neither one of us wants to CPE certain cards?**

A: Not an option. You've got to negotiate until one of you takes every card that is *valued* in your home. Remember, it's not a life sentence. If you're stuck because neither one of you wants to take a card, flip a coin! And then re-deal as needed.

Q: **What if we both want to hold a card because there are aspects of it that we both enjoy, like showing up for our son's basketball games?**

A: For a lot of people, the joy is in the Execution—both of you showing up at the game and sitting together in the bleachers to cheer on your son. There is no harm in this, and by no means am I suggesting that by taking the lead on a card, your partner is boxed out or left out of the fun. This system is designed for inclusion. Still, one of you must take the lead on every card in your deck or risk the consequences of doubling up or breaking up. In this basketball example, I suggest one of you hold the "extracurricular (sports)" card while the other holds "showing up and participating." That way, you both get to share in this feel-good moment that creates meaningful connection within your family, but only one of you is responsible for driving carpool and bringing snacks to the game, while the other just *shows up*.

Q: **If we have more than one child, how should we deal or "split" the kid-related cards?**

A: In the event that your kids both have playdates to attend or sports games on the *same day and time*, it is permissible for both parents to hold the *same card* for different kids so long as the full Conception, Planning, and Execution for the separate events stays with the cardholder. This is called a **Kid Split** when both you and your partner are holding the same card *at the same time* . . . just for different children. The Fair Play cards most typically split because there are two or more children in your home going in myriad directions on any given day—"birthday celebrations (other kids)," "extracurricular (non-sports)," "extracurricular (sports)," "friendships and social media," "packing and unpacking (local)," "transportation (kids)," "tutoring and coaching," "watching," and if your children attend different schools, you may split "school forms," "teacher communication," and "school service."

Note! Splitting cards for different kids is not mandatory but permissible.

Q: What's "fair"? How many cards should each person hold?

A: What is fair is not always equal and what is equal is not always fair, so don't expect a 50/50 split. **The goal of Fair Play is equity, not equality.** Minimum: One person cannot hold all the cards, even in a marriage where one partner does not work outside the home. Both players hold the adult friendships, self-care, and Unicorn Space cards *plus*, at a minimum, each partner must hold a fair share of Daily Grind cards, preferably one from each suit. This ensures that both of you are digging in to the most time-sucking aspects of domestic life across the board and are responsible for labor-intensive duties that you typically cannot CPE on your own timetable.

Q: **Why not aim for a 50/50 split of the cards?**

A: Fair Play is not about score-keeping but customization. And anyway, when I asked women what makes the biggest difference in their marital satisfaction, they said that it depends far less on whether tasks are split 50/50 in the household, and far more on whether their partners perform full Conception, Planning, and Execution of those cards in their hands with competence and care. "My husband taking full CPE ownership of the 'auto' card was worth ten cards to me because that one card relieved me of so many mental minutes. Not having to plan, remind, or even *think* at all about DMV registration, renewing insurance and oil changes is liberating!"

Here's the game-changing news, ladies: The gender revolution can be measured in CPE.

Truly, one card can be transformative. When my husband took over "extracurricular (sports)" for Zach and Ben, I gained back *eight hours a week*. Just from re-dealing a single card! One, I might add, that Seth enjoys holding because he loves sports and watching his kids engage on the field. Once my husband understood how CPE ownership invites him to step into a stronger and more fulfilling parenting role, and also puts him in the driver's seat of aspects of domestic life that he values, he willingly built his hand.

Q: **But really, and to be fair, how many cards should men hold?**

A: After testing the Fair Play system extensively, a magic number revealed itself—couples felt the division was equitable when the man CPEs 21 cards. **Blackjack!**

Regardless of the fact that 21 cards is mathematically only one-fourth of a typical deck—far from a

50/50 split—when men held a "blackjack" or beyond, their wives reported that the division of labor was equitable and fair. And not in a settling-for-less, she-fault kind of way. Most every woman I spoke to whose spouse held a minimum of 21 cards at a time felt supported, and no longer drained from daily resentments and fatigue. (This goal applies in all households regardless of who works or doesn't work outside the home.)

"I've always appreciated my husband's willingness to Execute, but once he took over Conception and Planning, I felt like a free woman," reported my friend Chelsea.

The deepest resentment lives in the "C" and "P" because therein lies the bulk of the mental and emotional weight. So when our partners completely take Conception and Planning off our minds, suddenly the heaviest aspects of the domestic workload are lifted. What's more, the men who report feeling the most confident, invested, and happiest in their relationships are those who have the full backing and trust of their partners to take a full CPE lead!

My advice to the women: As you and yours negotiate and split your deck, don't expect and certainly do not demand that your man take 50 cards. Holding more than he had *yesterday* is a gain, and working toward a blackjack or beyond is often a gradual and incremental build, depending on your starting point.

My advice to the men: Resist any urge to overstack your hand in this first round. Carefully consider what you're holding before you willingly take another card. As you continue to play and renegotiate cards week after week, your hand will likely build. And then one day, like Gene, a general surgeon, you may realize you're happily holding a whopping 46 cards!

Q: What's the difference between CPE and MSC?

A: Conception, Planning & Execution (CPE) unveils all of the invisible steps required to complete a task. Minimum Standard of Care (MSC) is the expectation that you will follow through on the steps with your family's standard for competence and care, and on a timetable that works for your family.

Q: What if I don't trust my partner to play fair?

A: Fair Play only works when both parties align expectations and adhere to a mutually agreed-upon Minimum Standard of Care. If you can, discard some cards, but if you both decide to play a card, it must be done with a MSC. Revisit Chapter 6 for a refresher on establishing your values and standards.

9.

RE-DEALING
THE DECK

Stay in it to win it.

Congratulations! You and your spouse have begun the Fair Play system. You've strategically dealt the Fair Play cards between the two of you in accordance with your shared values and mutually agreed-upon expectations, while also taking into consideration your individual strengths, preferences, and abilities. Now that you've rebalanced the domestic workload and are playing for time equality, enhanced efficiency, equity and fairness...

What happens next? You will continue the conversation. There's no going backward, right?

THE ALL-IMPORTANT CHECK-IN

Within the first week of implementing Fair Play in your home, **set a date to return to the table for your first check-in.** Every system needs maintenance, and within the rules of Fair Play, preserving fairness requires direct and open communication. Before too many days pass, schedule a future date, place, and time where you will again lay all your cards on the table. Prioritize your check-in like it's the next episode of *The Bachelor*. I'm not kidding—do not miss it! Across the board, couples who make regular time to exchange feedback about the Fair Play system achieve maximum efficiency and happiness. In fact, it's the number-one predictor of long-term success.

INVITATION TO CHECK IN

Date:

Place:

Time:

>> The Power of Feedback

Within the professional world, hiring managers and organizational team leaders love to debate the most effective method for delivering feedback to employees and teammates. Direct. Warm and fuzzy. Careful framing. Turning critiques into questions. Whatever the method, many successful organizations agree on one thing: Feedback is vital to progress. It's the reason for Monday-morning staff meetings and regular performance reviews. Without consistent feedback, how do you know what's working and what needs correction? The same holds true in the home. The weekly check-in is your opportunity to receive and exchange valuable feedback with your partner. It creates the time and space needed to clarify roles, assignments, and expectations, ultimately allowing you to refine the system to ensure you both continue to win.

After all, Fair Play isn't like a crash diet; it's a lifelong shift in how you approach your relationship.

>> Wait for It

Within the home environment, many of us aren't accustomed to waiting to provide feedback to our partners or spouses. We may mutter under our breath. Nag and complain, and sometimes shout. On occasion, we might storm out of rooms. Slam doors. Throw jabs and deliver RATs. And when our voices aren't heard or our expectations aren't met, some of us withhold sex until all the dishes are out of the sink.

These are all examples of feedback in the moment and I implore you—hold your temper, hold your tongue, and *wait for it*.

Delivering feedback in the moment is never helpful, not really. Sure, there can be merit to saying how you feel when you *feel* it. But within the Fair Play system, it's not recommended unless there is an imminent danger, like your spouse is about to apply tush paste to your infant's face as a substitute for sunscreen. When you communicate during what behavioral economist Dan Ariely calls "emotional cascades," you can easily derail the long game—two happy people who feel valued, heard, and treated with fairness.

When we spoke over the phone about this topic, he pointed me to this quote in his bestselling book *Predictably Irrational: The Hidden Forces That Shape Our Decisions*:

> I think romantic relationships best illustrate the danger of emotional cascades. As couples attempt to deal with problems—whether discussing (or yelling about) money, kids, or what to have for dinner, they're not only dis-

cussing the problems at hand, they're also developing a *behavioral repertoire*. This repertoire then determines the way they will interact over time.

I've seen this "behavioral repertoire" play out in polar reverse with couples testing the Fair Play system. Those who continue to give feedback in the moment tend to remain in a competitive dynamic, ultimately losing trust in the process, whereas couples who create a new habit of *waiting* to provide thoughtful feedback exemplified more collaborative interactions over time.

World-renowned psychologists John and Julie Gottman promote the advantage of waiting to provide feedback. They found that couples in conflict who take a short cooling-off period have better cognitive perspective. Professor Darby Saxbe offers the neurological explanation for doing this:

> It's hard to think clearly when you're feeling stressed or upset. Your prefrontal cortex, which helps you reason out a logical argument, may work less effectively when the threat response centers of your brain, like the amygdala, are fired up. In my own research, I found that unhappily married couples were more physiologically reactive to each other—that is, they showed more strongly linked levels of the stress hormone cortisol. This finding suggests that stress can be contagious; when one partner gets upset, it's easy to get caught up in their emotion. So, if you can't respond calmly in the moment, then back off and find another time when you're both in a good mental state.

Kim Davis, my former colleague from JPMorgan Chase

who advised its chairman and CEO and is now a senior executive at the National Hockey League and who has managed hundreds of employees, mirrored Saxbe's recommendation. "I go by the saying 'when emotion is high, cognition is low.' My advice is to come back to the table when you can have a calm conversation and really be heard."

>> Big Feelings

The suggestion to withhold your feedback in the early days of Fair Play may feel challenging. Many of my female beta testers, specifically, reported the stirrings of negative chatter within the first weeks of testing the system:

> "I'm worried my partner won't 'play' his cards; what if he just doesn't do it?"
>
> "What if he screws them up?"
>
> "What if he forgets? Should I remind him?"
>
> "I'm scared 'playing fair' won't work and we'll be back to where we started—*fighting*."
>
> "Even though I've handed over some of my cards, I'm having a hard time letting go."
>
> "I'm trying to trust the process, but I'm secretly watching to see if my partner fails."
>
> "What if . . . we can't change?"

As you wait for your check-in date to roll around, acknowledge that change tends to bring up big emotions. Expect to feel both subtle and strong feelings of:

- Resistance
- Discomfort
- Fear and anxiety
- Sadness
- Loss of control
- Impatience
- Discouragement
- Distrust and doubt

"If you're wrestling with any of these feelings," advises clinical psychotherapist Marcia Bernstein, "remind yourself that where you are is in the process of change, and making corrections along the way is part of this process."

YOUR WEEKLY CHECK-IN

Step 1. Set a Check-In Date

Step 2. Take Stock

Step 3. Re-Deal or Hold

Step 4. Plan Ahead

STEP 1: SET A CHECK-IN DATE

Ideally, schedule your check-in when you and your partner are alone as a couple, and at a time that can be easily replicated week after week (or more than once a week if needed). Late in the afternoon on Fridays, up pops a calendar reminder on my phone: > Seth weekly check-in 5–5:30 p.m. My husband and I meet at our favorite taqueria and each order a plate of two-dollar tacos, and a half hour later, we know exactly what cards we're playing with and who will be responsible for each one. Our check-in is a great kick-start to the weekend; it aligns us in the spirit of collaboration. Other couples in the Fair Play system do their weekly check-in over coffee, while walking the dogs around the block, or snuggled up in bed after the kids have fallen asleep. Having this conversation in person is preferable but not mandatory. You can check in face-to-face via Skype or simply talk over the phone. The *when, where,* and *how* isn't as important as providing each other with your dedicated attention. While your first check-in may take some time, these meetings will grow shorter as you become more familiar with the system and settle into a new domestic rhythm and routine.

> *Tip!* **Fridays over Sundays.** *Many couples report that a check-in on Friday is preferable to a Sunday because by the end of the weekend, most couples are toast. Starting a conversation about rebalancing the workload when you're both likely tired and overextended can open the door to an argument. Couples who have been through the Fair Play system tell me that on Fridays they're exponentially more willing to participate in conversations that require a collaborative mind-set.*

STEP 2: TAKE STOCK

Next, you and your partner will review your household deck. Review each card that is currently in play in your home and determine whether the assignment of that card still makes sense for your family. If there are any cards that are no longer relevant or hold value, toss them aside. This is another opportunity to trim your deck. Remember: The fewer the task cards, the more manageable each person's workload, so **trimming your deck is an advantageous move.**

RE-DEALING THE DECK

COUNT YOUR COLLECTIVE CARDS AND ENTER YOUR TOTAL:

_____

Now, review the task cards that you are separately holding across all five suits—**Home, Out, Caregiving, Magic,** and **Wild.** This is the appropriate moment to remind your partner—*nudge, nudge*—which cards you each agreed to handle.

COUNT YOUR CARDS AND ENTER YOUR TOTALS:

Player 1: _____

Player 2: _____

Tip! *Recognize this as the perfect moment to credit your partner or spouse for all the cards he or she is playing right.*

Point out the positive! At a recent check-in with Seth, I acknowledged: "Babe, thank you so much for holding the 'electronics and IT' card and fixing our spotty cable connection before the Golden Globes started."

Seth returned the compliment with: "Thanks for being so 'on it' with daily homework. I know that's a grind and I appreciate all the time you spend sitting with Zach and Ben."

Within the corporate environment, there's a popular feedback method referred to as the "compliment sandwich" that packages criticism in between two compliments. When it comes to providing feedback in the home environment, I suggest an open-faced sandwich. At check-in, lead with something positive and then shift the conversation toward areas that need fine-tuning (see Step 3).

STEP 3: RE-DEAL OR HOLD

After you've reviewed the cards you're each holding separately and playing well, have a discussion where you consider three things during the "re-deal or hold" process:

> Are there any cards that are eligible for a re-deal because they're meant to be "shared" but not at the same time?
>
> Are there any cards where you and your partner fell into a Both Trap?
>
> Are there any Cards of Contention?

>> Cards Meant to Be Shared (The Daily Grind Cards)

Remember: There are no strangleholds. It's not forever that you or your partner will be holding any one card (unless you want "dishes" to be your lifetime job). Fair Play is fluid. Meaning the pre-negotiated window for every card in your deck can always change as desired or needed.

That being said, look at the Daily Grind cards that are an everyday or highly repetitive occurrence. These cards should be re-dealt frequently, and now is the time to pre-negotiate any handoffs for the week ahead. Remember: There are a handful of cards that may be re-dealt midweek, or even day to day. If holding the "meals (school lunch)" card for more than a few days at a time feels like an unbearable grind, re-deal for fairness. When it comes to middle-of-the-night comfort, no one person should be sleep-deprived for years. In Fair Play, no one has exclusive ownership of any one card, and by frequently swapping the Daily Grinds, you each have a chance to experience all that's entailed in the responsibility. Lucky you!

Three days after Alan took on the "transportation (kids)" card, he confessed to his wife: "I'm so sorry you've been stuck in this never-ending carpool line every day. I had no idea how much time this one job requires."

> *Tip!* *Before re-dealing any Daily Grind cards, you and your partner must agree on what it means to Conceive, Plan, and Execute every aspect of the domestic task at hand.*

Provide each other with context; this is the opposite of "figure it out." Also, determine with your partner the intended time frame for holding the card(s) before the next re-deal. Schedule the intended time frame for every re-deal during weekly check-in and have the "calendar keeper" make a note of the day-to-day or hour-to-hour handoff of the card in the shared calendar. Of course, plans change and sometimes you have to make adjustments in the moment. Still, some advance notice is better than none.

NAME ANY DAILY GRINDS ELIGIBLE FOR A RE-DEAL BECAUSE THEY'RE MEANT TO BE SHARED:

Card 1: _____

Card 2: _____

Card 3: _____

etc.

DO NOT Re-Deal to Offload Cards!

Weekly check-in is an opportunity to trim your collective deck, but it does not grant permission to simply off-load cards to your partner. **The chief objective is to re-deal or hold.** There are 30 Daily Grinds and no one person should be responsible for them all. Hold your ground as you negotiate these cards to ensure that neither one of you becomes the default cardholder in this category. **Each partner should hold a fair share of Daily Grind cards, preferably one from each suit.** This ensures that both of you are digging into the most labor-intensive aspects of domestic life across the board that cannot typically be done on your own timetable.

>> Cards That Fell Into a Both Trap

After you've renegotiated the Daily Grinds and reviewed the cards you're each holding separately, **single out any cards where you and your partner fell into a Both Trap**—the very common mistake when one person oversees Conception and Planning of a card (for example, "pets") and then asks for help with Execution (texting you to pick up cat food), causing a CPE Break-Up. Or a CPE Double-Up, when partners attempt to both "hold" a card. Laundry? Bills? School forms? Oh, we *both* do it. Nope. That's a recipe for disaster. (See page 233 for a refresher.)

Stop yourselves before you begin blaming, shaming, or pointing fingers.

"I thought *you* were handling that card!"

"All I asked *you* to do was . . ."

"I told *you* I was taking the lead!"

"I was only trying to help *you* . . ."

Replace "you" statements by taking personal responsibility and owning the part each person played in a Break-Up or a Double-Up. After you and your partner have identified any missteps or balls dropped (again, without blaming or shaming), reflect and revise. Have a thoughtful and collaborative conversation about what it means to Conceptualize, Plan, and Execute the particular card(s) in question. CPE for a given task card resides with one lead at a time, so clarify who will take full ownership of the card(s) going forward. The question to ask yourself is: Do I want to continue to "hold" this card or renegotiate who takes the lead?

Since onboarding Fair Play, or since your last check-in, you may have discovered that there's a card in your hand that doesn't play best to your individual capabilities or availability. It wasn't likely your intention, but if a task is falling through the cracks, recognize this as a potential detriment to your household—and more important, your relationship. To maintain harmony in the home, negotiate to re-deal the card(s) to the person best equipped to handle full CPE.

ASSIGN ALL CARDS THAT HAVE FALLEN INTO A BOTH TRAP:

Break-Ups:

Name the card(s) _____ and who will take the lead

_____

Double-Ups:

Name the card(s) _____ and who will take the lead

_____

>> Cards of Contention (System Fail)

Finally, ask yourselves: Do we have any Cards of Contention? As you're working out the kinks in your system, expect imperfection. Allow for mismatched socks. However, hit the pause button if either of the following glitches occur:

CPE Fail: Your partner doesn't complete crucial steps of the task at hand, or doesn't play his or her card at all. (*I forgot! You were supposed to remind me! I didn't have time. I was going to, but . . .*) For example: You have an empty fridge because the "groceries" cardholder never made it to the store this week. You open the fridge and complain, "What are we supposed to eat around here!"

MSC Fail: Your partner doesn't do his or her card in a reasonable time period or *with care*. For example, the "groceries" cardholder does shop for groceries but does not adhere to the mutually agreed-upon grocery list. Many of the food staples your family counts on for breakfast are not in the pantry. However, a party tray of buffalo wings found its way into the cart, tipping your household food allowance over budget. And there's not even a game this weekend!

In the event of a CPE or MSC Fail, the questions to be answered are:

o Is this a reasonable, one-off mistake?
o Is this a repetitive, unreasonable pattern?

In other words: How pissed should I be? If it is a reasonable, one-off mistake, drop it. Don't bring the house down over every unintentional misstep. Of course, you can still be disappointed that there's no cream for your morning coffee and now someone has to go back to the store, but rather than give negative feedback in the moment, save it for the check-in when you can both calmly discuss the reasonable standard for this card and mutually agree upon who is best to take the CPE lead. Perhaps a re-deal of this card is in order?

BONUS POINTS!
Follow Through on the Mistake

"Repair can only come when someone takes personal responsibility for their actions," advises Dr. Phyllis Cohen. So if you've gaffed, own it and then make it right. Get back to the grocery store with list in hand (and don't come home until you've checked off every item)! Correct your error before your partner concludes: *I might as well do it, or re-do it myself.* Following through on a mistake not only remedies a situation but also rebuilds trust with your partner. Remember: Long-term trust rather than long-term resentment is the long-term goal.

In the early days of Fair Play, some degree of forgetfulness or failure to follow through is reasonable. However, if a repetitive pattern of "I forgot" or "I didn't have time . . ." becomes routine, or if not adhering to the Minimum Standard of Care becomes *the standard*, sound the alarm! Taxes not filed on time. The rent check going out late. Failure to pick up your child from school. Not only will your piss-o-meter go into the red zone in these instances, but also **you're potentially facing a system breakdown because trust is critically compromised.** The gavel must come down! And by that, I don't mean introducing monetary consequences such as what one woman told me: "He didn't empty the dishwasher again, so I bought myself a new pair of shoes with his credit card." Rather than slap your partner with a penalty, invite him or her back to the table and express the following:

> In order for me to drop the nagging, score keeping, finger-pointing, and proclivity to control you, **I have to trust you to follow through on your cards.** That means taking full CPE ownership of every task in your hand, along with meeting our explicitly defined expectations and adhering to our mutually agreed-upon standards of care.

Again, if you or your partner do not feel equipped to handle full CPE of a card, re-deal for maximum efficiency. If there is a card where you have a disagreement over the MSC, or a standard is still not defined, collaborate on what is reasonable within your own home. If you get stuck, remind yourselves why you value the task at hand. For every Card of Contention, thoughtfully address them at check-in. Repeat every week until playing for fairness is your new normal.

?

POP QUIZ
How Would You Rule?

Imagine this scenario: You hold the "extracurricular (sports)" card. This means that to CPE this job, you're responsible for researching the sport, signing your kid up, and paying all dues. Because this card pairs with "packing and unpacking (local)" and "transportation (kids)," you are also responsible for providing her with the proper shoes, uniform, and equipment and getting your kiddo to regular practices and games, along with snacks, proper hydration, a possible clothing change, and about a million other things you'll forget if you don't have a system in place. This is a lot, no doubt, but if you hold this card, the Conceiving, Planning, and Execution of all of these to-dos are on you.

Now, what happens if in your scramble to make it out the door and get to practice on time, you pick up your daughter's equipment bag parked by the front door but forget to check if her batting helmet is inside (it isn't) and a week later you discover that her head is swarming with lice from the one she had to borrow from the equipment shed? Did this simple oversight of forgetting a helmet mean that all the other work you did on this task nonetheless resulted in a CPE or MSC Fail? If you and your partner agree that spending the day laundering everything in the house and delousing the whole family *sucks*, then, yes, the forgotten helmet is an example of not meeting expectations. However, it is a reasonable mistake and one your partner, babysitter, parents, or in-laws could have easily made, too.

Q: How do you reconcile this situation?

A: You own your mistake and take the lead on scrubbing your daughter's head with lice shampoo and washing and folding all the deloused laundry.

Q: How does your spouse react?

A: If this is a one-off mistake, initial annoyance quickly dissipates once you've taken responsibility for the unintended creepy-crawlies. Your spouse lets it go.

Q: At check-in, do you negotiate to re-deal the "extra-curricular (sports)" card?

A: No. You don't feign helplessness. You assert, "I got this." Your simple mistake has helped you refine what it means to CPE this card and you feel totally equipped to handle it next time.

Q: Will your partner trust you to pack all items necessary for the next practice?

A: Absolutely.

Q: In this situation, what are the consequences for your relationship?

A: Fair Play is about minimizing disappointment and maximizing ownership and trust. You have won this round! Keep playing!

STEP 4: PLAN AHEAD

After you and your partner have reviewed all the cards in your deck and have re-dealt for fairness and efficiency, plan for the week ahead. The person who holds the "calendar keeper" card will lead this point of the discussion by referencing any upcoming events on the schedule that may impact specific cards. For example, a birthday party, a school transition, a visit from extended family, or packing for an upcoming weekend getaway will be brought to the attention of the person holding those particular cards. If the cardholder requests feedback or buy-in, this is the time to solicit input from your partner in the Planning stage of your cards. For example: *Should we invite the whole class or just a few friends to the birthday party? What's the best day to schedule a school tour so we both can attend? In which restaurant would your parents enjoy having dinner on Saturday night?* If the cardholder needs extra support Executing the full card or a subtask of the card (like picking up the birthday cake and delivering it to the party), this is the time to solicit help or re-deal full CPE of the card. If it's the former, nudge your partner to ask someone other than *you* to lend a hand with Execution. Just remember: Delegating Execution is the responsibility of the cardholder. And when it comes to singing the "Happy Birthday" song, the person holding the card is ultimately responsible for dishing up cake with candles on top.

> **Note!** *The "calendar keeper" only keeps a record of events to be made visible and accessible on a shared family calendar. The scheduling of events falls under Conception and Planning and belongs to the cardholder of the particular event.*

And finally, when planning for the week ahead or until your next check-in, be prepared to reassign cards if your family is faced with a **Wild** card or a **Daily Disruption**. You can never plan ahead for a flat tire, a chirping smoke detector that needs a new battery, or when your kid gets bounced early from a playdate. These daily disruptions must be handled by someone, so before you become the default cardholder who presumes "it's on me," pre-negotiate with your partner who may be better equipped to step in and handle the unexpected between today and the next check-in.

NAME ANY BIG CARDS IN PLAY THIS WEEK:

Card 1: _____

Card 2: _____

Card 3: _____

*Wild Card: _____

*In the case of a Daily Disruption, the default cardholder will be: _____

>> Stay the Course

The endgame of the Fair Play system is not perfection from you or your partner. Things can and *will* go south as you navigate a busy life with kids. Doing so in the context of a partnership that respects each of your sometimes-not-so-perfect contributions requires that you stay the course, and course correct when needed.

When the drudgery of taking out the kitty litter threatens to kill your mojo and derail your commitment to the system, remember the *shared values* and *set of standards* you and your partner have placed on each of your cards. And finally, remind yourselves of the long game for playing fair.

Oddly enough, candy corn is my Fair Play reminder. Let me explain—I recently found my third-grade composition book. On page 17 I'd written: *Eve's favorite food: candy corn.* I was so tickled to discover that all these many years later, my tastes remain the same. My husband will tell you that I have bought bags of candy corn off the CVS clearance rack in November and inhaled half a bag before I get home. But after having kids and intentionally setting a standard of healthy eating in our home, I've modulated my habits. While I adore those striped kernels of pure sugar, I'm aware that a candy corn diet may well lead to type 2 diabetes, or, at the very least, grumpy sugar crashes. When Halloween rolls around and my favorite candy is available in every store checkout line, I buy one bag instead of ten and remind myself of the long game— serving as a healthy role model for my children and keeping all my teeth.

>> How Will You Keep Yourself in a Long-term Mind-set?

In law school, I learned that economists are obsessed with long-term incentives, so I turned back to Professor Ariely and asked him: What incentivizes people to think long-term? He named four things: (1) a set of rules (check! You've already learned the Four Rules for Fair Play); (2) imagining yourself at a later date (I want to be happily married in 10, 20, 30 years); (3) maintaining a positive reputation (you're regarded as a good partner by friends, family, your community, and most importantly *your spouse*); and finally (4) reward substitution.

On this last point, many of my early adopters of Fair Play reported that dropping short-term rewards into the system motivated them to stay the course.

> "At Friday night check-in, we re-deal our cards and then enjoy a delicious dinner together."   —Carl

"Once a month, my husband and I reward ourselves for sharing the work at home by getting a his-and-hers foot massage."   —Susan

"We let ourselves binge watch our favorite series *only after* we've completed our weekly check-in."
                                        —Miriam

"Our regular 'date night' keeps us going throughout the week and has kept us connected long-term."
                                        —Robert

"Sex means we've played our cards right!"   —Caitlin

10.

THE TOP 13 MISTAKES COUPLES MAKE—AND THE FAIR PLAY FIX

Keep your house of cards standing.

Systems need beta testers, and Fair Play is no different. Initially, I sat down with small groups of friends to help facilitate the "100 Cards of Fair Play" and onboard willing participants into the system. From there, I spoke with couples all over the country and internationally, conducting onboarding sessions over the phone and via Skype. From those interviews and interactions, this home organizational system has been fine-tuned by real-life experiences—by couples like *you* who have practically applied the Four Rules for Fair Play and played the game. From their feedback, I've learned what works best and what common hurdles and mistakes threaten to stall or even fail the system. Below are the Top 13 Mistakes couples make, along with the Fair Play Fix to ensure that you and your partner continue playing fair and winning for a lifetime!

1. THE CPE BREAK-UP

Mom says to Dad on Saturday morning: "Michael's mommy-and-me swim lesson is at the same time as Lucy's birthday party. How about you take Lucy to her friend's party and I'll take Michael to the Y?" What happens? Lucy never makes it to the party because Dad doesn't have the host's new address or a contact number, and when he texts Mom for clarification, she's already in the pool and not checking phone messages. His fault? No! This is a classic case of inefficient project management. As the primary cardholder of "birthday celebrations (other kids)," Mom took the lead on the Conception and Planning (answering the party RSVP, managing all communication with the party planner, and buying a gift for Lucy's friend), but then at the last minute, she fell through and failed to Execute by not delivering Lucy to the party on time with gift in hand. Without proper context, Dad was set up to fail, and what's worse, Lucy missed out on all the fun.

>> The Fair Play Fix

Keep Conception, Planning, and Execution with one person. If it feels like I've been hammering this point home, it's because it's *so* important. Once you become a parent, juggling your kids' playdates, birthday parties, and extracurricular activities can consume your entire weekend, so the "divide and conquer" strategy makes sense. Still—there must be a clear division of labor to maximize efficiency and minimize disappointment.

Only one person is assigned to each of the cards in your deck, and the cardholder takes full responsibility for Conception, Planning, and Execution of the task at hand. In this situation, Mom knew ahead of time that she wouldn't be free to take Lucy to the birthday party because in addition to the "birthday celebrations (other kids)" card, she also holds the "informal education" card, which means she scheduled Michael's swim lessons to occur every Saturday at 11 a.m. Understanding in advance that there would be parallel events, she ought to have re-dealt the "birthday celebrations (other kids)" card *in its entirety* to Dad during weekly check-in, providing him with all the CPE details. Where you may be tempted to hand off Execution by asking your partner to "just" take her to the birthday party, resist! By keeping Conception, Planning, and Execution with one person per card, your home will be ruled by more context and less control, and by clarifying assignments and clearly dividing roles, both partners are set up to consistently succeed.

> *Tip!* **Kid Split.** *In the event that your kids both have playdates to attend or sports games on the same day and time, it is permissible for both parents to hold the same card for different kids so long as the full Conception, Planning, and Execution for the separate events stays with the cardholder. For example, if Lucy and Michael have separate birthday parties to go to at the same time, Mom and Dad can both hold the "birthday celebrations (other kids)" card—for this day alone. Mom takes the full CPE lead on Michael's party and Dad handles all the details of Lucy's party, start to finish.*

2. THE RAT F*CK

It's three o'clock in the afternoon and Mom calls Dad at the office: "Hey, babe, can you pick up some glue on your way home after work?" As her husband hears it, the request comes out of nowhere and he resents being asked to carry out his wife's instructions. A few hours later, he's forgotten all about the call, and when he walks through the front door at six o'clock with no glue in hand, his wife huffs, "But it was just glue! I've done everything else for Zoe's school project; I only asked you for one thing." He feels nagged. She feels overextended. A fight ensues.

>> The Fair Play Fix

I smell a RAT! Once you let one in the house, more are bound to follow. If you want to invite your spouse to become a collaborator who is capable of succeeding, **you must retire your habit of issuing RATs, the Random Assignments of Tasks.** "But all I needed was glue" is a one-off, random directive that is easily forgotten by your partner because there is no context to the request. Moreover, asking for glue in the eleventh hour is a classic Break-Up and a failure to Execute on the "homework, projects, and school supplies" card. It is your responsibility to follow through on Execution. Don't ask your spouse to save the day. Get the glue yourself! If you need help with Execution or with a detail of the assignment, then ask someone other than your spouse to step in and lend a hand by providing clear directives. Or, ideally during weekly check-in, Mom would have solicited Dad's help by pre-negotiating a re-deal and handing off full CPE of the "homework, projects, and school supplies" card, if even just for this one project.

Random assignments become a thing of the past when C, P & E stay together because tasks are no longer random. After pre-negotiating and specifically assigning all the cards, both partners know in advance what they are responsible for so nobody is caught off guard with a random request like "Can you just . . ."

3. THE CPE DOUBLE-UP

"Where is the babysitter? We're about to be late for dinner!" In this case, there is no sitter coming because there was a Double-Up of the "childcare helpers" card and thus no clear delineation of responsibility. Each person thought the other was handling the Planning for this date night and guess what—neither did! When no one person takes the lead, the blame game is easily played—*I thought* you *were doing it? No! You said* you *were handling it!*

>> The Fair Play Fix

Delineate cards and roles. Even when partners double-up in an attempt to share the work or because "we like doing things together," when you approach tasks as the royal "we," efforts are duplicated, big and small details tend to fall through the cracks, and neither person is absolved of the task or off the hook. Someone has to claim the card or inefficiency will likely ensue. On a recent date night with my husband, two waiters took our dinner order. Guess what happened? I didn't get my meal because both servers thought the other had entered it into the computer. This type of Double-Up plays out tenfold in our homes!

4. THE ELEVENTH-HOUR VETO

"Wait a minute! I just spent two weeks of my 'off time' researching elementary schools, going on school tours, meeting teachers and principals, talking to other parents, filling out a mountain of application paperwork, and updating vaccination records—all required to get Vivian enrolled in kindergarten before the first day of school. And now *you* decide that you'd prefer she go to a school across town? You said that you'd stand by my school choice and now you're vetoing my decision in the eleventh hour?!"

>> The Fair Play Fix

Opt out or buy in. In the Planning stage of your cards, always solicit input from your partner. At your weekly check-in, make it very clear to your partner that this is the best time to offer insights or weigh in with feedback about any cards you are holding. If the non-cardholder has a strong opinion or preference for how a task should be Executed, he or she should make their voice heard in the Planning stage. And then forever hold your peace. When you make eleventh-hour changes on a card you aren't holding, you undermine all the work your partner has completed to date, which compromises your relationship and the efficiency of the system. A critical part of Planning is consulting with other stakeholders (particularly your partner, but perhaps your kids, caregiver, in-laws, etc.) for their opinion and buy-in. If the non-cardholder "doesn't care" how a card will be Executed, then he or she can opt out of the Planning. Whatever the case, you must be united on how all cards in your deck will be Executed before the train leaves the station.

5. GOING ROGUE

Dad says, "I just got off the phone with my mother and she says you're planning Sam's bar mitzvah ceremony in Israel. Are you crazy? First off, I can't get that much time off from work. Second, my parents are too old to travel that far; and lastly, what you're proposing is a huge expense! We have to make this decision *together*."

Mom argues, "When we played for value, you said you don't *value* the 'spirituality' card, so I hold this one alone. I take the lead on Shabbat, I'm the one who gets the kids to synagogue, and I plan for all the High Holidays. So I alone decided that traveling to Israel for Sam's bar mitzvah is an important component of our son's spiritual growth."

Dad counters, "But you've gone rogue. You can't make a decision like that alone! We're partners, aren't we?"

>> The Fair Play Fix

If a card is important to only one of you, that person claims it. However, **you must include your partner in the Planning, even if you hold a card he or she doesn't value.** Fair Play is not a game of solitaire; you must play as a team. Consulting with stakeholders is always a part of Planning, especially when it affects other cards. In the example above, Mom did not consider or consult with her husband on many of the cards in his hand—"money manager," "travel," "parents and in-laws"—that would need to be played alongside her "spirituality" card. During your weekly check-in, consider *all* cards in play.

5A. THE HERO FAIL

Dad surprises Mom: "Honey, I found a local junior college student to babysit so we can have a regular Thursday night out. I already paid for the next 12 weeks!"

Mom says, "Honey, that's really sweet, but Ally is about to start rehearsals for the school play on Thursday nights. We won't get home until after nine and that's too late to go out."

Dad's well-intentioned effort to take the lead on the "marriage and romance" card fell flat because he hadn't checked in with his wife before Conception and Planning. His fail alone? No! Mom, who holds the "extracurricular (non-sports)" card, hadn't told Dad ahead of time that play rehearsals were about to begin.

>> The Fair Play Fix

The Hero Fail is the well-intended version of Going Rogue and the same fix applies: **Always consult your partner in the Planning stage of your cards.**

6. STANDARDS SLIP

It's Sunday afternoon and Dad is holding both the "watching" and "meals (weekend)" card. Mom comes home from the grocery store and both kids are melting down. There's strong evidence that Dad has done well entertaining his daughters—a craft project on the dining room table, dress-up clothes scattered throughout the living room, and glitter in his preteen daughter's hair—and yet, something has gone sideways. When the five-year-old emerges from the pantry scarfing a bag of M&M's, they both look at the clock and realize it's 2:30

and the girls haven't yet had a proper lunch. As Dad frantically throws together sandwiches, arguing that he does things on a different timetable than she does, Mom stops herself from responding: "You mean, the *on-time* timetable?"

In this case, Dad has failed to adhere to the Minimum Standard of Care. Mom and Dad *mutually* agreed that lunch on weekends should happen by noon and no later than one in order to dodge midday cataclysmic fits that can stretch into dinnertime and even disrupt nighttime sleep.

>> The Fair Play Fix

Reestablish your Minimum Standard of Care. During your weekly check-in, after you've reviewed the cards you're each separately holding, have a discussion where you ask of yourselves and each other:

Are there any cards in play where we need to reestablish the MSC?

Are there any cards in play where we have a disagreement over the MSC?

Redefine the standard by coming to a collaborative agreement on what is reasonable. For example, "I notice when the kids don't eat before two o'clock they turn into hangry monster-children who scare everyone entering our home, including the cats. To stay on the safe side, can we agree that lunch is washed down with milk no later than one?"

7. BLOWING DOWN THE HOUSE

"By the end of the day, I felt like I'd been holding my breath by not giving feedback in the moment. Before my husband went to bed, I started listing, rapid-fire-style, all the things he'd forgotten or not done to the 'standard.' I started with, 'I wasn't going to say anything, but I got really pissed when you didn't . . .' When I finally finished, he said, 'Great talk,' and turned out the light."

>> The Fair Play Fix

Remember, when emotion is high, cognition is low. Thoughtfully decide when to communicate before you blow the house down. **Ideally, *wait for check-in*.** "If you just can't hold your feedback, move up your check-in date," suggests Dr. Phyllis Cohen, "so that you can return to the table and engage in collaborative dialogue." **Pay careful attention to tone, brevity, and word choice as you thoughtfully discuss any Cards of Contention.** Start with something positive. Share with your spouse all he or she is doing right. Then, if a redeal of a card is in order, negotiate in the spirit of partnership, recalling your agreement to explore a new way to work together as a team to create more efficiency and fairness in the home.

8. TOXIC TIME MESSAGES

"My husband now recognizes that our time is equal, but the last two times our son was sick, he said, 'I don't have time to take him to the doctor.' So I did. Not only that, but I had to stay home from work for two full days when our son was diagnosed with the crappy flu. I was happy that I could take the time off to be home and care for my son, but when push came to shove, why was this job *on me*?"

>> The Fair Play Fix

Stand up for your time equality. Daily disruptions can easily trigger Toxic Time messages, such as those said to you:

o I don't have time.
o I have to go to "work," so can you . . . ?

And said to yourself:

o It's on me since my partner [makes more money, doesn't have the time, goes to work early, etc.].
o I don't really have the time, but I'll *make* the time.
o I don't want to bother him, so I'll just do it.
o This is more of a "me" job anyway.

Don't become the default cardholder. Every daily disruption must be handled by someone, so before you presume "it's on me," remind yourself that your time and your partner's time are created equal. Because *every* domestic task requires time, fairness is sharing the workload. At your next check-in, pre-negotiate with your partner, who may be better equipped to hold the "daily disruption" card the following week.

9. BELIEVING SYSTEMS AREN'T FUN

"Doesn't 'organizational management' in the home take the fun and romance out of the relationship? I worry that a regimented approach to our domestic life will kill our spontaneity! We'd rather go with the flow."

>> The Fair Play Fix

Reality check: Chaos isn't fun. Disappointment and resentment aren't either. **Systemization allows for fun and fulfillment.** It's only when you and your partner reclaim your time by putting a system in place that you create room (that likely wasn't there before) for fun together, not to mention the Happiness Trio: adult friendships, self-care, and Unicorn Space. Truly, the more you invest in unpacking the details of your domestic workload, setting clearly defined expectations and mutually agreed-upon standards, the more you will be rewarded by the Fair Play system. Prickly indictments like "You're so not fun" and "You really ought to lighten up" will be words of the past because once you've systemized the domestic workload and are playing for time equality, enhanced efficiency, fairness and *fun* will return to your lives. As Jill from Montana discovered, "Once we got in the flow of the Fair Play system, my husband and I finally had time to enjoy our time together!"

10. PLAYING BY THE NUMBERS

"I told him—you *have* to take 21 cards."

If you find yourself lying in bed at night, privately keeping score with your partner, stop right there. If you've become obsessed with the card count and swapping totals with your girlfriends and demanding your partner "take his fair share," remember: Fair Play is *not* a score-keeping exercise.

>> The Fair Play Fix

Do not play by the numbers; play for fairness. Counting your cards or tallying your list in an effort to measure how much more you do in relation to your spouse encourages competition over collaboration, which doesn't help to alleviate resentment or the workload. While my research discovered that both women and men feel increased equity and contentment in the relationship when the man holds a minimum of 21 cards, holding more than he had *yesterday* is a gain. Re-dealing just *one card* can be transformative, as it was when my husband took the lead on "extracurricular (sports)." Re-dealing that single card was a game changer in my marriage because it alone freed up several hours of my time per week and offered my husband an opportunity to take the lead on an aspect of raising our children he really enjoys.

What is fair is not always equal and what is equal is not always fair. **Couples will only win at this game by emphasizing fairness,** and the division of labor need not be split 50/50 down the middle to create that sense of fairness. If, however, you do feel the division is unfairly lopsided, negotiate for a re-deal at the next check-in.

11. CURRENCY OF CONSEQUENCES

"He didn't empty the dishwasher again, so I bought myself a new pair of shoes with his credit card as 'damages awarded to me' because he didn't follow through on his cards."

In the beginning stages of testing Fair Play, I considered introducing rewards and damages into the system because so many women were establishing their own penalty box within their homes when, in their estimation, cards weren't properly or fairly played. "He owes me," "Hit him where it hurts—the wallet," or "There should be consequences for failing to meet the standards *we* set for our family" were common arguments. But it quickly became clear that establishing a currency for good and bad behavior led to even more scorekeeping and misaligned incentives. "A system of punishment and revenge is not a system that creates closeness," stresses Professor Dan Ariely.

>> The Fair Play Fix

Substitute consequences with a re-deal. It's the only viable solution. Within the Fair Play system, even in the event of a CPE or MSC Fail, the preferred course of action is to own your mistake, and then have a thoughtful and collaborative conversation about reasonable standards and what it means to Conceptualize, Plan, and Execute the Cards of Contention. To avoid a future "fail," agree to take full ownership of the card or go back to the table with your partner and re-deal the card(s) based on individual strengths, preferences, and abilities.

12. RESENTMENT OF THE HAPPINESS TRIO

"I know I should take care of myself, but I'm already taking care of a house, the kids, and an endless list of mental chores. Even when I schedule 'me time,' I rarely get to it. It's just one more thing *to do*. Of course, my husband found time for a long run this weekend."

Ironically, the three cards that make us the happiest outside family life (adult friendships, self-care, and Unicorn Space) can be the cards most resented by our partners. If you're resenting the time your partner spends on the Happiness Trio, you're likely not claiming or carving out equal time for yourself, inevitably triggering feelings of jealousy and creating even more contention within your marriage.

>> The Fair Play Fix

Happiness is an equal right. Both of you deserve and need time for friendships, self-care, and Unicorn Space. When I ask what makes men and women most happy, many name simple pleasures such as "quiet time for a book," "walking my dog on the beach," and "freshly cleaned teeth." What does self-care look like for you? Self-help author Brianna Wiest suggests: "True self-care is not salt baths and chocolate cake; it is making the choice to build a life you don't need to regularly escape from." Amen! Creating time for personal care and fulfillment will likely feel like an impossible choice to make until you and your partner rebalance the workload. Encourage and support each other's essential need to allocate more time and space for these three cards by trimming your deck and rebalancing the division of the remainder of the cards. The Happiness Trio is vital to your individual contentment and a happy marriage and unless you have a Kid Split, they are the only three cards you should both be holding at the same time.

13. SKIPPING THE VALUES STEP

"I just needed to get things off my plate, so I skipped ahead to dividing cards with my husband. Going through all the preliminary steps just felt like *more work* than I'm already doing!"

Slow your roll! I appreciate your eagerness to begin rebalancing the workload by dealing cards to your spouse, but skipping the values step (#2 of Playing the Game) will only set you up to fail at Fair Play. And anyway, the quickest way to lighten your load is by playing for value because this will determine what cards are "in" or "out" of your deck.

>> The Fair Play Fix

Always play for value. You and your partner must regard this as an all-important value-setting exercise where you thoughtfully discuss the aspects of domestic life that are a priority to you each individually and collectively for your family. For every card, ask yourselves: *Does this card add value to our lives?* Only by assigning *value* to every task that benefits your home will you be able to determine what cards are in play in your house. Good news—assigning value to the cards often results in a lighter deck and less work for you and your partner. Remember, you do not have to do it all! This is your opportunity to decide what is important to avoid living a burned-out life. For example, when Jenny and Ken realized that sending out the annual holiday card was something they always did but didn't necessarily want to do, they scrapped it. "Taking this one task off our list was transformative," said Jenny. "We used to spend hours and hours on this one project: scheduling and getting a photo taken, designing the card, addressing envelopes, buying the right stamps, and finally sending them out on time. Now, we have those hours back to spend on holiday events our family enjoys more!" **Bottom line: Simplify your lives by playing only the cards that hold value to you and your family.**

BONUS ROUND: PLAY FOR LIFE

"We played a few rounds over a couple of months and then we got lazy and went back to our bad habits."

>> The Fair Play Fix

The duration of play is a lifetime. If you stop playing, you risk a slip backward, resuming your old patterns of inefficient communication. Nagging. Blaming. Controlling. Reminders. RATs. Unwelcome feedback in the moment. You go back to what wasn't working to begin with! "In my experience," said marriage counselor and the Reverend Stephen Treat, "when couples stop communicating well, the women get sick and the men get drunk."

Don't let this happen to you and yours! Play the long game. As you continue to pre-negotiate and re-deal cards with forethought as needed, you will refine a life-management system that promises to keep both your individuality and partnership strong. Seth and I play the game—discussing each card and whether the assignment of that card still makes sense for our family—every week over tacos and margaritas. We consider this time together as a gift to ourselves, each other, our partnership, and our family.

11.

LIVING IN YOUR UNICORN SPACE

The real win is a happier, healthier you.

CLAIM YOUR UNICORN SPACE

So now you've done it. You've laid your cards on the table, you've rebalanced the deck, and you've re-dealt that deck a few times with your partner to find that sweet spot in the division of labor within your home. You feel happier. Your spouse feels empowered. You're crushing Fair Play.

Now what?

Remember the goal of Fair Play? No, not just fewer fights or even better sex with your significant other (though those are nice perks). The endgame here—what you're really working for—is time and space to reclaim, or discover and nurture, the natural gifts and interests that make you uniquely **you**, driving you to be *the fullest expression of yourself and make* *life worth living.* Unicorn Space! But sometimes finding the space that, as Marie Kondo might say, "sparks joy" is surprisingly difficult.

A quick refresher—

Unicorn Space is *not*:

o Going to Pilates, spin class, or cozying up with a good book. Self-care is essential to your brain and body function and gives you a mental lift, but it does not count as Unicorn Space unless it's connected to a larger goal that can be *shared with the world*, such as getting trained and certified as an exercise instructor or leading story time at your local library.

o Unwinding at the local wine bar with your BFF. This is "adult friendships" and it's absolutely valuable and essential to happiness but in a category of its own.

o Getting a manicure or visiting the hair salon. The "beauty" card can be a wonderful example of back-to-me time that deserves a regular slot in your crowded schedule. And still, be mindful of confusing beauty appointments with activities that fuel *a deeper sense of purpose.* Adding fresh color to your curls may make you feel more buoyant, but I encourage you to think much bigger than your hair. In a greater sense, how do you want to define yourself? How can you use your Unicorn Space to reclaim or discover what makes you uniquely you *under the surface*?

o Binge watching the latest series on Netflix, watching sports, or uploading pictures to your social media feed. While often an entertaining use of time, this is not Unicorn Space.

○ Your job or career, unless your work delivers a Category 5 storm of passion to your life (take the Pop Quiz on page 286).

○ Just for the rich.

STEP 1: IDENTIFY A PASSION

What would you like to create more time and mental and physical space for *today*? Don't hold back; allow yourself to dream. It may seem like a fairy tale to carve out time to play piano again or research the business idea that you've back-burnered for five years, but reclaiming Unicorn Space *is* worth your time. I encourage you to sideline any doubts or concerns you have about what's "realistic" or how you'll actually "find time" to do it. (This line of thinking is likely the reason you relinquished your Unicorn Space to begin with.) For that to change, give yourself permission to let your desire resurface and make itself known. Once you've given yourself permission to dream, all the things you want to do given the time may stream into your consciousness like flooding water. If you struggle with identifying that *one* magical thing that gives you mental relief and a natural lift, understand that whatever stokes you today will likely change over time and as you change. At that point, you can use your Unicorn Space for that something else. Today, identify one passion to pursue.

If you're not sure what your passion is or what it once was, try brainstorming with the following questions:

I would like more time for _____

Or

I want to get back to _____

Or

I have always wanted to _____
(If you have more than one, pick one for now.)

Or

When doing _____ or thinking of doing _____
I feel at least two of the following:

- o Exhilarated
- o Content
- o Fulfilled
- o Focused

If you're still drawing a blank, consider the following visual prompts to spark an idea. Are you more drawn to activities that utilize your *hands*, build *heart* connections or *heart*-pumping adrenaline, or challenge you to use your *head* and/or align with a *higher* purpose?

Pick one category that appeals to you today and drill down to identify a trade, skill, sport, art, practice, or class that you want to commit to exploring, developing, or completing over the next **six months**. It's not forever—*whatever you choose today can change*. Delmi, a high school PE teacher, told me, "For 30 years, my job was my Unicorn Space, but now I want something new."

- o **Hands**—building, making, crafting, cooking, baking, drawing, painting, gardening, design, decorating, scrapbooking, pottery, knitting, flower arranging

○ **Heart (connection)**—volunteering, charity work, civic engagement, politics, dance, friendly competition through group sports or training groups, animals, travel, music, the arts

○ **Heart (pumping)**—adventure sports, car racing, surfing, rock climbing, skydiving, skiing, cycling

○ **Head**—learning, extended education or training, teaching, speaking, writing, being an influencer and thought leader; engaging in mind-building games such as chess, mah-jongg, and cards

○ **Higher**—church, synagogue, or mosque groups; group meditation; spiritual teaching and learning

If you're still stuck, take some more time to think on it. It'll come to you—*I promise!* Once you identify your "something," write it down or mentally tuck it away. Eventually, you and your partner will share and discuss what you each need to make your Unicorn Space a reality, but for now, this awareness is for you alone.

POP QUIZ
Is My Job Unicorn Space?

If you're not sure if your job doubles as Unicorn Space, take this pop quiz.

Ask yourself: *Do I think about my work with joy and enthusiasm on a Sunday night? If I won the lottery tomorrow, would I still do the same work, or a version of it?*

If your answer is no, then whatever provides you with a paycheck is presumably not your Unicorn Space. Even if your for-pay work is deeply fulfilling, but you answered no to one of the above questions, then it likely doesn't qualify as Unicorn Space.

If your answer is yes, and you find yourself doing the same "job" in your free time, then you are working in your Unicorn Space. Consider yourself lucky! When I posed this question to Jason, an antiques collector living in Hudson, New York, he jumped at the idea, "Absolutely! If I won the lottery, I'd have *even more time* to dedicate to my trade."

STEP 2: PLAN TO SHARE IT WITH THE WORLD

When I began my interview process of asking individuals what passion they wished they had time for again or to pursue and explore for the first time, I borrowed language from an exercise I'd read about in a business magazine. I asked: *What interesting thing do you want your obituary to say about you?*

My question landed with a thud. Not unlike a fresh body in a grave.

Asking people to face their own mortality over lunch wasn't inspiring the type of purposeful answers I was searching for, so I shifted my approach. This time, I adopted a line from a guy who runs innovation camps for kids and who'd been invited to speak in Zach's third-grade classroom during science week. He'd asked the class of young innovators: How can you *share what you are passionate about* with the world? I watched as his question inspired the class of nine-year-olds. Their collective eyes went wide as nearly all of their hands shot up. When I asked my adult interviewees the same question, their responses took a notable turn from grim and glum toward animated, excited, and often joyful. "What a fun question!" one woman exclaimed. "It's now *me* connected to a bigger *we*." I quickly discovered that when you pair passion with a "share with the world" mind-set, when that thing that you do for you is extended outward to include others, it becomes more meaningful, purposeful, and therefore even more fulfilling.

Professor Darby Saxbe was not surprised by this finding. She said, "These interviewees are discussing 'eudaimonic well-being'—feeling fulfilled and finding life to be meaningful. It derives not from passive pleasure, like sitting on a beach drinking a margarita, but from building quality relationships and working toward goals that matter. Eudaimonic well-being is linked with the best long-term health outcomes and inspires what you could also call 'joy.'"

>> Share Yourself with the World

Meet Amy. She was an avid runner, but she set aside her sneakers for the sandbox when her baby was born. Once she and her husband rebalanced the workload in their home, she began running again. But this time, rather than returning to her solo practice of doing laps throughout her neighborhood, she began training for a marathon. This immediately connected her with a community of runners with a shared goal and who supported one another every step of the way toward race day.

Meet Adam. Experimenting in the kitchen had always been the most delicious part of his day, until his kid-friendly mac 'n' cheese became the most popular dish on his menu. Once he gave himself permission to reclaim his Unicorn Space, he checked out a stack of cookbooks from the local library on

Moroccan cooking. Adam's turmeric-and-honey granola and cardamom-stuffed dates were such a hit with his kids that he decided to *share* his passion by teaching them how to cook. At a recent school bake sale, Adam's daughter proudly presented a traditional Moroccan orange cake.

Meet Ana. She'd always been passionate about helping people. Once she and her partner renegotiated how to more efficiently balance the workload between them at home, she signed up to train as a volunteer firefighter. Ana is now the head of the department and she's created a curriculum to better train other counties. She's also become the beloved "fire mom" at her children's school and visits regularly to teach about fire safety.

Meet Graham. A trained guitarist, he stopped playing, even just for fun, after his first child. Now, with the support of his husband, who's taken ownership of a good portion of the Fair Play cards, he's practicing 20 minutes a day and slowly building toward his big debut—a small house concert where he will perform for some of their closest friends and family.

Meet Keisha. When her neighbors had their first baby, she organized a meal train to help them out. Keisha found the experience so rewarding that she wanted to keep cooking for "good." She invited other families in her church community to continue the free service. This inspired a community effort, and after six months, Keisha's meal train had expanded to include distributing meals to low-income families throughout her county.

All of these people, and many more I interviewed, reported that when others either witnessed and observed, participated in, similarly experienced, or positively benefited from their passion, something magical happened—they rediscovered a purpose beyond marriage and parenting.

Q: **Does what I do in my Unicorn Space have to be shared with the world? Why can't this space be just for me?**

A: As I said earlier, back-to-me time deserves a regular slot in your schedule, but what I learned is that time spent on strictly internal pursuits like self-care do not produce the same level of happiness and joy as external pursuits that can be shared with the world. In other words, when your Unicorn Space goes beyond yourself, it becomes so much bigger and that much more fulfilling. Ancient scholars and modern thinkers alike believe that we are each stamped with a uniqueness, and with that comes a responsibility to share with others. Alexis Jemal, PhD, and assistant professor at Silberman School of Social Work, reflected, "The value of what you do in your Unicorn Space is derived from sharing." Of the individuals and couples I spoke to, those who share their passion with family, friends, their community—or the world at large—report great happiness. This struck me as a really interesting finding, so I did some digging around, searching for other studies to support my own research. I stumbled upon a wellspring of data by leading psychologists who report something similar: The pursuit of meaning, where one connects with and contributes to something beyond the self and purpose, where one feels directed and motivated by valued life goals, is the true path to happiness and joy.

If reclaiming time and space for the passions that fuel your greater sense of meaning and purpose aren't a strong enough motivator to rebalance the domestic workload in your own

LIVING IN YOUR UNICORN SPACE

home, then consider new research that links meaning and purpose to a number of positive health outcomes, including better sleep, fewer strokes and heart attacks, and a lower risk of disability and dementia. A study into aging and cognitive longevity by scientists at Rush University Medical Center in Chicago found the brains that function better belong to people who indicated more purpose in life. The authors concluded that those with higher levels of purpose tend to be goal-oriented and resilient, which likely enhances the strength and efficiency of neural systems. Bottom line: Unicorn Space will not only give your life more meaning and purpose and increase your happiness, but it will also keep you healthy and sharp long-term.

STEP 3: SET A GOAL

Once you identify a passion that can be shared with the world, put yourself on a committed schedule that includes a specific timeline by which you will reveal it to others, such as: *By December I will learn to play "Stairway to Heaven" on the ukulele and perform it at a dinner I will host for friends.* Then commit to your goal by voicing it aloud. In other words, *set the dinner party date and invite people!*

Around the time that I had the inspired idea to take the "Sh*t I Do" list and expand it into a values-based system modeled on organizational-management principles that could be shared with couples who were also searching for a solution to rebalance fairness within their own homes, I stumbled upon this quote from the Hay House Writer's Workshop: "A dream written down with a date becomes a goal. A goal broken down into steps becomes a plan. A plan backed by action becomes reality." These words of encouragement spoke loudly to the project manager in me, and I immediately set a date for when I hoped *Fair Play*, the book, would be published. Back then, what you now hold in your hands was just a dream, but once I outlined for myself the series of steps I believed were necessary to reach my end goal (write a book proposal, find a literary agent, and meet with book editors) and took action (actually wrote a book proposal, found a literary agent, and scheduled meetings with editors), my dream started to become *a reality.*

When the day came for me to pack my suitcase and fly to New York and pitch my book idea, Seth was right by my side. Literally, he was helping me pick out my clothes. I asked him, "What jacket should I wear? The leopard or the royal blue?"

"Definitely the royal blue," he said without hesitation.

"Really? What makes you so sure?"

"Because it clearly says 'I'm not f*cking around.'"

SIGNAL SERIOUSNESS

Take your next serious step toward discovering and claiming your Unicorn Space by identifying, planning, and setting an actionable timeline with a specific goal in mind. This intentional step creates urgency to combat procrastination and acts as your insurance policy, so to speak, by keeping you accountable to follow through on your commitment and achieve your dream.

>> Beware of Unfulfilled Dreams

As I mentioned earlier, in my study of couples who embrace their right to be interesting, when you signal seriousness in pursuing a passion and ask for Unicorn Space to do so, your partner is very likely to support you.

To the contrary, if your dream stagnates for too long in the idea phase, your partner is far less likely to encourage you or be willing to provide you with the time and space you need today, and in the days ahead, to fulfill your dream. My finding was that **our partners and spouses respond poorly to unfulfilled dreams**. In many cases, they find them insufferable.

"She ordered five boxes of craft supplies months ago and they still haven't been opened," offered Kyle, who initially supported his wife's longing to return to her passion for jewelry making but who had become frustrated when she didn't act on her desire. "She keeps spending money on beads and tassels and the boxes just stack up in the hallway. At this point, I don't think her 'dream' is anything more than a fantasy."

Stephanie from Lafayette, Louisiana, had a similar complaint of her husband, who'd turned their garage into a workshop filled with tools, piles of raw materials, sketches, and plans that were indefinitely under construction. "I'm so tired of hearing about all the woodworking projects he's 'going' to do. If he can't follow through on something he says he 'wants' to do, then what other things around the house won't he follow through on that I need his help with?"

This charged reaction to unfulfilled dreams was consistent with men and women in nearly all interviews I conducted regarding Unicorn Space, leading me to conclude that in order to elicit support from our partners, **we must signal seriousness by going beyond the idea and taking action-**

able steps that can be recognized by our loved ones. When Clare from Taos showed her husband the working website for her photography, he felt a renewed appreciation for her artistic side. When Nathan from Knoxville signed up for a three-day mountain bike intensive, his wife registered his real commitment to ride the Great Smoky Mountains. And when Sara hired and met with a business coach to help her build a personal training and fitness business, her husband enthusiastically jumped *all in*. He helped register new clients to her first boot camp experience.

>> Level Up Your Life

If you've ever played a video game, you know that the goal is to keep playing by using what you learn along the way to "level up" as you get better and better. Whether you're playing an old-school favorite or the latest trend, the rules have basically stayed the same; you don't want to die on level one! The same holds true with Unicorn Space. Once you've identified your "must share with the world" goal, take it to the next level. Signal seriousness by taking actionable steps forward, and then track how you're leveling up in your Unicorn Space in a succession of visible ways—brainstorming with a trusted friend, meeting with a new business partner, sharing your journey through social media. Whatever your end goal, continue to push yourself forward, and as you do, give yourself permission to be ambitious about succeeding in your Unicorn Space. Challenge yourself to reframe ambition, not as a dirty word that's often used to explain why women succeed less often professionally than men, but as accomplishing something meaningful that you value and want to purposefully share with the world.

STEP 4: FACE YOUR FEARS

At some point after setting your goal, fear will likely get in
your way. And when it does, "What I'm telling you is not to
let fear stop you from going after [it,]" heeds Reshma Saujani,
colleague and author of *Brave, Not Perfect*. "I'm telling you
not to give up before you try."

CONSIDER: THE CASE OF HIGH PERFORMANCE ANXIETY

At the peak of her before-married-with-children prime, Carrie
was a successful voice-over artist and Hollywood commercial
actress, and she'd also sung on Broadway. She was a sought-
after performer who was paid generously—and even more for-
tuitous for Carrie, her work inspired and fulfilled her. Being
onstage and in front of an audience was *her* Unicorn Space. But
after her first child was born, Carrie decided to walk off stage.
She rationalized that she'd put her entertainment career on temporary hold while she settled into a new role at home.

Fast-forward ten years and Carrie was still performing center stage, typecast as the quintessential mother of three kids.
In what had evolved into a permanent, full-time role as the
PTA president and a SAHM (Stay At Home Mum), Carrie
admitted she no longer identified with her former self.

"I really missed the feeling of being onstage, but that's not
who I was anymore," she expressed with equal parts resignation and regret.

That all changed when, out of the blue, Carrie was invited
to perform in her daughter's middle school talent show.

"I remember reading the letter from the school," Carrie
recalled. "I totally panicked. As the PTA president I was al-

ready planning a big portion of the show. Did I also have to *perform*? A big part of me wanted to, but it had been so long. I wasn't sure I could sing again."

For a decade, Carrie had been an *object at rest*, and over that period of time, she'd lost confidence in her natural talents and gifts. Singing had always come easy to her, and yet Carrie felt frozen in place, fearful to step back into the spotlight and reclaim an essential part of herself.

"But you love to sing, don't you, Mom?" her daughter asked when she heard Carrie call the school and decline the offer.

Yes. I always did. Carrie reconsidered, and with additional encouragement from several friends on the PTA and support from her husband, who took the "bathing and grooming (kids)" and "bedtime routine" cards, Carrie recovered a full 90 minutes of her evening time to practice. Two weeks later, she walked onto the small auditorium stage, "nervous and pumping with adrenaline," and sang "Defying Gravity" from *Wicked*. Carrie recalled how she felt the moment she started to sing: "It felt like riding a bike. It didn't matter how long it had been; I was singing! And suddenly, I didn't care what the audience thought of my performance. I understood that this wasn't about external validation, but internal gratification. I relaxed and let go. I gave all of 'me' to the moment."

Carrie said she found herself again onstage. "More like I found my *soul*," she clarified, "and it was like an electric jolt of joy. Oh, there I am!"

Newly electrified, Carrie was poised for a new goal. A few days after she'd defied her fears and rediscovered a meaningful part of herself, another school friend approached her on campus and asked if she'd like to join a few musicians who performed private house concerts. She accepted—this time, without hesitation.

"He brought in another mom from the school to sing harmony and a dad who played trumpet, and before I knew it, I was in a community of musicians who were also parents. These relationships encouraged me to continue 'feeding my unicorn,'" she recollected with a smile. "And I haven't stopped since."

Beware the Ten-Year Passion Gap

Comparable to the "pay gap" that disproportionately affects women after their first child is born and grows larger with each additional child, the following trend emerged in my interviews: Those women who'd sidelined their unique talents and interests in order to focus more time and energy on their families felt the "passion gap" widen with each child and every passing year. As was the case with Carrie, the women who'd relinquished their Unicorn Space for more than ten years felt proportionally much more reticent, and often fearful, to rediscover and reclaim it.

>> The Antidote to Fear

Fear is a great paralyzer, which is why supportive relationships are so vital to discovering, or refinding and claiming, your Unicorn Space—and especially, if you're experiencing a "passion gap." Through personal experience and backed by my conversations with hundreds of people, I identified two types of *spiritual* friendships worth cultivating at this stage of the game. My friend and Rabbi Jill Zimmerman explains it best: "A spiritual friend is someone who wakes you up when you go to sleep, so to speak, and who reminds you of who you are in your core, and who can help you navigate through difficult times by lifting your spirit and guiding you back to *you*."

Spiritual Friend #1: Sharing the Journey. These are the friends who occupy the same Unicorn Space as you and share your journey toward a similar goal. For example, your marathon-training partner. Jazmin from Florida asked her best friend to join her in training for a local 5K run raising research money for pancreatic cancer. "My father died from the disease, so that was my initial reason for training," recalled Jazmin. "That and shedding some unwanted pounds. But after my friend Issa started running with me, I really got into it. After the first 5K, we set our goal on a 10K. On and on we went until we'd eventually raised over $10,000 for pancreatic cancer research and qualified for the New York City marathon."

Spiritual Friend #2: Supporting the Journey. The second type of spiritual friend is someone who's doing their own thing separate from you but who is still with you every step of the way by either offering you loving words of encouragement and advice, providing you with resources and connections to help you reach your goal, or by giving you their valuable time. Though this friend may not be running the race with you, she is nevertheless at the finish line with a bottle of electrolyte water and a "You're My Hero!" sign.

While your spouse's support is necessary because he or she will allow you more time and space for you to reclaim your Unicorn Space, your spiritual friendships are an inspiring additive. These friends will provide you with the uplifting soul support you'll likely need to untangle yourself from the tentacles of self-doubt and fear that can threaten to stall your progress, or knock you backward and away from what you're hoping to achieve. In addition to arming you with fear-busting courage, your spiritual friends will encourage you to share your special talents, gifts, and desires with the world because they *see* you and already know what you're capable of.

As I climbed the levels of book authorship, I called on many friends to talk me off the ledge. I had moments (and still do) where I was seized by the fear of vulnerability and failure inherent in writing a personal book. After *you* identify a passion that can be shared with the world, anticipate flashes of acute fear the closer you get to the sharing part. Putting yourself out there, up front and on the big stage of life, can be scary. In preparation for such tender moments, if you haven't already, designate a spiritual friend—or two or three or four—who will either metaphorically or quite literally hold your hand and keep you steady as you ascend from level to level. I'm forever grateful to my friends who have supported my book-writing journey and shepherded me along the way, including my longtime friend Lori, who loves to drop Eleanor Roosevelt's oft-repeated quote into her girl-to-girl pep talks: "Remember, Eve: Do one thing every day that scares you." We laughed together the afternoon we were out shopping for a birthday gift for a mutual friend and happened upon a coffee mug that tweaked the famous line: *Do one thing every day that scares **your family**.* We bought three—one for each of us and another for our friend. Seth looks at me sideways when I drink out of it, which, admittedly, I like.

STEP 5: GET YOUR PARTNER'S SUPPORT AND SUPPORT HIM IN RETURN

Our spouses and partners *must* have Unicorn Space, too. One at a time, you and your partner will discuss what your respective Unicorn Space goals entail and require—time, money, and kid-coverage-wise. Remember: Before you can discover and reclaim your Unicorn Space, you will likely need to negotiate the redistribution of a significant number of childcare and household tasks with your partner. Some ground rules:

>> Don't Claim the Same Space

Throughout my interviews, I began to track an inclination by some couples to choose the same Unicorn Space, rather than designate a unique space for him- or herself. I wondered: Is this because these couples were initially drawn together over a shared passion? A similar joy? Or is something else going on here? "My husband, Mike, has always loved to golf, but over the years he's cut his games short," explained Jacqueline. "In fact, he hardly plays anymore. When I shared with him the concept of Unicorn Space, he was quick to say: I want more time on the green! I thought, *Why not learn the game myself and join him?* That way, I'm supporting his passion and we're doing it together. A win-win."

My antennae shot up when I heard this. I believed that Jacqueline was enjoying more kid-free time with her husband. But it didn't sound like golf was *her* passion. Were the hours they spent on the course every Saturday truly fulfilling to her? Did she really want to climb the levels with Mike and compete in a community tournament as he'd outlined as his "share with the world" goal?

What I unraveled after speaking to Jacqueline alone was that she'd confused support of her husband's Unicorn Space with forfeiting her own. Sure, she enjoyed learning a new sport and boasted, "I'm actually pretty good," but in truth, what she'd rather do, she said, "is join a knitting group."

I leaned forward and said, "Did you read Khalil Gibran's *The Prophet* in high school? Remember that great quote: 'Fill each other's cup but drink not from one cup'?"

Jacqueline squinted with vague recollection.

"What I mean to say is—you get to take your *own* time and space. Ditch the golf and use your time to spin some yarn."

"Be my own unicorn," she acknowledged.

"That's right."

>> In This Case, Keep Score

Once you have both identified your Unicorn Space, determine how many hours each week are required to make these separate territories a reality—and feel free to keep score in this part of the system. **Reminder: This is the only card for which 50/50 time management is encouraged**; you need to get granular or your Unicorn Space will remain a fantasy. If you set aside three hours a week for writing, then your spouse may also set aside three hours weekly to learn Spanish. If your partner likes to take Saturdays "off" to mountain bike, then you get to pick Sundays, or another full day during the week that goes to you. And here's the sticky wicket: If your partner's job is his or her Unicorn Space, it gets trickier to divide equal time, so be thoughtful as you talk it through. With Unicorn Space, you must pre-negotiate how much time is required, *down to the hour*. My finding was that the couples who don't allow each other equal time in their respective Unicorn

Space resent each other. And because fathers, research and my own studies show, continue to take significantly more time, and with more frequency, for leisure, hobbies, and creative outlets than mothers, you don't have to guess who's feeling the bulk of the bitterness.

>> Unicorn Space Gone Wild

"People are always impressed by the pictures of John on Facebook, training for his treacherous open water swims, but what they don't see in the picture is me out of the frame—left alone at home with the kids for sometimes days at a time," said Patty from Fremont, California.

I spoke with many men like John who, soon after they became fathers, took up various time-consuming, arduous, and often dangerous endeavors such as climbing Mount Everest, competing in Ironman Triathlons, and building the Temple at Burning Man. After introducing them to the concept of Unicorn Space, they all easily identified their extreme-adventure sports as fulfilling the need for personal time and space. Agreeably, an outlet is important, and yet, the idea of *extremism* got me thinking.

Were there instances where Unicorn Space could be taken *too far*? As I continued to collect more data and study my growing number of Cases of the Triathlete, a pattern emerged that proved unhealthy to most partnerships. Of the dozens of men (and a handful of women, too) who were engaging in what I now identify as Unicorn Space Gone Wild, their motivation for choosing these types of grand activities typically fell into one of two camps: escapism and extremism.

Escapism. When his son was still a newborn, Matt acted alone when he signed up for a civilian training class with the

Navy SEALs. The commitment was for two weeks, and at the end of his training, he accidently shot himself in the upper groin, which left him hospitalized and immobile for an additional six weeks.

"A big part of me wanted to just leave him there in the hospital writhing in pain," his wife, Dana, expressed with no apology. "He'd sold me on the training as 'something I need to do for me.' Well—shooting himself in the dick turned out to be a very convenient way to escape the responsibilities of having a newborn at home." (And likely to ensure another one didn't come along soon after.)

Extremism. The second strain of Unicorn Space Gone Wild emerges in reaction to extreme deprivation. Remember that "passion gap" I spoke about earlier? Individuals who have lost touch with their natural talents or interests for an extended period of time will sometimes set a goal to make up for lost time by reidentifying with an extreme version of themselves. Where novelty and surprise are good for most relationships, setting limits is important. Case in point— Oliver, a veterinarian living in Chicago, was encouraged by his wife, Elaine, to take some time for himself outside the animal hospital. He brushed off her suggestion at first, and then finally acquiesced by purchasing ten acres of land in Oregon.

"I thought about it and realized that beyond caring for animals, my passion is raising them," Oliver announced with zeal over lasagna one night. "So I bought us a farm in Oregon! I can use all my vacation and holiday hours to work on it!"

Elaine had encouraged Oliver to find himself, but—*a farmer*? In all the years she'd been married to him, she'd never picked up on his passion for herding goats. Oliver's extreme interpretation of Unicorn Space gave her a stress stomachache that continued for several months until she finally demanded he sell. "You're traveling for weeks at a time when I need you at home, and the cost for upkeep of the farm is depleting our savings," she reasoned.

"But this is my dream," he argued.

A dream that bankrupts your marriage is the wrong vision.

BEWARE OF UNICORNS IN DISGUISE

Discovering or recommitting to the interests that stoke your passion and drive you to be the most fulfilled version of yourself is the endgame. But don't overlook the primary objective of Fair Play: staying together, happily, as a couple.

Thoughtfully consider your underlying motivation for seeking Unicorn Space, and carefully steer clear of escapism and extremism. Sadly, a sizeable number of women I spoke to admitted they'd had affairs as a method of rediscovery. Psychotherapist and author Esther Perel uncovered a similar finding in her article titled "Why Happy People Cheat." Perel writes: "As I listen to [my female client], I start to suspect that her affair is about neither her husband nor their relationship. Her story echoes a theme that has come up repeatedly in my work: affairs as a form of self-discovery, a quest for a new (or lost) identity. For these seekers, infidelity is less likely to be a symptom of a problem, and more likely an expansive experience that involves growth, exploration, and transformation."

If your Unicorn Space provides you with a method of escape from your responsibilities at home or even *hints* at threatening your relationship with your partner, go back to the drawing board and conceive another idea. Ask yourself: *What about this extreme experience or method of escapism*

*attracts me? How can I mimic or re-create a similar feeling
and experience in my own home or community?* Is there a
way to localize or scale down your solo race to the South
Pole so that your partner can carve out an equal amount of
time for him- or herself?

Reclaiming Unicorn Space requires careful consideration
of the calculated risks, along with strategic planning and
consulting with your partner. When one person goes wild
and the other doesn't, it's not Fair Play.

STEP 6: STICK TO YOUR SCHEDULE

You've established that you will be taking the time for it, so
it's up to you to build Unicorn Space into your schedule and
stick to it. Don't allow guilt, shame, or "domestic encroachment" to cause you to miss your scheduled time.

CAUTION!
Watch Out for Domestic Encroachment

Consider this scenario:

You block out 2 to 4 p.m. to practice the instrument you've
been meaning to pick up again since you stopped playing
freshman year of college. Your eye catches the time on your
phone—2:45 p.m. You think: *Even though I arranged for
after-school care, I might as well leave now to pick up the
kids at three o'clock.* And—*poof!*—your Unicorn Space and
your dream of playing music are *gone.*

As you create, or begin to dream and imagine more creative space in your life, you will be at your most vulnerable to the darkening clouds of domestic encroachment powered by heavy winds of guilt and shame blowing in to remind you of all the things you "should be doing" to benefit your family or to bring order to your personal sh*t storm at home. Resist as best you can. Remind yourself that the result of listening to Toxic Time messages that tell you to feel badly for reclaiming a greater sense of passion and purpose in your life will prevent you from making gains, and ultimately erode your Unicorn Space. Recognize that you are likely using excuses like, "I might as well unload the dishwasher rather than work on my watercolor painting" as a Shame Shield to ward off critical comment and also forestall feelings of fear (refer back to Step 4: Face Your Fears). Imagine if everything you want is on the *other* side of fear?

>> Finally, Give Yourself Permission to Be Unavailable, Too

Our partners love it when we give ourselves permission to be interesting. And, in a nod to grandma wisdom everywhere, they also can't help but ultimately respond positively when we're *unavailable*—when we take time away from the marriage to work on our more passionate, vibrant selves.

Back to Carrie—PTA president, stay-at-home-mum, and rock star . . .

Not too long after she was invited to perform at house concerts with her new community of parent-musicians, Carrie ran into an old friend who was looking for a background singer for their 1970s cover band. "Can you learn 'Gimme Shelter' by the Rolling Stones in ten days?" he challenged her.

"Heck yes!" Carrie remembers thinking. "But I didn't want to be backup. I wanted to sing lead vocals."

She knew what *she* wanted, but Carrie didn't run off with the band until she sat down with her husband, and together they discussed what this new goal would entail and require—even more practice time in the evenings and longer blocks away from the family on show weekends. Reclaiming that much personal time was only possible if Carrie's husband agreed to be even more engaged in family life by taking on even more childcare and household cards. Because she'd accommodated his participation in a community basketball league for years, he readily said yes. More important, because he *picked up on her passion* and her strong *signal of serious-ness*, Carrie's husband was eager to support her and agreed to do whatever he could to help make her dream become a reality. (Do not discount the joy of watching someone claim and thrive in his or her Unicorn Space!)

She recalled with excitement one of her first shows singing lead at a local venue. "My oldest daughter, Jane, sat with the audio engineer in the back of the room and watched me perform. At one point, she and I locked eyes and she shaped her hands into the sign of a heart. She told me later that she was proud of me and how 'cool it was' that moms can be onstage, too. My Unicorn Space has taken some of the time I used to reserve for my family," Carrie admits, "but I don't feel guilty about it because I know I'm a good mom and I see the positive effect my Unicorn Space has had on my kids, especially Jane. She now says she wants to be a singer and a songwriter . . . and a mom like me."

Beyond inspiring her kids to connect with their own passions, Carrie revealed the benefit of being less available to her husband. "The sex is way better the nights I come offstage in my red leather pants."

CONCLUSION

HOW ROSITA FOUND HER UNICORN SPACE

It was Friday night and Seth and I were snuggled on the couch with the kids watching one of our family favorites, *Sing!* For those of you who haven't seen the movie (it's worth watching once you reclaim some of your time), Rosita the pig was a beautiful singer. But with the passage of time and the birth of many piglets, Rosita had completely lost touch with this important pastime; her life was entirely consumed by her identity as a wife and mother who unclogs toilets and gets dozens of piglets fed each day. In the narrative, though devoted to their family together, Rosita's husband failed to really *see* her. When she bravely seizes the opportunity to participate in a singing competition, Rosita rediscovers her voice, along with a greater sense of personal fulfillment and purpose. Her knockout vocal and dance performance at the end of the movie draws a standing ovation and enthusiastic cheers from the crowd and her little ones, and even more so when her husband storms the stage and kisses her passionately.

At this heart-swelling moment of the movie, Ben, my then-six-year-old, turned to me and said, "Rosita found her Unicorn Space!" I swelled even more and put my hand to my heart. Ben, my son, had finally put it together.

Though he'd seen the movie many times before, this time, after hearing my side of countless phone conversations with interviewees and passively listening to many of my casual conversations about Unicorn Space with friends like Carrie, the real-life embodiment of Rosita, Ben understood what it looks, sounds, and feels like to witness someone express themselves fully, and also how valuable it is to reclaim that essential part of yourself. The next morning at the breakfast table, Ben asked Seth and me if he might start taking singing classes. "I'd like to start a band," he said innocently. I looked over at Seth. That's the 'extracurricular (non-sports)' card," I said with a wink. "You wanna take it?"

"I'm in." He turned to Ben and leaned forward. "Buddy, you are my witness that Daddy now holds 23 task cards and ten regular re-deals. Tell Mommy to put that in the book."

"Mom," Ben asked, "who's the hero in your book?"

Ever since I'd begun writing, Ben had wanted to know—what kind of book is it? Instead of boring him with a category description like personal growth or gender studies, I'd explained it simply: "It's about the dynamics between moms and dads . . ."

Ben jumped in, "You mean like how superheroes battle?"

"Yeah, sort of like that."

This description had satisfied him for the past six months. And now, Ben wanted to know who was *the* hero.

I looked across the table at Seth and smiled. "We both are."

After much trial and error, engaging in regular dialogue, negotiating with intention, and re-dealing cards, my husband and I are playing fair. And by watching us, our kids are learning what it means to have an equitable and collaborative partnership, one where both Mommy's and Daddy's individual time is respected and valued, household work is shared, and everyone in the family is encouraged to feed their unicorn.

A win-win-win.

FAIR PLAY GLOSSARY

BOTH TRAPS: The inevitable pitfalls—wasted time at the top of the list—when you both try to CPE a card at the same time. Opposite of a re-deal. Includes the Break-Up and the Double-Up.

BREAK-UP: When one person oversees Conception and Planning and the other handles Execution.

THE CARDS: 100 tasks, or "task cards," organized into the following suits: Home, Out, Caregiving, Magic, Wild, and Unicorn Space.

CARD PAIRING: When two task cards in the Fair Play deck are meant to be held by the same person.

CPE: Conception, Planning, and Execution.

DAILY GRINDS: Fair Play cards that represent nonnegotiable labor-intensive tasks that typically cannot be CPE'd on your own timetable.

DOMESTIC ENCROACHMENT: Household labor and child-care tasks that encroach on "me" time for work, self-care, friendship, and Unicorn Space (akin to clouds encroaching on a beautiful sunny day).

DOUBLE-UP: When partners "share" a task card, akin to two colleagues at work tackling the same assignment.

GLOSSARY

HAPPINESS TRIO: Friendship, Self-Care, and Unicorn Space. All three cards of the Happiness Trio are vital to your individual contentment and a happy marriage, and yet most couples report a glaring deficit in at least one and often all three categories.

KID SPLIT: In the event that you have more than one child, both parents may hold the *same card* for different kids so long as the full Conception, Planning, and Execution for the separate events stays with the cardholder.

MSC: Minimum Standard of Care.

RAT: Random Assignment of a Task. Something to avoid.

REASONABLE PERSON TEST: The legal concept based on a simple question—*Given our community's agreed-upon standards, would a reasonable person have done this?*—on which the Fair Play Minimum Standard of Care is based.

RE-DEAL: The Fair Play–approved pre-negotiated handoff of a card to a partner explicitly given with full CPE. Opposite of a Both Trap.

SHAME SHIELD: A woman's defensive reaction in person or online when either unconsciously or consciously anticipating criticism or judgment for being unavailable in the home.

SHE-FAULT PARENT: A woman serving as the default parent for household labor and childcare tasks.

TIME TAX: A woman's compulsory time contribution to household work and childcare with significant costs to her career, identity, health, and marriage.

TOXIC TIME MESSAGES: Verbal messages said *to* women by their partners or society at large or *by* women to themselves

that internalize the concept that a man's time is more valuable than a woman's time.

UNICORN SPACE: Time and space to reclaim, or discover and
nurture, the natural gifts and interests that make you uniquely you, stoking your passion and driving you to share those
passions with the world. (Unicorn Space is separate from self-
care and adult friendships.)

100 cards of FAIR PLAY ™

HOME

childcare helpers 🍵

cleaning

dishes 🍵

dry cleaning

garbage 🍵

groceries

home furnishings

home goods & 🍵
supplies

home maintenance 🍵

home purchase/
rental, mortgage &
insurance

hosting

laundry 🍵

lawn & plants

mail 🍵

meals (weekday 🍵
breakfast)

meals (school lunch) 🍵

meals (weekday 🍵
dinner)

meals (weekend)

memories & photos

money manager

storage, garage &
seasonal items

tidying up, organizing 🍵
& donations

OUT

auto

birthday celebrations
(other kids)

calendar keeper 🍵

cash & bills 🍵

charity, community
service & good deeds
(adults)

civic engagement &
cultural enrichment

electronics & IT

extracurricular 🍵
(non-sports)

extracurricular 🍵
(sports)

first aid, safety &
emergency

packing & unpacking 🍵
(local)

packing & unpacking
(travel)

points, miles &
coupons

returns & store
credits

school breaks
(non-summer)

school breaks
(summer)

school forms

social plans
(couples)

transportation (kids) 🍵

travel

tutoring & coaching

weekend plans
(family)

CAREGIVING

bathing & grooming 🍵
(kids)

beauty & wardrobe
(her)

bedtime routine 🍵

birth control

clothes &
accessories (kids)

dental (kids)

diapering & potty 🍵
training

estate planning & life
insurance

friendships & social
media (kids)

grooming &
wardrobe (him)

health insurance

homework, projects
& school supplies

medical & healthy
living (kids)

morning routine 🍵

parents & in-laws

pets 🍵

school service

school transitions

self-care (her) ☺

self-care (him) ☺

special needs & 🍵
mental health (kids)

teacher
communication

MAGIC

adult friendships ☺
(her)

adult friendships ☺
(him)

birthday
celebrations (your
kids)

discipline & screen 🍵
time

extended family

fun! & playing

gestures of love
(kids)

gifts (family)

gifts (VIPs)

hard questions

holiday cards

holidays

informal education

magical beings

marriage & romance

middle-of-the-night 🍵
comfort

partner coach

showing up &
participating

spirituality

thank-you notes

values & good deeds
(kids)

watching 🍵

WILD

aging/ailing parent

death

first year of
infant's life

glitch in the
matrix/daily
disruption

home renovation

job loss & money
problems

moving

new job

pregnancy &
baby's birth

serious illness

UNICORN
SPACE

UNICORN ☺
SPACE

BIBLIOGRAPHY

Alksnis, Christine, Serge Desmarais, and James Curtis. "Workforce Segregation and the Gender Wage Gap: Is 'Women's' Work Valued as Highly as 'Men's'?" *Journal of Applied Social Psychology* 38, no. 6 (2008): 1416–1441. https://doi.org/10.1111/j.1559-1816.2008.00354.x.

Altintas, Evrim, and Oriel Sullivan. "50 Years of Change Updated: Cross-National Gender Convergence in Housework." *Demographic Research* 35, no. 16 (2016). https://dx.doi.org/10.4054/DemRes.2016.35.16.

Ariely, Dan. *Predictably Irrational*, Revised and Expanded Edition. New York: HarperCollins, 2009.

Baumeister, Roy F., and Mark J. Landau. "Finding the Meaning of Meaning: Emerging Insights on Four Grand Questions." *Review of General Psychology* 22, no. 1 (2018): 1–10. https://doi.org/10.1037%2Fgpr0000145.

Baxter, Janeen, Belinda Hewitt, and Michele Haynes. "Life Course Transitions and Housework: Marriage, Parenthood, and Time on Housework." *Journal of Marriage and Family* 70, no. 2 (2008): 259–272. http://dx.doi.org/10.1111/j.1741-3737.2008.00479.x.

Biehle, Susanne N., and Kristin D. Mickelson. "First-Time Parents' Expectations About the Division of Childcare and Play." *Journal of Family Psychology* 26, no. 1 (2012): 36. https://doi.org/10.1037/a0026608.

Blachor, Devorah. "How I Solved the Gender Labor Imbalance." *New York Times*, February 6, 2018. https://www.nytimes.com/2018/02/06/well/family/how-i-solved-the-gender-labor-imbalance.html.

Blake, Sherry. *The Single-Married Woman: True Stories of Why Women Feel All Alone in Their Marriages*. Atlanta, GA: Touchstone Psychological Services, 2011.

Borelli, Jessica L., S. Katherine Nelson-Coffey, Laura M. River, Sarah A. Birken, and Corinne Moss-Racusin. "Bringing Work Home: Gender and Parenting Correlates of Work-Family Guilt Among Parents of Toddlers." *Journal of Child and Family Studies* 26, no. 6 (2017): 1734–1745. https://doi.org/10.1007/s10826-017-0693-9.

BIBLIOGRAPHY

Borelli, Jessica L., S. Katherine Nelson, Laura M. River, Sarah A. Birken, and Corinne Moss-Racusin. "Gender Differences in Work-Family Guilt in Parents of Young Children." *Sex Roles* 76, no. 5–6 (2017): 356–368. https://doi.org/10.1007/s11199-016-0579-0.

Borresen, Kelsey. "What Divorced Women Wish They Had Done Differently in Their Marriages." *Huffington Post*, October 9, 2018. https://www.huffpost.com/entry/divorced-women-marriage-regrets_n_5bb4cfd5e4b0876eda9a2de0.

Boyle, Patricia A., Aron S. Buchman, Robert S. Wilson, Lei Yu, Julie A. Schneider, and David A. Bennett. "Effect of Purpose in Life on the Relation Between Alzheimer Disease Pathologic Changes on Cognitive Function in Advanced Age." *Archives of General Psychiatry* 69, no. 5 (2012): 499–504. https://dx.doi.org/10.1001%2Farchgenpsychiatry.2011.1487.

Brooks, Kim. *Small Animals: Parenthood in the Age of Fear*. New York: Flatiron Books, 2018.

Chesley, Noelle, and Sarah Flood. "Signs of Change? At Home and Breadwinner Parents' Housework and Child Care Time." *Journal of Marriage and Family* 79, no. 2 (2017): 511–534. https://doi.org/10.1111/jomf.12376.

Ciciolla, Lucia, and Suniya S. Luthar. "Invisible Household Labor and Ramifications for Adjustment: Mothers as Captains of Households." *Sex Roles* (2019): 1-20. https://doi.org/10.1007/s11199-018-1001-x.

Corner, Natalie. "Time Parents Spend Getting Their Children Ready for School Amounts to an Extra Day of Work a Week for Busy Mums and Dads." *Daily Mail*, October 19, 2018. https://www.dailymail.co.uk/femail/article-6293855/British-parents-completing-entire-day-work-week-getting-jobs.html.

Crittenden, Ann. *The Price of Motherhood: Why the Most Important Job in the World Is Still the Least Valued*. New York: Metropolitan Books, 2001.

D'Amore, Laura Mattoon. "The Accidental Supermom: Superheroines and Maternal Performativity, 1963–1980." *Journal of Popular Culture* 45, no. 6 (2012): 1226–1248. https://doi.org/10.1111/jpcu.12006.

Daniels, Arlene Kaplan. "Invisible Work." *Social Problems* 34, no. 5 (1987): 403–415. https://www.jstor.org/stable/800538.

Dey, Claudia. "Mothers as Makers of Death." *Paris Review*, August 14, 2018.

Donath, Orna. *Regretting Motherhood: A Study*. Berkeley, CA: North Atlantic Books, 2017.

Drucker, Peter F. *The Practice of Management*. New York: HarperCollins, 2006.

D'Souza, Karen. "Parenting: What you need to know about self-care for moms." *The Mercury News*, January 23, 2019. https://www.mercurynews.com /2019/01/23/parenting-what-you-need-to-know-about-self-care-for-moms.

Dube, Rebecca. "Moms Confess: Husband Versus Kids, Who Stresses Them Out More?" *Today*. October 14, 2016. https://www.today.com/ parents/moms-confess-husband-versus-kids-who-stresses-them-out-more-1C9884930.

Dufu, Tiffany. *Drop the Ball: Achieving More by Doing Less*. New York: Macmillan, 2017.

Dush, Claire M. Kamp, Jill E. Yavorsky, and Sarah J. Schoppe-Sullivan. "What Are Men Doing While Women Perform Extra Unpaid Labor? Leisure and Specialization at the Transitions to Parenthood." *Sex Roles* 78, no. 11–12 (2018): 715–730. https://doi.org/10.1007/s11199-017-0841-0.

Dutil, Caroline, Jeremy J. Walsh, Ryan B. Featherstone, Katie E. Gunnell, Mark S. Tremblay, Reut Gruber, Shelly K. Weiss, Kimberly A. Cote, Margaret Sampson, and Jean-Philippe Chaput. "Influence of Sleep on Developing Brain Functions and Structures in Children and Adolescents: A Systematic Review." *Sleep Medicine Reviews* (2018). https://doi.org/10.1016/j.smrv.2018.08.003.

Fisher, Roger, William Ury, and Bruce Patton. *Getting to Yes: Negotiating Agreement Without Giving In*. New York: Penguin, 2011.

Giallo, Rebecca, Melissa Dunning, Amanda Cooklin, Monique Seymour, Helen Graessar, Nikki Zerman, and Renzo Vittorino. "Acceptability of Wide Awake Parenting: A Psycho-Educational Intervention to Manage Parental Fatigue." *Journal of Reproductive and Infant Psychology* 30, no. 5 (2012): 450–460. https://doi.org/10.1080/02646838.2012.742999.

Gibran, Kahlil. *The Prophet*. Oneworld Publications, 2012.

Glover, Emily. "70% of Young Moms Are 'Most Defined' by Motherhood— and There's Nothing Wrong with That." *Motherly*, May 22, 2018. https://www.mother.ly/news/its-okay-to-feel-most-defined-by-motherhood-the-majority-of-mamas-do.

Goldberg, Abbie E., and Maureen Perry-Jenkins. "Division of Labor and Working-Class Women's Well-Being Across the Transition to Parenthood." *Journal of Family Psychology* 18, no. 1 (2004): 225. https://dx.doi.org/10.1037%2F0893-3200.18.1.225.

Gough, Margaret, and Mary Noonan. "A Review of the Motherhood Wage Penalty in the United States." *Sociology Compass* 7, no. 4 (2013): 328–342. https://doi.org/10.1111/soc4.12031.

Grissom, Nicola M., and Teresa M. Reyes. "Let's Call the Whole Thing Off: Evaluating Gender and Sex Differences in Executive Function." *Neuropsychopharmacology* 44 (2019): 86–96. https://doi.org/10.1038/ s41386-018-0179-5.

BIBLIOGRAPHY

Hartley, Gemma. *Fed Up: Emotional Labor, Women, and the Way Forward.* New York: HarperCollins, 2018.

Henderson, Amy. "Fatherhood Makes Men Better—at Work and at Home." *Slate*, June 15, 2018. https://slate.com/human-interest/2018/06/fatherhood-makes-men-better-at-work-and-at-home-research-shows.html.

Henderson, Angie, Sandra Harmon, and Harmony Newman. "The Price Mothers Pay, Even When They Are Not Buying It: Mental Health Consequences of Idealized Motherhood." *Sex Roles* 74, no. 11–12 (2016): 512–526. https://doi.org/10.1007/s11199-015-0534-5.

Hewlett, Sylvia Ann, and Carolyn Buck Luce. "Off-Ramps and On-Ramps: Keeping Talented Women on the Road to Success." *Harvard Business Review*, March, 2005. https://hbr.org/2005/03/off-ramps-and-on-ramps-keeping-talented-women-on-the-road-to-success.

Hochschild, Arlie Russell. *The Managed Heart: The Commercialization of Human Feeling.* Berkeley, CA: University of California Press, 1983.

Hochschild, Arlie Russell. *The Time Bind: When Work Becomes Home and Home Becomes Work.* New York: Metropolitan Books, 2001.

Hochschild, Arlie, and Anne Machung. *The Second Shift: Working Families and the Revolution at Home.* New York: Penguin, 2012.

Hook, Jennifer L. "Women's Housework: New Tests of Time and Money." *Journal of Marriage and Family* 79, no. 1 (2017): 179–198. https://doi.org/10.1111/jomf.12351.

"How Do Women Spend Their Time?" *Real Simple.* https://www.realsimple.com/work-life/life-strategies/time-management/spend-time?

Ingraham, Christopher. "The World's Richest Countries Guarantee Mothers More Than a Year of Paid Maternity Leave. The U.S. Guarantees Them Nothing." *Washington Post*, February 5, 2018. https://www.washingtonpost.com/news/wonk/wp/2018/02/05/the-worlds-richest-countries-guarantee-mothers-more-than-a-year-of-paid-maternity-leave-the-u-s-guarantees-them-nothing.

Jee, Eunjung, Joya Misra, and Marta Murray Close. "Motherhood Penalties in the US, 1986–2014." *Journal of Marriage and Family* (2018). https://doi.org/10.1111/jomf.12543.

Jeffries, DJ. "Intention Is One with Cause and Effect. Intention Determines Outcome. If You're Stuck Check the Thought and Action That Created the Circumstance." *Medium* (blog), January 15, 2019. https://medium.com/@TheDJJeffries/intention-is-one-with-cause-and-effect-intention-determines-outcome-if-youre-stuck-try-this-5dbe28c614a3.

Kamo, Yoshinori. "'He Said, She Said': Assessing Discrepancies in

Husbands' and Wives' Reports on the Division of Household Labor." *Social Science Research* 29, no. 4 (2000): 459–476. https://doi.org/10.1006/ssre.2000.0674.

Katz-Wise, Sabra L., Heather A. Priess, and Janet S. Hyde. "Gender-Role Attitudes and Behavior Across the Transition to Parenthood." *Developmental Psychology* 46, no. 1 (2010): 18–28. https://psycnet.apa.org/doi/10.1037/a0017820.

Kaufman, Michael. *The Time Has Come: Why Men Must Join the Gender Equality Revolution.* House of Anansi, 2019.

Kelton Global. "Bright Horizons Modern Family Index." Bright Horizons, 2017. https://solutionsatwork.brighthorizons.com/~/media/BH/SAW/PDFs/GeneralAndWellbeing/MFI_2017_Report_v4.ashx.

Killewald, Alexandra, and Margaret Gough. "Money isn't everything: Wives' earnings and housework time." *Social Science Research* 39, no. 6 (2010): 987–1003. https://doi.org/10.1016/j.ssresearch.2010.08.005.

Kitroeff, Natalie, and Jessica Silver-Greenberg. "Pregnancy Discrimination Is Rampant Inside America's Biggest Companies." *New York Times*, February 8, 2019. https://www.nytimes.com/interactive/2018/06/15/business/pregnancy-discrimination.html?smid=tw-nytimes&smtyp=cur.

Krueger, Alan B. "Where Have All the Workers Gone? An Inquiry into the Decline of the US Labor Force Participation Rate." *Brookings Papers on Economic Activity* 2017, no. 2 (2017): 1. https://dx.doi.org/10.1353%2Feca.2017.0012.

Lachance-Grzela, Mylène, and Geneviève Bouchard. "Why Do Women Do the Lion's Share of Housework? A Decade of Research." *Sex Roles* 63, no. 11–12 (2010): 767–780. https://doi.org/10.1007/s11199-010-9797-z.

Laney, Elizabeth K., M. Elizabeth Lewis Hall, Tamara L. Anderson, and Michele M. Willingham. "Becoming a Mother: The Influence of Motherhood on Women's Identity Development." *Identity* 15, no. 2 (2015): 126–145. https://doi.org/10.1080/15283488.2015.1023440.

Laughlin, Lynda Lvonne. "Maternity Leave and Employment Patterns of First-Time Mothers: 1961–2008." US Department of Commerce, Economics and Statistics Administration, US Census Bureau, 2011. https://www2.census.gov/library/publications/2011/demo/p70-128.pdf.

Lawrence, Erika, Alexia D. Rothman, Rebecca J. Cobb, Michael T. Rothman, and Thomas N. Bradbury. "Marital Satisfaction Across the Transition to Parenthood." *Journal of Family Psychology* 22, no. 1 (2008): 41. https://dx.doi.org/10.1037%2F0893-3200.22.1.41.

Lenz, Lyz. "I'm a Great Cook. Now That I'm Divorced, I'm Never Making Dinner for a Man Again." *Glamour*, November 26, 2018. https://www

.glamour.com/story/now-that-im-divorced-im-never-making-dinner-for-a-man-again.

Lusignan, Kerry. "Love Smarter by Learning When to Take a Break." The Gottman Institute, September 22, 2017. https://www.gottman.com/blog/love-smarter-learning-take-break.

Malos, Ellen. *The Politics of Housework.* Cheltenham, UK: New Clarion Press, 1995.

Mansbach, Adam. *Go the F**k to Sleep.* New York: Akashic Books, 2011.

Månsdotter, Anna, Lars Lindholm, Michael Lundberg, Anna Winkvist, and Ann Öhman. "Parental Share in Public and Domestic Spheres: A Population Study on Gender Equality, Death, and Sickness." *Journal of Epidemiology & Community Health* 60, no. 7 (2006): 616–620. https://dx.doi.org/10.1136%2Fjech.2005.041327.

"Marriage and Divorce." American Psychological Association. https://www.apa.org/topics/divorce.

McKeown, Greg. *Essentialism: The Disciplined Pursuit of Less.* New York: Crown Publishing Group, 2014.

Meyer, Joyce. *The Confident Woman: Start Today Living Boldly and Without Fear.* New York: Warner Faith, 2006.

Miller, Claire C. "Men Do More at Home, but Not as Much as They Think." *The New York Times*, November 12, 2015. https://www.nytimes.com/2015/11/12/upshot/men-do-more-at-home-but-not-as-much-as-they-think-they-do.html.

Murphy, Gillian, John A. Groeger, and Ciara M. Greene. "Twenty Years of Load Theory: Where Are We Now, and Where Should We Go Next?" *Psychonomic Bulletin & Review* 23, no. 5 (2016): 1316–1340. https://doi.org/10.3758/s13423-015-0982-5.

Nepomnyaschy, Lenna, and Jane Waldfogel. "Paternity leave and fathers' involvement with their young children: Evidence from the American ECLS-B." *Community, Work & Family* (2007). https://psycnet.apa.org/doi/10.1080/13668800701575077.

OECD Family Database. "PF2.5. Trends in Leave Entitlements Around Childbirth Since 1970." March 16, 2017. https://www.oecd.org/els/family/PF2_5_Trends_in_leave_entitlements_around_childbirth.pdf.

Organization for Economic Co-operation and Development. "Employment: Length of Maternity Leave, Parental Leave, and Paid Father-Specific Leave." https://stats.oecd.org/index.aspx?queryid=54760.

Perel, Esther. "Why Happy People Cheat." *The Atlantic*, October 2017. https://www.theatlantic.com/magazine/archive/2017/10/why-happy-people-cheat/537882.

Petersen, Anne Helen. "How Millennials Became the Burnout Generation." *BuzzFeed News*, January 5, 2019. https://www.buzzfeednews.com/article/annehelenpetersen/millennials-burnout-generation-debt-work.

Petersen, Sara. "Mama Bear Knows Best: The Enduring Problem with Children's Picture Books." *Washington Post*, October 22, 2016. https://www.washingtonpost.com/lifestyle/2018/10/22/mama-bear-knows-best-enduring-problem-with-childrens-picture-books.

Pollitt, Katha. "Day Care for All." *New York Times*, February 9, 2019. https://www.nytimes.com/2019/02/09/opinion/sunday/child-care-daycare-democrats-progressive.html.

Raley, Sara, and Suzanne Bianchi. "Sons, Daughters, and Family Processes: Does Gender of Children Matter?" *Annual Review of Sociology* 32 (2006): 401–421. https://doi.org/10.1146/annurev.soc.32.061604.123106.

Raley, Sara, Suzanne M. Bianchi, and Wendy Wang. "When Do Fathers Care? Mothers' Economic Contribution and Fathers' Involvement in Child Care." *American Journal of Sociology* 117, no. 5 (2012): 1422–1459. https://dx.doi.org/10.1086%2F663354.

Remes, Olivia, Carol Brayne, Rianne Van Der Linde, and Louise Lafortune. "A Systematic Review of Reviews on the Prevalence of Anxiety Disorders in Adult Populations." *Brain and Behavior* 6, no. 7 (2016): e00497. https://doi.org/10.1002/brb3.497.

Rodkinson, Michael L., ed. *The Babylonian Talmud*. Talmud Society, 1918.

Ryan, Richard M., and Edward L. Deci. "On Happiness and Human Potentials: A Review of Research on Hedonic and Eudaimonic Well-Being." *Annual Review of Psychology* 52, no. 1 (2001): 141–166. https://doi.org/10.1146/annurev.psych.52.1.141.

Saujani, Reshma. *Brave, Not Perfect: Fear Less, Fail More, and Live Bolder*. New York: Penguin, 2019.

Scarborough, William J., Ray Sin, and Barbara Risman. "Attitudes and the Stalled Gender Revolution: Egalitarianism, Traditionalism, and Ambivalence from 1977 Through 2016." *Gender & Society* 33, no. 2 (2019): 173–200. https://doi.org/10.1177%2F0891243218809604.

Shulman, Joyce. "Calling All Martyr Moms: You Are Not Doing Anyone Any Favors." *Huffington Post*, June 3, 2015. https://www.huffpost.com/entry/calling-all-martyr-moms-you-are-not-doing-anyone-any-favors_n_6981888.

Simms/Mann Institute & Foundation. http://www.simmsmanninstitute.org.

Sizensky, Vera. "New Survey: Moms Are Putting Their Health Last." *HealthyWomen.* https://www.healthywomen.org/content/article/new-survey-moms-are-putting-their-health-last.

Sobol, Donald J. *Encyclopedia Brown and the Case of the Midnight Visitor,* vol. 13. New York: Penguin, 2008.

Sorvino, Chloe. "Why the $445 Billion Beauty Industry Is a Gold Mine for Self-Made Women." *Forbes,* May 18, 2017. https://www.forbes.com/sites/chloesorvino/2017/05/18/self-made-women-wealth-beauty-gold-mine/#340434202a3a.

Stack, Megan K. "Women's Work: Paying for Childcare in China and India." *The New Yorker,* March 10, 2019. https://www.newyorker.com/culture/personal-history/womens-work.

Stone, Douglas, Sheila Heen, and Bruce Patton. *Difficult Conversations: How to Discuss What Matters Most.* New York: Penguin, 2010.

Telford, Taylor. "A Doctor Said the Gender Pay Gap Is Fair Because Women in Medicine 'Don't Work as Hard.' He Apologized." *Washington Post,* September 3, 2018. https://www.washingtonpost.com/health/2018/09/02/texas-doctor-says-gender-pay-gap-is-fair-because-women-dont-work-hard.

Tilly, Louise A. "Women, Women's History, and the Industrial Revolution." *Social Research* (1994): 115–137. https://www.jstor.org/stable/40971024.

UK Office of National Statistics.

UNICEF. "Girls spend 160 million more hours than boys doing household chores everyday – UNICEF." Press release, October 7, 2016. https://www.unicef.org/media/media_92884.html.

University of Manchester, www.manchester.co.uk.

UN Women. "Turning Promises into Actions: Gender Equality in the 2030 Agenda for Sustainable Development." 2018. http://www.unwomen.org/en/digital-library/sdg-report.

US Census Bureau. "Income and Poverty in the United States: 2017." 2018. https://www.census.gov/library/publications/2018/demo/p60-263.html.

US Department of Education. Institute of Education Sciences, National Center for Education Statistics. "Degrees Conferred by Postsecondary Institutions, by Level of Degree and Sex of Student: Selected Years, 1869–70 Through 2027–28," Table 318.10. Raw data. https://nces.ed.gov/programs/digest/d17/tables/dt17_318.10.asp?referrer=report.

Valenti, Jessica. "Kids Don't Damage Women's Careers—Men Do." *Medium* (blog), September 13, 2018. https://medium.com/s/jessica-valenti/kids-dont-damage-women-s-careers-men-do-eb07cba689b8.

BIBLIOGRAPHY

Van Bavel, Jan, Christine R. Schwartz, and Albert Esteve. "The Reversal of the Gender Gap in Education and Its Consequences for Family Life." *Annual Review of Sociology* 44 (2018): 341–360. https://doi.org/10.1146/annurev-soc-073117-041215.

Wang, Wendy, Kim C. Parker, and Paul Taylor. "Breadwinner Moms: Mothers Are the Sole or Primary Provider in Four-in-Ten Households with Children; Public Conflicted About the Growing Trend." Pew Research Center, 2013. http://www.pewsocialtrends.org/2013/05/29/breadwinner-moms.

Weisshaar, Katherine. "From Opt Out to Blocked Out: The Challenges for Labor Market Re-entry After Family-Related Employment Lapses." *American Sociological Review* 83, no. 1 (2018): 34–60. https://doi.org/10.1177%2F0003122417752355.

Westervelt, Amy. *Forget Having It All: How America Messed Up Motherhood—and How to Fix It.* New York: Seal Press, 2018.

Wiest, Brianna. "This Is What 'Self-Care' REALLY Means, Because It's Not All Salt Baths And Chocolate Cake." *Thought Catalog*, June 8, 2019. https://thoughtcatalog.com/brianna-wiest/2017/11/this-is-what-self-care-really-means-because-its-not-all-salt-baths-and-chocolate-cake/.

Wharton, Amy S. "The Sociology of Arlie Hochschild." *Work and Occupations* 38, no. 4 (September 16, 2011): 459–64. https://doi.org/10.1177/0730888411418921. Arlie Hochschild is one of the most influential sociologists of the twentieth and twenty-first centuries. Her many contributions include her research on emotion and emotion work, the gender division of labor in the household, work–family relations, and the global dimensions of carework. A less visible aspect of Hochschild's career involves her efforts to nurture, encourage, and engage those inspired by her work. This essay examines Hochschild's influence as revealed in a new book on work and family life edited by two of her former students. The book offers a look at "Hochschildian sociology" as practiced by those who have expanded and built on her ideas.

Wong, Ali. *Ali Wong: Hard Knock Wife.* Netflix special. May 13, 2018. https://www.netflix.com/title/80186940.

Woolf, Virginia. *A Room of One's Own.* London: Hogarth Press, 1929.

Yavorsky, Jill E., Claire M. Kamp Dush, and Sarah J. Schoppe-Sullivan. "The Production of Inequality: The Gender Division of Labor Across the Transition to Parenthood." *Journal of Marriage and Family* 77, no. 3 (2015): 662–679. https://doi.org/10.1111/jomf.12189.

Zimmerman, Erin. "The Identity Transformation of Becoming a Mom." *The Cut.* May 25, 2018. https://www.thecut.com/2018/05/the-identity-transformation-of-becoming-a-mom.html.

ACKNOWLEDGMENTS

Thank you to Reese Witherspoon, Sarah Harden, Lauren Levy Neustadter, and the entire Hello Sunshine team for believing in me and working so diligently and thoughtfully to champion the Fair Play messages. There is no place any first-time author (or any author, for that matter) would rather be than with you by their side. And who says you can't be funny and also game changing? Everyone in your orbit manages to achieve the impossible on a daily basis. Thank you for being the place where women can tell their stories.

Thank you to my writing partner and "work wife," Samantha Rose. Having a mind-meld with someone doesn't happen often and it's happened with you. Your professionalism, writing style, humor, and patience are unparalleled. You are the best. Let's keep working to change the world together!

Thank you to Yfat Reiss Gendell. This project is a testament to your belief in me and Fair Play. Your limitless talents for writing, deal making, editing, advising, and beta-testing the system make you a unicorn. And thank you to Bradley Gendell for not only being a willing player but a champion of Fair Play.

Thank you to the greater Foundry team including Sara DeNobrega, Sarah Lewis, Mike Nardullo, Claire Harris, Deirdre Smerillo, Jessica Felleman, Melissa Moorehead, Hayley Burdett, and Klara Schlotz.

ACKNOWLEDGMENTS

Thank you to my partners on the wonderful Putnam team. You had me at "hello" from the moment I walked in to your conference room holding a book proposal and binders full of emotional labor articles. Every step of the way you have gone above and beyond what I could have imagined possible. I'm eternally grateful to my editor, Michelle Howry. Your gifted organizational mind and thoughtful guidance have made the process of writing this book a true joy. Every line of feedback was extraordinarily meaningful and made the manuscript better and better. I am extremely thankful to the all-star team of editor-in-chief Sally Kim, president Ivan Held, and publisher Christine Ball, alongside director of publicity Alexis Welby, director of marketing Ashley McClay, and publicist Ashley Hewlett. A special thank-you to head of managing editorial Meredith Dros, managing editors Maija Baldauf and Mia Alberro, head of sales Lauren Monaco, marketing team members Emily Mlynek and Jordan Aaronson, copyeditor Jennifer Eck, production editor Claire Sullivan, design supervisor Tiffany Estreicher, art department directors Anthony Ramondo and Monica Cordova, subrights manager Bonnie Soodek, editorial assistant Gabriella Mongelli, publicity assistant Sydney Cohen, Pauline Neuwirth, and Sanny Chiu for the awesome cover design.

Thank you to Sarah Rothman, Meredith O'Sullivan Wasson, Anna Bailer, and Matthew Avento at The Lede Company for all your hard work amplifying the messages of the book.

Thank you to Rebecca Raphael. This project would have stayed a pipe dream without your early and critical support. Your insights into the publishing industry, introductions you made on my behalf, and written contributions to the manuscript, and especially to the cards, were priceless.

Thank you to Professor Alexis Jemal and Professor Darby Saxbe for your work as consultants on Fair Play. Your comments to the manuscript and insights based on your profound knowledge were invaluable.

Thank you to the following experts for taking time from your busy writing, teaching, and professional lives to speak to me for this book: Professor Mimi Abramovitz, Professor Daniel Ariely, Professor Orna Donath, Professor Caroline Forell, Dr. Tovah Klein, Dr. Pat Levitt, Professor Pamela Stone, Dr. Stephen Treat, Jen Waldburger, MSW, and Rabbi Jill Zimmerman. Your deep professional expertise informed the writing of Fair Play.

Thank you to two additional incredibly insightful mental health professionals—psychologist Dr. Phyllis Cohen (my incredible aunt and powerhouse of our extended family), and psychotherapist Marcia Bernstein, LCSW (my wonderful stepmother, who came into my life with love and candy fireballs and who never left).

Thank you to my brother, Josh Madison, for the shared experience of a childhood with a front-row seat to how hard it can be in a one-parent home. When I was scared at night, you and your Cabbage Patch Kid Tommy Lee always comforted me.

Thank you to my father, Michael Madison, for a lifetime of unconditional love and encouraging my passion for learning. I feel lucky to have the opportunity to share a deep connection with you as an adult. And thank you to my grandmother, Thelma Madison, may she rest in peace, for showing up every other Friday for me as a child with a hug waiting.

Thank you to my wonderful in-laws, Laurie and Terry Rodsky, for always being there to help Seth and me with so much E in our CPE. Your support and encouragement mean the world to me—and your unconditional love of Zach, Ben, and Anna is a priceless gift in their lives.

ACKNOWLEDGMENTS

Thank you to my brother-in-law, Eli Rodsky, and sister-in-law, Michal Cohen, for always being there for Zach, Ben, and Anna.

Thank you to our most wonderful nanny, Cecilia Interiano, who is living Fair Play with us every day.

Thank you to Dr. Victoria Simms for teaching me that how you connect is who you become. Your talents, unique expertise, and passion to change the world has inspired me to push forward no matter how hard it seems at the time.

Thank you to my spiritual friends who supported my journey by helping with early contributions, sourcing, editing, and writing of the "Sh*t I Do" list and Fair Play: Samantha Engel Azulay, Jessica Berman, Lauren Hammer Breslow, Sarah Hendler, Kristie Macosko Krieger, Elana Kutz, Heather Paulson, Lesley Kallet Rose, Natalie Sarraf, Zoe Schaeffer, Ryan Shadrick, and Liz Young. I feel so lucky to have each of you in my life. You have all meaningfully impacted this process.

Thank you to the following friends and colleagues for each of your special input, connections, and support: Hilary Angelo, Ami Aronson, Carol Auerbach, Rachel Bendit, Rachel Kravitz Boyle, Jennifer Brown, Natalie Silver and Micah Burch, Julie Buxbaum, Tait Chatmon, Peter Chung, Jason Clark, Dolores Concepcion, Kara Corwin, Kim Davis, Morgan Des Groseillers, Georgia and Breck Eisner, Samantha Ettus, Maisa Fernandez, Monica Leed and Jeff Fierson, Nan Bernstein and Paul Freed, Jenny Galluzzo, Lauren Gershell, Amy Glover, Jessica Goldin, Kirsten Green, Kathleen Harris, Andrew Heyman, Monica Mange Johnson, Jamie Kantrowitz, Gina Katz, Melanie Kraut, Sari Lehrer, David Lee, Ellen Lee, Carol Leif, David Lengel, Bianca Levin, Kadar Lewis, Hannah Linkenhoker, Jenny Louchheim, Emily Love, Sean McDonald, Heather Schlachter McGill, Megan Needleman, Rebecca

Nelken, Kim Shapira Ochacher, Helen O'Reilly, Zibby Owens, Merritt Paulson, Laurie Puhn, Avia and Doug Rosen, Jonathan Schaeffer, Dr. Andrew Schroeder, Amanda Schumacher, Gina Gagliardi and Todd Schwartz, Stacey Sibley, Jackie Smith, Hilary Thomas, Jim Toth, Gabi Tudin, Tracy and Justin Ward, Sheila Warren, Dara Weeden, Norah and Brian Weinstein, Jackie and Adam Winnick, Melissa Wood, and Court Young.

Thank you to Sharna Goldseker and the 21/64 team for teaching me the importance of cards as a tool to change the lives of families.

Thank you to my wonderful intern, Ian Nel, who thoroughly and diligently combed through the academic literature to support and verify the statistics and studies quoted in the book and much more.

And to the more than 500 men and women who took the time to speak with me in person, online, on direct message, on airplanes, in taxis, on the subway, on the playground, at little league, in grocery checkout lines, etc. . . . and for providing feedback and testing the Fair Play concepts . . . truth is always more interesting (and yes, sometimes stranger than fiction) . . . thank you for your stories.

INDEX

INDEX

INDEX